Temporal Experience

OXFORD STUDIES OF TIME IN LANGUAGE AND THOUGHT

General Editors

Kasia M. Jaszczolt, *University of Cambridge* and Louis de Saussure, *University of Neuchâtel*

Advisory Editors

Nicholas Asher, Université Paul Sabatier; Johan van der Auwera, University of Antwerp; Robert I. Binnick, University of Toronto; Ronny Boogaart, University of Leiden; Frank Brisard, University of Antwerp; Patrick Caudal, CNRS; Anastasia Giannakidou, University of Chicago; Hans Kronning, University of Uppsala; Ronald Langacker, University of California, San Diego; Alex Lascarides, University of Edinburgh; Peter Ludlow, Northwestern University; Alice ter Meulen, University of Geneva; Robin Le Poidevin, University of Leeds; Paul Portner, Georgetown University; Tim Stowell, University of California, Los Angeles; Henriëtte de Swart, University of Utrecht

Temporal Experience

The Atomist Dynamic Model

GIULIANO TORRENGO

OXFORD
UNIVERSITY PRESS

Great Clarendon Street, Oxford, OX2 6DP,
United Kingdom

Oxford University Press is a department of the University of Oxford.
It furthers the University's objective of excellence in research, scholarship,
and education by publishing worldwide. Oxford is a registered trade mark of
Oxford University Press in the UK and in certain other countries

Published in the United States of America by Oxford University Press
198 Madison Avenue, New York, NY 10016, United States of America

British Library Cataloguing in Publication Data
Data available

Library of Congress Control Number: 2024908219

ISBN 9780192845580

DOI: 10.1093/9780191937804.001.0001

Printed and bound by
CPI Group (UK) Ltd, Croydon, CR0 4YY

MIX
Paper | Supporting
responsible forestry
FSC® C013604

Acknowledgements

In strict alphabetical order, and without the slightest pretence to be exhaustive, here is a list of people who have helped me with discussion, criticism, suggestions, and comments in written or spoken form: Giacomo Andreoletti, Emiliano Boccardi, Davide Bordini, David Braddon-Mitchel, Clotilde Calabi, Craig Callender, Claudio Calosi, Daniele Cassaghi, Daniel Deasy, Silvia De Bianchi, Natalja Deng, Marco Facchin, Florian Fischer, Graeme Forbes, Yazan Freij, Akiko Frischhut, Carl Hoefer, Christoph Hoerl, Samuele Iaquinto, Dave Ingram, Klaus Kiefer, Cristian Mariani, Teresa McCormak, Giovanni Merlo, John Michael, Kristie Miller, Alvaro Mozota Frauca, Francesco Orilia, Elisa Paganini, Laurie Paul, Grame Peeples, Oliver Pooley, Simon Prosser, Sven Rosenkranz, Adam Sennett, Matthew Seteriou, Jonathan Tallant, Stephen Torre, Emanuele Tullio, Achille Varzi, Federico Viglione, Daria Vitasović, Gottfried Vosgerau, Nick Young, and Sandro Zucchi.

Special thanks go to Kasia Jaszczolt and Joshua Mozerski who have believed in this project from the beginning and to my editor at OUP, Julia Steer.

For financial support, I wish to thank the Department of Philosophy 'Piero Martinetti' of the University of Milan under the Project 'Departments of Excellence 2023–2027' awarded by the Ministry of University and Research (MUR); the project Chronos/PID2019-108762GB-I00, funded by MCIN/AEI/10.13039/501100011033; and the projects PRIN2022 2022NTCHYF_003 and PRIN2022PNRR - P20225A73K_003 awarded by the Ministry of University and Research (MUR).

Contents

General Preface

The series *Oxford Studies of Time in Language and Thought* identifies and promotes pioneering research on the human concept of time and its representation in natural language. Representing time in language is one of the most debated issues in semantic theory and is riddled with unresolved questions, puzzles, and paradoxes. The series aims to advance the development of adequate accounts and explanations of such basic matters as (i) the interaction of the temporal information conveyed by tense, aspect, temporal adverbials, and context; (ii) the representation of temporal relations between events and states; (iii) human conceptualization of time; (iv) the ontology of time; and (v) relations between events and states (eventualities), facts, propositions, sentences, and utterances, among other topics. The series also seeks to advance time-related research in such key areas as language modelling in computational linguistics, linguistic typology, and the linguistic relativity/universalism debate, as well as in theoretical and applied contrastive studies.

The central questions to be addressed concern the concept of time as it is lexicalized and grammaticalized in the different languages of the world. But its scope and the style in which its books are written reflect the fact that the representation of time interests those in many disciplines besides linguistics, including philosophy, psychology, sociology, and anthropology.

In *Temporal Experience: The Atomist Dynamic Model*, Giuliano Torrengo takes up the topics of experiencing time and beliefs about time, focusing on the sensation of change that is commonly interpreted as a sensation of the passage of time. He asks the big question as to what it is like to live in a world that provides one with the experience of change. In addressing this question, he focuses on the first-person nature of experiences, and as such on the intimate connection between time and the self, arguing that, in a sense, humans are time: what we are aware of is our inner time, where the past and the future are inherently connected with the present experience—the present is, in his words, 'all we have'. This focusing on the self leads him to propose 'the tenseless sunshine of the conscious mind' model on which the past and the future are always where we are not but are in themselves static properties of the block universe. Time does not flow but the flow is more than an illusion: the flow is firmly entrenched both in phenomenology and in metaphysics, for the reasons progressively revealed in the book.

While the topic of the book is placed at the 'thought' rather than 'language' end of the spectrum covered by the *Oxford Studies of Time in Language and Thought* series, there is something for everyone here: readers interested in linguistically representing human experience of time can join the author in addressing the question as to why, considering that time flow comes entirely from the human perspective on reality, natural languages abound in devices to lexicalize and grammaticalize time flow and to capture it in metaphors.

Kasia M. Jaszczolt and Louis de Saussure

Prologue

> Thought is of the past and future;
>   when it is emancipated from these two, the difficulty is solved.
>   Jalal al-Din Rumi, *Masnavi*, Book II, 177 (ca. 1260)

Investigating the nature of time is difficult. Investigating the nature of temporal experience, doubly so. If caution and humility are in general good virtues for a scholar, they are of paramount importance to those who enter such an intricate subject. In this book I defend a view that is likely to be controversial, but probably not much more than others in the present landscape. It also has some ambition at being complete, in the sense of touching on the main types or aspects of our experience of time: qualitative change and movement, awareness of one's own experience unfolding in time, awareness of the present moment, and feeling the passage of time. Roughly, according to my *atomist dynamic model*, we are aware of our own temporality in virtue of the intrinsic features of our present life. Temporal experience is not confined to perception or introspective knowledge of change, but it involves structural elements of both cognition and phenomenology. The model is atomist because according to it we experience our own temporal position as simple and unextended, and it is dynamic because it gives a central role to the feeling that experience is renewed as time goes by.

The chapters of this book are not self-contained. Indeed, I doubt that a book whose chapters are really self-contained is worth writing or reading. However, this does not mean that the reader who wants to jump directly to this or that chapter will not understand a thing. In fact, I intended this book to be as friendly as possible to such a reader and have added many internal references to previous (and sometimes subsequent) parts. Hopefully, those references will prove useful also to the diligent reader who opts for reading the chapters in their rightful order.

Although it contains many references to empirical literature in contemporary psychology, this book is an investigation of temporal experience primarily with respect to the nature of its phenomenology, namely the 'what it is like' to be a conscious being who is phenomenally aware of many temporal aspects of reality. Maybe one day we will reach a point at which there will be no use for phenomenology or metaphysics. However, at least until then there is room for hypotheses about reality and experience that goes beyond what is immediately relevant to the empirical sciences, and for considerations about conceptual negotiations.

Chapters 4, 5, and 6 contain material from articles that I have previously published. 'Feeling the passing of time', *The Journal of Philosophy*, 114, 4: 165–88 (2017); 'Perspectival tenses and dynamic tenses', *Erkenntnis*, 83, 5): 1045–61 (2018); 'Flow and presentness in experience' (with D. Cassaghi), *Analytic Philosophy*, online first (2022); 'The way of presentness' (with D. Cassaghi), *Erkenntnis*, 88: 2787–805 (2021). Thanks to the publishers for permission to reuse. The translation of Rumi's epigraph is from *The Mathnawi of Jalal'uddin Rumi* by Reynold A. Nicholson, Volume II, 1926, p. 231.

1

Introduction

In this chapter, I introduce the main notions that I will use throughout the book and discuss certain methodological presuppositions of my inquiry. In Section 1.1. *The ontology of the mental and the metaphysics of experience*, I give an overall idea of the terminology and concepts that I am going to use to talk about temporal experience in the rest of the book. In Section 1.2. *Cogent and interpretational phenomenology*, I explain an important difference between having an experience at the centre of one's attention, with a fully determined phenomenology, and having an experience whose phenomenology is amorphous and indeterminate. In Section 1.3. *Experience-based claims*, I lay down a central methodological tool of my investigation. When we talk about the world around us—for instance, when we say that there is a red rose on the table—we often indirectly characterize our own phenomenology, for instance when we say that because we see a red rose on the table. I will use this idea to argue that different types of temporal phenomenology are to be accounted for differently, depending on what those indirect descriptions capture of them. In Section 1.4. *Transparency and phenomenal objectivity*, I discuss the issue of transparency, and the relation between outward-directed experiences and inner-directed experiences. In Section 1.5. *Believing, experiencing, and projecting time*, I introduce the idea, specific to temporal experience, of overarching phenomenology, namely those phenomenal aspects that, although pertaining to our presently occurring experiences, somehow put us in contact with our past and future. In Section 1.6. *Temporal Experience: an overview of what follows*, I give a quick overview of the main tenets of my theory of temporal experience, to help the reader navigate the rest of the chapters. Almost everything I say in this Introduction will be further elaborated in the rest of the book. Therefore, contrary to what happens in the rest of the book, where cross-references abound, I shall avoid referring to future chapters altogether.

1.1 The ontology of the mental and the metaphysics of experience

Talking about experience is a bit like building a sandcastle on top of another sandcastle. It is impossible without having built the first sandcastle, and how

Temporal Experience. Giuliano Torrengo, Oxford University Press. © Giuliano Torrengo (2024).
DOI: 10.1093/9780191937804.003.0001

the second castle will look partly depends on how we have shaped the first one. Decisions must be taken concerning the foundations of our theorizing. I begin with the observation that we humans are the subjects of experience, in the sense that we have or undergo experiences. Plausibly, we are subjects of experience because we have a mind, and this is why experiences are often taken to essentially involve mental *states*. However, I will rarely and only derivatively talk of having, or being in, a mental state. I will take mental *events* (or episodes) to be the fundamental ontological category to use when we talk of experience. Experiences are things like perceptions, sensations, or thoughts and are mental events which have people (or other entities with minds) as main participants.

When talking of experience, I will distinguish between experience in the *strict* sense, and experience in the *broad* sense. An experience in the strict sense is the mental event that is occurring now and involves me. It is what I can experience 'in one go', as it were. Experiences in this strict sense have *phenomenal character*, namely there is something that it is like to have them. Experiences typically also have *presentational phenomenology*, namely they present us things as being in a certain way. By attributing a *content* to an experience, I characterize its presentational aspect as what can *track* a feature in the world. Roughly, an experience tracks a feature when it correlates with it in such a way that if the feature is in contact with our sensorial systems in the right way, we have the experience. Whether to present things in some way is all that there is to have an experience with a given phenomenal character, or whether there may be aspects of experience that are left out, is an open question.[1] I am inclined to think that there are sensations and feelings that exceed the presentational aspect of the phenomenal character.

Experience in the broad sense refers not merely to our occurring mental life, with its individuating phenomenal character, but also to our cognitive life in general, including memories and thoughts about the future. Part of our experience in this broad sense is beliefs, desires, inclinations, whether they have phenomenal character or not, and what I will call our *commonsense narrative* about reality, the totality of implicit beliefs and assumption on how things are, such as that there are objects around me and, perhaps as we will see, that time passes.

Besides experiences as mental events that have us as the main protagonist, I will also talk of us being aware of this and that, or of there being *awareness* of various things. As with almost all words about the mental, awareness is

---

[1] Cf. Dretske (1995); Byrne (2001) for positions of the first kind, and Block (2003); Boghossian and Velleman (1989) for positions of the second kind. Papineau (2021) defends a more radical view, according to which there are no intrinsic presentational aspects in experience.

ambiguous between a phenomenal and a merely cognitive, or psychological, reading. The mere cognitive reading does not entail any specific phenomenology and involves experience in the broad sense rather than in the strict sense. Examples of cognitive awareness are when we say that we are aware of the current situation at the office, or that the Euro is rising again after it dropped. Unless otherwise specified, I will use the term as phenomenally charged and involving experience in the strict sense. When used with a complement, as in being aware of the rose in the vase in front of me, I take it to entail that something, the rose in the example, is *presented* to me; it is made phenomenally accessible to me in some sense. However, sometimes awareness has a complement without clearly having an object, as when I am aware of a sensation or of a feeling, such as being cold, or moody. Sometimes, I will slightly stretch the meaning and talk of awareness *that* something is such and so, even if I am not referring to a cognitive form of awareness. In those cases, one should understand the *that*-clause following the expression as characterizing the phenomenal character the whole expression aims at referring to.

Experience in the strict sense is traditionally the focus of attention of philosophy and psychology in the form of *perception*, or perceptual awareness. Although there are mental events that are functionally very similar to perception but occur without a phenomenology (for instance, when we 'calibrate' the opening of our hand in grabbing something, or we react to the visual stimuli by positioning so to catch a tennis ball), as a conscious event perception is usually distinct from other phenomenally charged mental events. At the least, the received view distinguishes perceptions from *sensations*.[2] Roughly, perceptions are understood as more stable and correlate with external stimuli in a way that makes them suitable to be described as 'about' objects and their properties. If I look at the sheep on the hill in the distance, while the sun goes down, and fire crackles nearby, I am having visual and auditory perceptions of the sheep in the distance, and of the fire on my left. Sensations are more intimate, and do not correlate so stably with external stimuli. I can feel warm, and in a relaxed mood, while sitting next to the fire and looking outside, without there being anything that is presented to me in feeling warm and relaxed. I will say that perceptions have *outward-directed* presentational phenomenology, they present us something as being in a certain way, whereas sensations lack presentational phenomenology; what it is like to have a sensation is not captured by saying that something is presented to us.

---

[2] The *locus classicus* is James (1890: chap. XIX). See also Tayler Burge's distinction between *sensory registration of information* and *perceptual representation* (2010: 367 and ff.).

Somewhat in between perception and sensation there is *mental imagery*, not merely of the visual sort, but also auditory, tactile, and so on, like when we visualize a green apple next to the red one that we see in front of us. Mental images can present us with things being in a certain way, but their presentational aspect can be *inward-directed*, like when we 'replay' a tune in our head. More disputed is the phenomenal status of *propositional thought*. Some think that it is only by having a certain accompanying phenomenology regarding something other than the propositional content, for instance that of an utterance made in inner speech, that there is a 'what it is like' to entertain a thought. Others argue that there is a specific ('proprietary', as they put it) phenomenology of thought, that there is a distinctive 'what it is like' to think that Paris is the capital of England, say, and it is indeed in virtue of the specificity of the phenomenal character in question that we know what we are thinking. I will not enter this debate. For the purposes of this book, it suffices that propositional thought occurs, and its phenomenology is *at least in part* characterized by the propositional content and the attitude (believing, desiring, etc.) that identify the thought in question, regardless of how it is characterized (via accompanying phenomenology or proprietary phenomenology). I will say that propositional thought has non-presentational phenomenology, while being neutral with its nature exactly.

Although perceptions are typically about objects, when it comes to the temporal aspects of experience, it makes sense to talk about events as what is presented to us in perceptual experience. It may be that perception of events is still fundamentally perception of the objects involved in those events, and indeed I am inclined to think that awareness of events and their properties is derivative of objectual awareness. Just to fix terminology, I will talk of experiences presenting us with *moments* and *intervals* (or periods). Forcing slightly ordinary usage, I understand moments not as purely temporal entities, like instants, but rather as *qualitative* events with virtually no temporal extension. Intervals are composed of moments. Propositional thoughts may also be about the same moments and intervals that are involved in perception, and typically they involve larger periods and various temporal connections (such as this happen before that, etc.).

1.2 Cogent and interpretational phenomenology

The phenomenal character of a given mental episode is always, or at least usually, complex. As James pointed out, simple sensations are abstractions, rather than the starting point of experience (James 1890: chap. XVII). I will sometimes talk of *phenomenal field*, as the plurality of elements or ingredients that can constitute the phenomenal character of an occurring experience. Phenomenal characters are varied not only because different sensory modalities often contribute at once to them, but also because within the same sensory modality there are aspects that we can distinguish, usually by attending separately. Besides, there are various experiences that do not clearly pertain to any specific sensory modalities, even bracketing the fact that how many, and which, sensory modalities there are is an empirically open question.

But what does it mean that an experience has different aspects, elements, or ingredients? I shall leave it open as to whether those aspects are better understood as parts of experience (what are sometimes called moments, or tropes), or whether they constitute the experience, or are features of experience. For the purpose of this book their ontology is not crucial. What is important is the way we individuate them. I have already pointed out that we can direct attention towards each of them individually. I will also assume that we can talk about the experience by *describing* them, either in a direct way or indirect way. Different descriptions can capture, or perhaps refer to, those different aspects or ingredients. I will come back to indirect descriptions later when talking of experience-based claims and their methodological role in the book. Here I want to introduce another important conceptual tool that will show up throughout the book: the distinction between *cogent* and *interpretational* phenomenology.

I take for granted that we know what a description of a phenomenological character is, namely a sentence or a turn of words that aims at individuating an aspect of a certain experience. More precisely, a description targets an aspect of the phenomenological character (which sometimes, talking loosely, can be referred to simply as the phenomenal character in the context) in the focus of interest. For instance, we can describe directly an experience of drinking a wine by using words such as 'it tastes like there is a hint of strawberry', or an olfactory experience by saying 'it smells like gasoline', or a visual one by saying 'I clearly see a pink stripe in the banner'. In all such cases the experiences described will also possess other aspects besides the one described. A cogent description is a description that it is faithful to the experience, one that captures what the experience is like at face value. If I cogently describe my experience to you, and you understand my description, you have a fairly clear idea of what it would be like to have that experience. If you describe my experience cogently, I will concur that you have spoken truly of what it was like to have it. Although the term cogent applies primarily to descriptions (of experiences), I will mainly talk of *cogent phenomenology* or cogent phenomenal character. A cogent phenomenology is a phenomenal character that allows unambiguously, or almost, for a cogent description. It is an experience that has, *with respect to the aspect in question*, a fully determined phenomenal character, such that we can correctly say that it has motivated a cogent description.

By contrast, an *interpretational phenomenology* is a phenomenal character that we cannot determinately associate with a single cogent description. It is such that it is widely a matter of interpretation, due to extrinsic and often temporally posterior factors, that we describe it in one way rather than another. If we say that the phenomenology has motivated or caused the description, we are either lying or confabulating (*viz.*, we think it has, but it has not). Either way, we are wrong. And yet, if the phenomenology of an experience is interpretational with respect to a certain aspect, we cannot really be wrong with respect to its description, or at least we cannot in a wide range of cases, because how to describe the aspect of that experience is largely up to us. Largely, since an interpretational phenomenology does not need to be a 'postmodernist' phenomenology, one that is entirely unstructured; it is just one that is largely undetermined and amorphous.

In the literature, the distinction between those two kinds of phenomenal character is often understood as a distinction between two radically opposite ways to understand phenomenology, rather than two coexistent phenomena. Although the parties to the debate would not put it in this way, the opposition is that of two metaphysical views of what phenomenology is like: the realist side and the deflationist or antirealist side about phenomenology itself. For instance, on the antirealist side, Daniel Dennett has at length defended the thesis that it just does not make sense to talk about what an experience is really like, independently of how one (the person who is having it) takes it to be. There is nothing more to phenomenology than the judgement we make about the experience we are having; there is nothing those judgements are based on. Here is a significant passage:

> Some people [...] are under the impression that they actually observe themselves judging things to be such as a result of those things seeming to them to be such. No one has ever observed any such thing 'in their phenomenology' because such a fact about causation would be unobservable (as Hume noted long ago). (Dennett 1991: 133)

I think that both the ideas that phenomenology is essentially cogent or essentially interpretational are problematic. If one goes for the cogent understanding, they have to say that in a situation in which two ordinary subjects in optimal conditions disagree about their descriptions, one of the two is simply wrong about their own phenomenology. We could thus in principle correct them and tell them what they really experienced. This seems wrong. However, if we go for the view that phenomenology is essentially interpretational, we end up with undesirable consequences too. Suppose we are in optimal conditions and see a red dot moving from left to right. Another subject, in the very same conditions, however, reports observing a rotating pink star moving from right to left. If phenomenology is interpretational, we would have no ground for thinking that there is something wrong with them (or that they are not really in the same conditions in which we are). This seems wrong too. Trite as it may be, we need to take the distinction with a grain of salt and allow for both kinds of phenomenological character. Sometimes a phenomenal character imposes on us, and we cannot but describe it in a certain way, given the conceptual resources we are endowed with. Other times the situation is not so clear-cut, and there is leeway for different interpretations of what it was like to undergo the experience.

My hypothesis is that *attention* is crucial in the way this distinction is to be understood. When a certain aspect of our experience is under our full attention, its phenomenology, the 'what it is like' to experience it, will usually be determined. Perhaps when attention is used for action, the role of phenomenology is not to be taken for granted, since there is a lot of processing that is done by the cerebellum, very fast and totally unconscious. But there is a sense of attention according to which if we are attending to a certain phenomenological aspect, then it is in the focus of our phenomenology, is the thing that we cannot miss, as it were. Although no description or judgement is sacrosanct, I take it to be methodologically sound to take those aspects of our phenomenology as cogent, and thus as being suitable for a correct description. However, very often there are aspects of our experience that fall off the focus of our attention, and sometimes, for instance in the case of peripheral vision, they cannot be in the focus of attention, unless we change the context (for instance, we move our gaze or our head), and yet they are not entirely void of phenomenology. In these cases, it is safe to assume that there is no cogent way to describe those phenomenal aspects, and their phenomenology will be largely interpretational. Depending on different contextual hints, and often posterior inputs, we will tend to describe the experience in different ways, or be open to competing descriptions, or perhaps more liable to be influenced by extraneous factors, such as beliefs.

1.3 Experience-based claims

In the previous sections I talked of descriptions of experiences, or reports about them, in a somewhat vague way. In order to make the notion of direct and indirect description of an experience (or, more precisely, of an aspect of an experience) more precise, I introduce the notion of *experience-based claims*; that is, ordinary claims such as 'there is a red apple on the table in front of me', or 'the ball is rolling down the slope', which are usually prompted by perceptions of the environment around the speaker, or other phenomenologically charged experiences. While there is a long tradition, in philosophy of science, of attempts to individuate observational sentences (Popper 1935; Reichenbach 1938; Van Fraassen 1980), my aim here is not securing an empirical base for scientific knowledge, but rather individuating a pre-theoretical way to characterize the elements of our experience under study. Certain ordinary claims are, on the one hand, *directly* connected with sensorial experience, in the sense of not being the outcome of an overt inferential process, and on the other hand *indirectly* descriptive of the experience that originated them, in the sense of not being overtly about how the experience *feels* or *seems* to us, but rather *about the world that the experience presents to us.*[3]

Given those connections between the experience-based claims, phenomenology, and worldly beliefs, we can attempt to explain why we make certain claims rather than other (e.g. why, in a given circumstance, we say that there is a red apple rather than a yellow lemon) in terms of a *theoretical characterization* of the experience that purportedly grounds them. More precisely, the aim of the explanation is not to investigate the causes of given utterances of experience-based claims. This would be a complicated and somewhat vague empirical enterprise. Rather, the aim is to explain why, assuming that certain claims have the status of perception-based claims (they express pre-theoretical beliefs about the world and are non-accidentally connected to experience),

---

[3] It is worth noting that the beliefs that are connected to such claims (for instance, the belief that there is an apple on the table, or that the ball is rolling down the slope) are *neutral* with respect to further theoretical characterization of the objects and properties they are about. For instance, I can believe that there is a red apple on the table and believe it because I see a red apple on the table in front of me, but be an antirealist with respect to the existence of colours, because I maintain that they are properties of experience that we project onto reality. In other words, accepting an experience-based claim about coloured objects does not commit me to colour realism, and even less to any of its specific variety.

they have that status. Is it the phenomenological character in question that makes the indirect description cogent, or are there external factors to the phenomenology that are somehow predominant, and motivate a certain interpretation of the phenomenology? By resorting to tools from contemporary philosophy of mind (e.g. Crane 2009; Bayne 2010), I will distinguish three strategies we may endorse to account for their experiential base.

The *content* strategy is to maintain that, for instance, there is a red apple on the table (rather than a yellow lemon), because the concurrent experience has a red apple as content. In this book I use a quite strict notion of content. Roughly, something is part of the phenomenal content of an experience, only if there is a phenomenal aspect that tracks a feature of the world. The notion of tracking here must allow for misperception. It is not important which theoretical background one adopts. For instance, we may assume that in normal circumstances the phenomenal feature is present if, and only if, the corresponding feature causally impinges on the relevant sensory receptors of the subject. According to the *representationalist* variety of the strategy, the experience in question has a red apple as its content because it represents a red apple. This content is individuated by its correctness conditions, to which we are committed if we take the experience at face value (and we do not doubt, for instance, to be under the influence of some drug). This version of the content strategy is a clear application of the idea that that aspect of the phenomenology is cogent. The representationalist conception as a general view on experience is a popular position in philosophy of mind. We can further distinguish between *intentional representationalism*, which is the more traditional form, according to which the phenomenal character of an experience depends on its representational content, and a more recent version—*phenomenal representationalism*—according to which representational content depends on the phenomenal character. In both, understanding the link between the phenomenal character and the representational content is close, and this suggests that the phenomenology is taken to be cogent. As I said, I am not defending or attacking any of those general views, I am using some of their conceptual tools to model the idea that there are aspects of our phenomenology that are cogent, for which a certain description imposes on us.

The content strategy can be articulated also along the link of a *relationist* variety. Roughly, according to this strategy, when we see a red apple, the experience of a red apple has a content because our mental state is in a certain relation with a red apple. Relationism comes in a weak and a strong variety. Neither takes experience to be committed to correctness conditions for its content, as representationalism is. The weak variety is the closest to the idea that the phenomenal character in question is cogent. According to this, the experience-based claim captures a certain determined aspect of the phenomenology, one that is there because there is a relation between the mental event and the physical object. In other words, the relation with the external entity at least partially explains the phenomenology of the experienced content. For instance, an experience of noticing something moving, as opposed to simply staring at a stationary object, is triggered by certain stimulus conditions with which the subject enters in a relation that determines a specific movement phenomenology. The phenomenology is cogent, and we can say that in it movement is presented to us, even though there is no representational character, with well-determined correctness conditions, that individuates the experience (cf. Hoerl 2013: 399). The strong variety leans more towards an interpretational understanding of the phenomenology. According to this, there is no specific phenomenological character associated with or determined by the relation that individuates the experience. Experience does not commit us to correctness conditions and neither presents us with things as being one way or another. 'It is in making out, or trying to, what it is that *we* confront that we take things, rightly or wrongly, to be thus and so' (Travis 2004: 65); that is, it is how we interpret the phenomenology that establishes its content.

The *sensationalist* strategy is to appeal to intrinsic features of experience to explain the connection between the experience-based claim and the phenomenological character. For instance, according to a certain tradition that dates back at least to Galileo, colours are intrinsic features of our visual field that we project onto the world as we experience it. According to this strategy, the phenomenal character in question is likely to be cogent, since by using the experience-based claim we correctly describe a determined 'what it is like' to undergo a certain experience. The main difference between the content strategy and the sensationalist one is that certain aspects of the phenomenology can be cogent and yet not part of what is presented to us, for instance feeling cold, feeling moody, or having an after-image. For those aspects, unless we take their phenomenology to be merely or largely interpretational, a sensationalist strategy seems more apt.

Finally, the *error-theoretic strategy* is to maintain that the experience-based claims in questions are a *mis*characterization of our phenomenology. For instance, during a famous experiment, professional wine tasters were given white wine coloured with a tasteless substance that makes the wine look like a typical red wine does. The vocabulary that they used to describe it, and with it indirectly their experience, was in large part the vocabulary that they would have used for red wines. This strategy is compatible with the idea that the phenomenology in question is cogent. For instance, in the example of the wine tasters, the subjects are under the influence of a belief (that the wine is red) and thus simply misinterpret their own phenomenology, even though it is perfectly determined. Note that if the belief in some way penetrates or percolates into the phenomenology then their phenomenology would be altered, and thus their description may turn out to be cogent after all. In this case the example would no longer be a good example of the error-theoretic strategy to explain experience-based claims. However, it is also possible that the phenomenology in question is not cogent, but interpretational. If so, the error would be in taking it to be determinate, while it is largely unspecified and compatible with a large range of descriptions, for instance one including words for red and white wines alike. Perhaps in the case of the wine tasters experiment this is not so plausible, since it is assumed that the subjects pay as much attention as possible to the taste of the wine. However, in other cases it may be more likely. For instance, perhaps our experience is less smooth and continuous of how we ordinarily describe it, because we are often nonattentive towards many aspects of it, and thus our phenomenology has more 'interpretational gaps' than we like to admit. If so, when we focus on what just happened—for instance, on how many knocks at the door we just heard, after a loud 'they are knocking at the door!' from upstairs makes us emerge from an engrossing reading experience—we may take as perfectly determinate a succession of experiences that was actually largely amorphous in its phenomenology. But an error-theoretic strategy can also be applied in the framework of an eliminativist take on the phenomenological character at issue. For instance, according to certain deflationist accounts of the experience of the passage of time, there is no specific phenomenology of the passage of time itself, but we mistake the phenomenology connected to change and movement for one.

1.4 Transparency and phenomenal objectivity

Transparency is a thesis about *perception* and not the phenomenology of experience in general. In its broader formulation *transparency* is the thesis that awareness of (properties of) what we are presented with through our perceptual systems is in some sense *prior* to the awareness of (properties of) our own experiences (if any). Transparency can be tuned along at least two pairs of distinctions.

The first is the distinction between *positive* transparency and *negative* transparency (cf. Martin 2002: 380–92, 418). Positive transparency is the thesis that introspection of our perceptions is awareness of properties of external objects. Negative transparency is the thesis that introspection of our perceptions is not awareness of (the properties of) our experiences themselves. I will call *full transparency* their conjunction, namely the thesis that external entities and their properties are the *only* thing we are aware of when we introspect our perceptions.[4] Note that positive transparency is compatible with being aware of the properties of the experiences themselves, though only while also attending external objects, or in some sense vicariously. There are various ways to capture this idea. For instance, one may argue that we can be aware of intrinsic properties of experience only within our peripheral attention, but the focus is always on external objects (cf. Martin 2002: 380); or one may maintain that awareness of properties of our experience is only obtained *through* awareness of properties of external objects (cf. Benovsky 2013: 4).

The second distinction is between the *metaphysical* and the *phenomenal* readings of transparency (cf. Gow 2016). In the metaphysical reading, transparency is the thesis that we are *de facto* only aware of properties of external objects, even if we may think otherwise. In the phenomenal reading, transparency is the thesis that *it seems to us* to be only aware of properties of external objects. The metaphysical reading is compatible with the claim that people can make the 'internalizing content' mistake, that is attributing to experience itself properties of its objects; the phenomenal reading is compatible with the 'externalizing content' mistake, that is attributing to external objects intrinsic properties of experience (cf. Millikan 1991).

It is important to note that it is only transparency in its phenomenal reading that captures an aspect of the idea that perception, as opposed to other sensorial mental episodes, such as imagination and abstract thought comes with *phenomenal objectivity*, namely a feeling of being presented with an 'external world', through different and possibly integrated modalities (sight, smell, touch, etc.). Experience prominently presents us with things that inhabit the

---

[4] I am departing from more orthodox formulations of the transparency debate by distinguishing negative and full transparency. In most of the literature the negative thesis is taken to entail that we perceive *only* external objects (and hence to be equivalent to what I call full transparency), but the entailment holds on the assumption that we perceive at least some external object. Although I am very sympathetic to that assumption, I think that it is conceptually clearer not to take it for granted, and thus distinguish between the mere negative thesis and full transparency (the conjunction of the negative and the positive theses). Also, the general characterization of transparency in terms of the priority of the external over the internal is unorthodox. However, it captures what is common to positive and full transparency, without being partial to either.

same *space* and *time* we also inhabit, but which are located—quite literally—outside our heads (cf. Smith 2002; Masrour 2012). The brightness of the peaceful and vast poppy field in front of us, the chirping of the birds in the trees nearby, the smell of the freshly cut grass on which we walk. *Almost* all of what is perceptually presented to us is *undoubtedly* a denizen of the external world. And *if* full transparency holds, then even *ephemeral experiences* such as after-images and phosphenes present us with things of the external world, albeit illusorily (cf. Siegel 2006; Phillips 2012). The reason why we *misjudge* (by making the internalizing mistake) them to be either pure sensations, or properties of the sensory field, or other inhabitants of an 'inner world', is that there are many *phenomenal defeaters* of their phenomenal objectivity that lead us down the wrong path: after-images tend to flicker and flutter as objects around us do not, they lack kinetic independence, that is they 'move' in relation to where we move and direct our gaze, they also do not appear constant in size, since they do not 'become bigger' if we walk towards them, and in general cannot be inspected from different perspectives. Whereas, if full transparency does not hold, not all that is phenomenally present in perception has phenomenal objectivity, and the possibility that mental events like after-images and phosphenes are indeed experiences of properties of the visual field (or are pure sensations, or other 'internal' objects) opens up.

Phenomenal objectivity is not to be identified with *presentational phenomenology*, which we have already encountered by distinguishing perception from sensation. Presentational phenomenology can be *outward-directed* or *inward-directed*. We can think of after-images and other ephemeral experiences as having outward-directed presentational phenomenology and yet lacking phenomenal objectivity. Certain mental imagery can have a similar status. When experiencing a mental image (not necessarily of a visual sort), we can say to be presented with something. In certain cases, we are presented with something that does not inhabit any external space (as when we follow a melody 'in our head'), but in other cases we can 'visualize' things as if they were denizens of the external world. When an experience with presentational phenomenology has also phenomenal objectivity it is a *worldly* phenomenal character, as the typical cases of perception are. A worldly phenomenal character corresponds to the 'what it is like' to be presented with the external world as being in a certain way, typically as containing objects and events located in space. Experiences such as feeling physical discomfort or having a headache, feeling cold or warm, are experiences that usually lack outward presentational phenomenology, but have phenomenal objectivity; they do not feel as if there is nothing in the world that they latch onto. Maybe also certain gustative, auditory, and olfactory experiences can be like that.

All such experiences, namely those that have at least one of the two aspects among phenomenal objectivity and outward-directed presentational phenomenology, are part of what I call the *outer flow*, the succession of experiences that put us in contact with the environment around us. An experience in the strict sense that has neither of those features is part of what I call the *inner flow*, the realm of our intimate subjectivity, which is either inward-directed or has non-presentational phenomenology. Perhaps the inner flow encompasses what is sometimes called proprietary cognitive phenomenology, the 'what it is like' to have an occurring thought of some kind, like a belief or entertaining a supposition. Desires and other emotional attitudes are also likely to have aspects that are entirely non-worldly, even if they can be directed to the world outside too. Bodily sensation like proprioception can also lack both outward-directed presentational phenomenology and phenomenal objectivity, and in that case, they are part of the inner flow. I am not taking a stance with respect to what constitutes the outer flow and the inner flow. Perhaps the inner flow is entirely constituted by bodily sensation with some sort of inner-directed presentational phenomenology, or perhaps there are phenomenological aspects of it, such as cognitive phenomenology, which lack presentational phenomenology altogether. I am going to leave many options open, because I am not interested in the metaphysics of experience here, but in accounting for its temporal aspects. And for that end, it is sufficient to distinguish the worldly aspects of our phenomenology from the non-worldly ones.

1.5 Believing, experiencing, and projecting time

Many aspects of our experience can be said to be temporal. Some of them have a more qualitative flavour and are more clearly part of what is worldly in our experience. We see things moving, feel them change temperature, and hear them getting far away from us. Others are less clearly worldly and seem to be somehow more independent from qualitative elements, for instance the awareness that a certain sound lasted for a few seconds, regardless of its pitch, or that there was a succession of notes or of coloured flashes, regardless of the exact variety that entered in the succession, as when we focus on the rhythm of the succession. Still others seem to involve our own experiences primarily, rather than the world. For instance, we are aware of the succession of our experiences, and also of their own duration. Whether we are aware of those things independently from the awareness of the temporal properties of the events we are presented to is an open, and not easy, question, that I will address in the book.

Here I want to point out that certain temporal experiences seem to lie somewhat in between the strict sense and the broad sense of experience, as sketched above. Phenomenological characters that are connected with temporal extensions and succession seem, in certain cases, not to be confined to what we can experience 'in one go', but maintain that element of immediateness that disqualifies them as experiences merely in the broad sense. I will talk of *overarching phenomenology* to discuss this idea of an experience that somehow exceeds its temporal limits. In other words, certain aspects of our phenomenology 'inform' us of the existence of the content of other experiences, or perhaps of their existence. More specifically, I will talk of *feelings of persistence* for those outward experiences that tell us that the objects that are phenomenally presented to us did not just pop up out of thin air, and they are likely not to disappear very shortly. And I will talk of *awareness of succession* for that phenomenology that puts us in contact with our past and our future, the feeling that the experience that we are presently having is not alone in the temporal dimension, but it was preceded by others and it is likely to be succeeded by others.

One of the experiences that will be investigated at length in this book is our experience of the passage of time, as the more 'pure' or less qualitative temporal experience. The passage of time can be experienced in many ways. First, a plausible starting hypothesis is that it is very common to have the *belief* that time passes or flows. Certain recent results in experimental philosophy have cast doubts on this assumption and tried to debunk it as yet another philosophers' (and psychologists') prejudice. However, those studies seem to target mainly what may be called the *Priorian Belief* in the passage of time (after Arthur Prior), namely a metaphysically heavyweight belief according to which 'the only events and objects that exist are those in the present moment' and 'which objects exist, and what properties those objects have, *changes*.'[5] The (partially) negative results are compatible with the hypothesis that it is indeed constitutive of experience to have what I call a *Metaphysically Lightweight*

---

[5] Examples of the vignettes that Andrew Latham, Kristie Miller, and James Norton have used to test the hypothesis that there is a folk belief in the passage of time (Latham et al. 2020b: 364).

belief in the passage of time—roughly, the awareness that we are constantly under an updating of our experience, that the temporal location that we experience is never the same. I do not think that one needs to put metaphysical flesh on the bones of such a belief to have it, and thus as such its content is compatible with various metaphysics of time and indeed indifferent to it, since it is not committed with respect to the nature of time itself. Is it, however, committed with respect to how time appears or feels to us?

In talking about the metaphysically lightweight belief, I have characterized it as an awareness involving our own experiences. I did not use the word awareness in a phenomenologically charged way, but as a mere cognitive awareness, as when we say that we are aware of the recent change in power. However, it is not implausible to think that we have such a cognitive awareness in virtue of having a phenomenologically charged awareness of the passage of time, namely in virtue of a phenomenal character of experience in the strict sense that suggests to us the metaphysically lightweight belief in the passage of time. In other words, there may be a cogent phenomenology of the passage of time, one that is correctly albeit indirectly described by experience-based claims such as 'time passes' or 'few seconds have passed since...'.

The conclusion is that the answer to the previous question may well be: yes. I do not think that it is plausible that our feeling that time passes has a perceptual nature, namely that our perceptual phenomenology somehow tracks the passage of time, as it tracks different colours, the distinction between movement and stasis, and whether there is a face looking at us. If so, experience-based claims about the passage of time are better explained by resorting to a sensationalist strategy. As far as we also find passage in the world then, it has to be because we somehow *project* it. It can be a direct projection, in the sense that we misattribute the phenomenal character to the content of our experience, when it is a feature of its vehicle. Or it can be an indirect projection. An example of indirect projection is when we say to someone that their belief in the existence of god is but a projection of their fear to die. It does not mean that they are mistaking a sensational element of their phenomenology for something that is presented to them, but rather that they are interpreting reality on the ground of what they feel. Analogously, we may come to believe that time passes in the world outside, because it makes sense to believe it, given our phenomenology. When it comes to temporal experience, both senses of projection are relevant.[6]

---

[6] I use the terminology that Bardon (2023) suggests adopting with respect to the distinction between what Kail (2007) calls *feature* projection (direct) and *explanatory* projection (indirect).

1.6 Temporal experience: an overview of what follows

Talking about temporal experience allows for no shortcut and providing a rough summary of a theory risks misleading rather than illuminating, perhaps even more often than with other topics also because of the 'instability' of the terminology. However, beginning to read a book without having an idea of where the author is going may be unilluminating, if not frustrating or outright boring. Therefore, I will now do my best to give an overall idea of the theory that is defended in the book.

Chapters 2 to 5, the core of the book, are each dedicated to various types of temporal experience: detection of change, awareness of having experiences in succession, awareness of the present, and experience of the passage of time. One may wonder why I choose a structure that follows a division in topics, rather than the various parts of my theory. One reason is that the various theses that constitute my theory are more or less dedicated to each of those types of temporal experience. More deeply, there is little agreement among scholars on what it takes to provide a theory of temporal experience. Therefore, it is necessary to specify the object of the theory while arguing for the theory itself.

As for the theory itself, the *atomist dynamic model* of temporal experience that I defend throughout the book is based on four central theses. First, experiences are temporally atomic, in the sense that they are not made up of parts that are themselves experiences. Our conscious lives are made up of moments that are isolated from anything that precedes or follows. I also argue that those moments are themselves not temporally extended, although they can contain dynamic information about a changing world. Second, there are overarching aspects of temporal experience, aspects that in some sense exceed the present moment and put us in contact with the past and the future. Even if each experience is isolated from the other, it comes with an awareness of continuity with the past and the future, such that it can be described as the intertwining of an inner flow and an outer flow of consciousness. Such a continuity should not be overestimated, since our experience has more gaps in full-blown phenomenology than we ordinarily tend to think. Although a succession of experiences can be perfectly determined phenomenally with respect to a detail that is in the focus of our attention, a lot of conscious aspects of our lives have an amorphous phenomenology, and sometimes it is only postdictively that we can interpret what we just experienced as an experience of this or that. For instance, imagine you are watching a fly flying around. The movements of the fly are in the focus of your attention and your awareness of them is fully determined. However, while watching the fly flying you also hear the whining of Petunia the guinea pig and in the distance the neighbour rehearsing the trumpet. Those aspects are not in the focus of your attention, and indeed *that* you were hearing the whining and the trumpet is something that you can realize only afterwards, maybe because Petunia got definitely louder all of a sudden, or because the neighbour is particularly annoying to you today. The consequence is that our stream of consciousness is much less smooth than the metaphor of a stream or flow may suggest. Third, all we experience we experience now, when also our experiences happen. But the present of our life does not appear in any specific temporal way; it does not appear *as* present, and certainly not as past or as future. It is only through thoughts and more abstract representations that we can give to our experience an explicit temporal structure, with a temporal focus on an ordered sequence of moments. Fourth, our belief that time passes is grounded in a modification of our awareness of succession. We are aware not only of occupying a temporal location that is connected with past and future ones, but also of the dynamicity of such a connection. Temporal experience is inherently unstable, because our experiences are constantly renovating themselves. We are aware that every experience we find ourselves in is inexorably destined to get old and be exchanged for an upcoming new one. This is something we are aware of in some intimate and phenomenally cogent way. The sixth and last chapter of the book is an attempt to explain how the theory that is defended in the previous chapters must be understood in the context of the austere metaphysics of the so-called block universe view.

2

Change and movement

It was a spot which returned upon the memory of those who loved it
with an aspect of peculiar and kindly congruity. Smiling champaigns
of flowers and fruit hardly do this, for they are permanently harmo-
nious only with an existence of better reputation as to its issues than
the present.

Thomas Hardy, *The Return of the Native*, Chap. 1 (1878)

In this chapter, I focus on the 'qualitative' aspects of temporal experience,
such as those involving phenomenal awareness of change and movement.
The thread will be how to account for the indirect characterization of our
phenomenology that experience-based claims about change and movement
provide. Examples of such claims are not difficult to find: 'The fork fell from
the table to the floor', 'the noise is getting louder', 'the smell of burnt pizza is
going away'. In Section 2.1. *The experiences of change*, I set up the explanan-
dum of the chapter, namely the phenomenology of detection of change, in
the context of the more general inquiry into temporal experience. In Section
2.2. *Pure and qualitative temporality*, I give a taxonomy of different temporal
elements that experience seems to present us with along the pure-qualitative
spectrum. In Section 2.3. *Snapshot views*, I discuss and criticize accounts
according to which neither our experiences nor our experiential contents are
temporally extended. In Section 2.4. *Specious present views* and in Section 2.5.
Molecularism and postdictive illusions, I discuss and criticize accounts according to which either our experiential contents or both our experiences and
our experiential contents are temporally extended. In the last two sections,
Section 2.6. *Dynamic instantaneous contents* and Section 2.7. *Change and
succession*, I elaborate my view, an atomist dynamic model in which the phenomenology of change and motion is linked to the idea that certain detection
systems present us with objects with dynamic state properties, namely properties that involve movement and change, but that are presented in temporally
unextended experiences.

Temporal Experience. Giuliano Torrengo, Oxford University Press. © Giuliano Torrengo (2024).
DOI: 10.1093/9780191937804.003.0002

2.1 The experiences of change

Our experiences follow one another in a smooth succession. Sometimes while remaining qualitatively constant, as when we stay put and watch over a still panorama, other times while being different from one another, as when we walk and shift our perspective on an otherwise motionless room, and still other times by presenting us with something that changes or moves, as when all of a sudden we hear a noise and see the cat jumping off the table, a glass shattered on the ground. Although it may be dubious that the first example is an experience of change at all, the second and third cases clearly show ways in which our phenomenology can be described in terms of change. The experience of our own experiences changing, as the one we have when walking in an empty room, can be labelled *awareness of succession*. The experience of things around us moving, varying in colour and size, producing rhythmic sounds, changing smell, and so on, can be labelled *detection of (displacement and) change*. This chapter will be mainly concerned with the phenomenology of the latter kind of experience, while the former will be the focus of the next one.

Traditionally, philosophers and psychologists have discussed the problem of how it is possible to experience change and movement, given that it seems natural to think that we are always presented with what happens at one time only.[1] To see the point, variations of the following considerations are made. There is a difference between realizing, on the basis not only of perception, but also memory and reasoning, that a fork *has fallen* from the table to the floor (we see it on the floor, we remember that it was on the table, and we infer that it fell), and seeing that the fork *is falling* on the floor, by attending to the very fall when it is happening. This phenomenological contrast strongly suggests that motion, and possibly change in general, is one of the features that shows up in perceptual experience. We do not just notice that our experiences have changed, but our experiences are often as of a world that changes. When this happens, we are *presented* with change, as we are with colour- and shape-properties of the objects around us. But while something can be red or round as it is at a virtually unextended temporal location, change involves more than one temporal location, and thus seems to require that our awareness be somehow spread across an interval of time. We do not just have successive experiences and then deduce information about motion and change from them via memory and reasoning, but we 'take on' whole successions in one breath, so to speak. Are we hence

---

[1] The references are basically most of the ones that I will give in the rest of the chapter. For recent *loci classici* of the puzzle, see Kelly (2005) and LePoidevin (2007). I am aware that my formulation can be seen as non-standard; but it is also true that there are almost as many formulations of the problem as discussion of it, so I am not sure there is a standard formulation to begin with.

mistaken in thinking that experience, at least perceptual experience, always presents us with what happens at one time only? Or are we mistaken in thinking that we perceive change in the same way we perceive 'static' qualitative features of objects?

There are various proposals to solve the tension between what the phenomenology of perception of change suggests and our naive understanding of how perception is temporally constrained, and wide disagreement about their efficacy among both philosophers and psychologists. We can distinguish three general ideas, which correspond roughly to three of the four strategies about the corresponding experience-based claims, which I introduced in Section 1.3. One can go *error-theoretic*, and deny that there is any perception of temporally extended entities, and a fortiori of change or movement. (This is the so-called *snapshot* view.) The difference between seeing the fork falling and realizing that it has fallen is not thus a difference in phenomenology, or at least not in perceptual phenomenology. One can endorse a *content* strategy in the *representationalist* fashion, and maintain that instantaneous or very short mental episodes can present us with temporally wider contents. The phenomenology of our perceptual contact with change and movement is thus accurately captured by experience-based claims like the ones above, but we are mistaken if we think that our experiencing is as well temporally extended. (This is the so-called *atomist* or *retentional* view.) Or one can interpret the content in a *relationist* way, and maintain that the phenomenology is accurate, but it is temporally extended experiences (albeit short-lived ones) that present us with temporally extended contents. (This is the so-called *molecularist* or *extensionalist* view.)

As we will see, the situation is more complex than this rough summary suggests. Moreover, although the focus of the chapter is detection of movement and change, I will inevitably also introduce certain considerations that concern the awareness of succession, which will be the primary focus of the next chapter. Partly this is because certain interpretations of the phenomenology of change conflate the two phenomena. But more importantly it is because my aim here is to investigate the phenomenology of detection of change and motion in the context of temporal experience at large.

2.2 Pure and qualitative temporality

Change is just one, although allegedly quite a central one, of the temporal features to which we have access through phenomenal awareness. To a first approximation, we can divide the temporal properties that experience presents us with into two classes, the *qualitative* temporal properties and the *pure* temporal properties. Roughly, qualitative temporal properties involve some relation between non-temporal properties of objects (and experiences) and temporal structure, while the pure ones involve temporal structure only. I take change to be a central feature of our perceptual experience because it is the prototypical qualitative temporal property. As the prototypical pure, non-qualitative, temporal property I take passage. Although I introduced the distinction in terms of two classes, it is probably better to think of those properties as distributed along a spectrum.[2] For reasons of simplicity and space, I will consider only the following: *change, movement, succession, persistence,* and *duration.*

Change is prototypically qualitative because as much as it requires distinct temporal locations (ordered in a succession), it also requires *distinct qualities* located there. And the nature of the 'requires' is similar in both cases. That is, it requires not as a mere matter of a conceptual link (assuming that the concept of change entails that there are temporally located qualities); rather, an *experience* of change must, loosely speaking, have parts that are experiences of distinct qualities: different colours, shapes, locations, and the like. I say 'loosely speaking' because both whether experiences are temporally extended and whether temporally extended experiences have parts that are themselves experiences are open issues in the contemporary debate, which I will discuss shortly. Hence, an experience of change is essentially 'impure' with respect to temporality. Maybe an experience of change is a *precondition* for any experience to count as having a temporal aspect whatsoever. If so (which is still not to say that any temporal experience can be *reduced* to an experience of change), our temporal phenomenology is never pure. However, it may still make sense of talking about a spectrum of more and less pure temporal experiences, and in that spectrum change firmly holds its position at (or very close to) the qualitative end.

At the conceptual level, *movement* seems to be merely a specific way in which things can change. Movement is change of (spatial) position, while what we may aptly call qualitative change is change of some other properties, such as colour, shape, pitch, intensity of pleasure, and maybe also quality of smell. Indeed, the example that I gave in the opening, that of a falling fork off the table, is an example of motion as much as of change. However, there are at least two good reasons to keep them separate from a psychological point of

[2] Even the conceptualization in terms of a unidimensional spectrum is probably a simplification. For one, it is not clear that there is a distribution without 'overlap' in the spectrum, and—more importantly perhaps—the allocation within the spectrum may be highly contextual, depending both on the aims of the psychological or philosophical inquiry at issue, and the sensorial modalities involved.

view. Firstly, it seems that experiencing change of location is *not* the same as experiencing movement, although the two phenomenal characters very often go hand in hand. While there may be a conceptual connection between movement and change of position, an experience of movement may not involve an experience of change of position. Certain experiences can be described as cases in which they come apart. For instance, the waterfall illusion (Crane 1988) and some of Wertheimer's phi-phenomena (Hoerl 2015: 7). Secondly, the timings of our neural processes underpinning our experiences of qualitative change are likely to be different from those underpinning our experiences of movement (Arstila 2015b, 2015c).

Succession is an interesting borderline case. Although there is a sense in which we can abstract from the qualitative, non-temporal elements involved in succession,[3] and see it as a pure temporal feature, the experience of succession is not a purely temporal one insofar as—like experiencing change—it involves an experience of different qualities. The point here is not where exactly to locate the experience of succession (remember, talk of a spectrum here is merely heuristics, and basically any claim about where to 'put' a property is a decision, and thus subject to negotiation); rather, I am interested in highlighting that the experience of succession can be phenomenally contrasted with two quite different foils. On the one hand, we can contrast detection of succession with detection of *persistence*. In order to articulate such a contrast, it is crucial to appeal to the qualitative aspects involved in the experience. Roughly speaking, the difference between succession and persistence is that in the first case we experience qualitative *variation* through an interval, whereas in the second case we experience qualitative *constancy* through an interval. On the other hand, we can contrast situations in which we experience information about a temporal order with situations in which we do not. For instance, we can come to know (or believe), on the basis of experience, that a certain event e_1 happened *before* a certain event e_2 as opposed to the case in which two stimuli are so close together temporally that it is not possible to distinguish which came first. And we can be in situations in which it is possible to discern that two stimuli are not simultaneous without having perceptual information about their order (Mitrani et al. 1986). In both cases the experience is not purely temporal. And both cases rely on the experience of succession coming with a *qualitative profile*, not merely a *temporal profile*. Think of the fact that there is a difference in qualitative content between an experience of succession as exemplified by

---

[3] If that is true, could we not do the same with change as well? Maybe, but then what exactly is the difference between an experience of 'purified' change and an experience of succession?

an arpeggio *do-mi-so* (say), and one exemplified by a structurally homologous arpeggio *do-so-mi*. We can think of an abstract temporal structure, made up of empty slots (slot^1, slot^2, etc.), each with a quasi-metric[4] index (m_1, m_2, etc.) that encodes their duration, and ordered by a relational 'skeleton'. Roughly something like the following:

$$\text{slot}^1{}_{m1} > \text{slot}^2{}_{m2} > \text{slot}^3{}_{m3}$$

While the temporal profile is given by the metric and the relational skeleton, the qualitative one is given by an assignment of qualitative content to the slots of a certain temporal profile. The qualitative and the temporal profiles together can be seen as the bearer of higher-order (or gestalt) properties. For instance, the *rate of change*, and the *rhythm* of change. Notice also that 'experience of succession' is ambiguous between experiencing a temporal structure as just described, and being aware that our own experiences succeed one another, what I have labelled awareness of succession in Section 2.1. And this is probably not entirely by chance, because it seems that we can come to know of a succession either in a very direct way, as by seeing or hearing it, or by recalling what we experienced, or yet by something in-between, namely by being generally aware of our own experience being constantly refreshed, as it were.

The experience of *duration* is analogous in many respects to that of succession. Firstly, there is also, in this case, an ambiguity between a direct presentation of durations and their sizes, and the more general awareness of how much time has passed, also concerning considerably long stretches of our lives. Consider first experiences that are somehow phenomenally 'unified' (Section 3.5.1). For instance, the experience of watching a plane on the runway start moving, and then following it by sight until it takes off and disappears into the clouds. Regardless of the problem of how exactly to account for the continuity that seems apparent in the whole experience, such experiences are expected to come with some information about their overall duration and the durations of their parts. Did the taxiing phase last more than the acceleration before take-off? Did the whole thing last more than the walk from the car to the fence outside the runaway? And the same is true also of experiences that are not phenomenally unified (or at least not trivially so). Although there are ways of 'chopping up' the experience(s) of a lazy afternoon in the countryside which are more natural than others, and although it may be easier for the more

---

[4] With 'quasi-metric' I mean what Peacocke (2004: 69) means when he talks of unit-free perceptual experiences of magnitude.

natural ways to assign a duration to each, the question 'how long did it last?' can in principle always receive an experience-based reply (although one which may be quite inaccurate).

I think that there are good reasons to put duration a bit more towards the pure end of the spectrum than succession also in the case of the more direct experiences of duration that concerns us here. Historically, duration has been taken as a very good candidate for the purely temporal, at the same level (because identical to?), or perhaps even more basic than passage.[5] But in the framework of this book, we should take it as purer than succession, but still not as paradigmatically pure. Two things should be noticed in favour of this decision. First, any *perceivable* duration has a qualitative aspect. The analogy with succession is instructively imperfect here. For succession, qualitative variation is essentially involved, if we contrast it with the case of detection of persistence. For duration, it seems plausible that at some level of description we individuate durations on the basis of a persisting quality. But the individuation of such a persisting quality is not sensitive to the difference between the case in which we are presented with qualitative variation (succession) and the case in which we are presented with qualitative constancy (persistence). It may be tempting to say that in perceiving durations we are presented with the persistence of *something* (regardless of its qualitative profile)—maybe the perceptual fields themselves (or their unity as the object of some 'sensorium commune').[6] But I think the temptation should be resisted; and this leads us to the second reason for taking duration not as paradigmatically pure. Second, every experience of duration comes with a metric or quasi-metric aspect to it. A 'quasi-metric' aspect is one in virtue of which one is aware of at least some rough comparisons between experienced durations, even when such awareness is not very accurate. It is crucial here to realize how ubiquitous our experience of duration is. As we have seen, at long timescales, there is a metric or quasi-metric aspect in our being aware of something having had a duration. But also at very short timescales, differences in experienced durations are present. This metric or quasi-metric element is what makes the experience of duration impure with respect to temporality. In what follows, I will treat change and movement as prototypical 'impure' qualitative temporal experiences.[7]

---

[5] For different reasons, Kant (1782 [1989]) and Bergson (1889 [2003]) come to mind.

[6] If so, it would be quite natural to take duration as a paradigmatically pure temporal property. See Chapter 3 on the temporal *dis*unity of consciousness, though.

[7] As mentioned at the beginning of this section, I take the experience of the *passage* of time to be the prototypical 'pure' one. I will talk extensively about it in Chapter 5.

2.3 Snapshot views

Let us then come back to experience-based claims about change and movement. What kind of indirect characterization of our phenomenology are we giving when we say things like 'the fork fell (I saw it)', 'I am hearing the ambulance getting closer', or 'the smell of burned pizza is diminishing; thanks for opening the window'? In this section I discuss and criticize views that share the atomist structure of the view that I will defend, in that they are based on the assumption that experiences are virtually instantaneous, but which differ from my atomist dynamic model in that according to them dynamicity is a feature only of sequences of experiences, and not of individual experiences.

Early modern empiricists have traditionally appealed to a theory of change and motion experience that strongly suggests an error-theoretic strategy. Here is an often-quoted passage by Scottish 'philosopher of common sense' Thomas Reid:

> [...] if we speak strictly and philosophically, no kind of succession can be an object of the senses, or of consciousness; because the operation of both are confined to the present point of time. [... O]n that account the motion of a body, which is a successive change of place, could not be observed by the sense alone without the aid of memory. (Reid 1785 [2002]: 270)

Reid does not comment on the phenomenological contrast I mention above, between the direct experience of movement (seeing a second hand of a clock moving), and the indirect one (realizing from what we see and remember that the hour hand of a clock has moved). Hence it is not clear whether he would think that talking of a specific phenomenology of movement (as opposed to stasis) as legitimate. If he did not, the traditional cinematic view entails a form of error-theory strategy with respect to experience-based claims involving movement and change: they are not accurate indirect descriptions of the phenomenology of change and movement (as opposed to the perception of static scenes). Regardless, Reid is clear on the claim that *perception* (alone) does not present us with changes or movements. More up-to-date versions of this *snapshot* view do not deny the relevance of the phenomenological distinction. In those forms of snapshot theory, the instantaneous perceptual content is either permeated by information from short-term memory (Le Poidevin 2007) or used downstream by some resemblance mechanism that monitors the transition between the snapshots (Watzl 2013; Chuard 2017). Hence even if the experience-based claims are misdescriptions of the perceptual content (and therefore, we are in the range of an error-theoretic strategy), there is a phenomenological distinction between a succession of 'static' experiences, such that we would report that nothing is changing or moving, and a succession of gradually changing experiences, such that we would report that something is changing or moving. However, it would be a mistake to characterize the difference in phenomenology as a difference in mere *perceptual* content. While the memory theory version of snapshot construes the phenomenological difference in terms of influence from short-term memory, the one based on the resemblance mechanism, which I will call the *cinematic* theory for brevity, construes it in terms of similarity constraints between the experiences. I will dwell on the latter and return to the former in the next section, discussing the atomistic specious present view.

How exactly, then, does the cinematic view explain the phenomenology of change and movement? Here is Philippe Chuard:

> [T]he phenomenology we seem to introspect when enjoying successive experiential states not only *supervenes upon*, but *reduces* to, those features of successions of snapshot [. . .]: the experiential properties of snapshots, their temporal arrangement, the gradual transitions in their successive contents, [. . .] and inability to detect small gaps and jumps [. . .]. (Chuard 2017: 125; emphasis in the text)[8]

Chuard is implicitly subsuming the phenomenology of change and movement to the awareness of continuous succession. This cannot be seen as a problem in this framework, since, according to the cinematic view, there are *no* perceptual experiences of change and movement.[9] This does not mean that there is no difference between having a (continuous) experience of succession and the mere fact that we have successive experiences. Indeed, it is precisely *this* difference that the theory aims at accounting for in terms of the features that Chuard mentions, specifically the relation of resemblance between the snapshots. The phenomenology of succession reduces to the succession of snapshots with *certain features*: if the succession does not have those very features, our phenomenology would be different, and indeed in pathological cases, in which the succession of experiences does not have those features, it *is* different (Heywood

---

[8] Chuard lists also 'our memories of previous experiences' in this passage, but this seems to be in tension with what he says just a few lines above: 'Memories, too, play a role: *not* in accounting for the dynamic phenomenology of sequences of snapshots, but our cognitive access to it [. . .]' (2017: 25; my emphasis).

[9] Cf. 'To be clear, the snapshot view isn't trying to explain how we do, in fact, have temporal experiences. We don't, the snapshot theorist surmises' (2017: 126).

and Kentridge 2009). As Christoph Hoerl pointed out, appealing to the *recognition* of similarities between the snapshots is problematic here. If the aim is to explain our awareness of the similarities between what we are presented with in each snapshot, appealing to our awareness of the similarities between the snapshots themselves seems to be of little explanatory power (2017: 179). But even setting aside this problem, my point here is that the explanation cannot be *merely* in terms of the resemblance between the contents of the snapshots. Even if an experience of movement is partially constituted by the successive presentation of the same object at two slightly different locations on a similar background, it also requires features that involve *relations between the snapshot themselves*. More precisely, it requires sensitivity to the rate of intake of information.

Here is Chuard again: '[t]he *pace* of succession of experiential states [. . .] is crucial in accounting for their phenomenology, *provided* such pace falls within certain limits' (2017: 125; emphasis in the text). Although it is rarely noticed, this last feature puts the cinematic view in tension with the thesis of transparency (Section 1.4). Negative transparency, the idea that we are not introspectively aware of the features of our perceptual experiences themselves, but only of what we are perceptually presented with, seems violated. At least, that is so if the explanation of the dynamicity of the phenomenology of succession requires *awareness* of such relational features of our own snapshot experiences. I will discuss in the next section this aspect in relation to an analogous problem (also rarely noted) for the molecularlist take on the specious present approach. Here I comment on a strictly related problem for the cinematicist. As the last quote makes clear, the phenomenology of continuity is said to depend on there being certain *temporal boundaries* within which the succession of instantaneous experiences, given their pace, happens.

But how are those temporal boundaries supposed to be *relevant* for the difference in phenomenology? It seems plausible that the fact that a sequence of experiences (or the unfolding of an experience) happens within those temporal boundaries is what determines our 'inability to detect small gaps and jumps'. Consider for instance the slow movement of the hour hand in a clock. We cannot detect it because the displacement between the twelve position and the one position (say) happens through a minute interval. If it happened through a second interval (as does for the aptly named swift hand), we would notice it.[10] But given that those boundaries *cannot* be the boundaries of the

---

[10] Cf. Delia Fara's argument (Fara 2001), discussed in Phillips (2011) and Hoerl (2013).

content of our experiences, since the boundaries of our experiences are supposed to be much shorter in the cinematic view, it looks like the theory has to take their effects on the overall phenomenology as a brute fact, which it cannot explain any further (unless we appeal to a higher-order monitoring mechanism). Everybody has to accept brute facts sooner or later, but arguably, this brute fact does not sit very well with the general spirit of the proposal, because it involves what seems to be an awareness of a temporally extended content. In the next section, I comment on positions that take those boundaries to be the very boundaries of the content of our perceptual experiences.

2.4 Specious present views

Contrary to the snapshot views, other approaches consider the presence of a phenomenal contrast between the contemplation of a static scene (which may prompt the judgement that something mov*ed*) and the vivid, dynamic experience of change to be evidence that change and movement should be taken as part of the *content* of perception. Those views differ from mine since they entail that detecting change and motion entails experiencing a relation between features instantiated at different times along a temporal interval. Whether they differ also in not embracing an atomist, but rather a molecularist conception of the structure of experience depends on further details. As we have seen, traditional empiricist accounts of change and succession downplay the perceptual aspect of the phenomenology of change, in favour of the intuition that perceptions are always instantaneous. Other accounts see the phenomenology as a sign of the sui generis nature of the contribution of the recent past to present perception. In general, it is not universally agreed that phenomenology speaks in favour of change being part of the content in exactly the same manner as colour or shape, say, are part of the content of a static visual experience. Let us call the views that entail that we are perceptually presented with extended entities *specious present views*.

Specious present views maintain that the *phenomenal present*, what we can take on all at once in experiencing (Section 4.1.2.1), is 'saddle-back shaped', to paraphrase James (1890: Chap. XV). Those views are thus in line with the content strategy for experience-based claims about change and movement, according to which claims such as 'the ball is rolling down the slope' are cogent indirect characterizations of the perceptual content of experience and not mischaracterizations of the phenomenology (Section 1.3). The specious present is (or rather corresponds to) a *short temporal width* in which movement and

change that are quick enough to be discernible, but not too fast to be undetectable, can thus be experienced directly. The temporal width has a *lower
boundary*, below which lies the 'perceptual instant' or 'window of simultaneity',
that is an interval in which it is not possible to discern two successive stimuli as
successive, and an *upper boundary*, above which we are no longer *perceptually*
presented with a continuous movement or change (although iconic memories
or short-term memories may occur). Whether we can be said to be aware of
the boundaries of the specious present is a matter for Chapter 4; here I want
to stress the explanatory import of the existence of those boundaries. It is in
virtue of the fact that the phenomenal present has lower and upper boundaries
that we perceive change and movement, although only short ones. This point
is very important, so let me repeat it in different words. The core hypothesis
of the specious present view is that the lower and upper temporal boundaries
in which movement and change detection happens are boundaries of the content *of experiences*. And this hypothesis is taken to have explanatory import
with respect to the phenomenology of movement and change perception,
as opposed to that of experiences of static scenes, which can be experiences
of change and movement only in the sense that from them, together with
memory, we can *infer* that change or movement occurred.

The core hypothesis is compatible with at least two varieties of the specious
present view. This is so, because the thesis that the present of our perceptual
experience is specious does not entail (although it does not exclude either) that
the experiences themselves follow the same fate. Even if in experiencing movement and change we are presented with temporally extended contents, it is not
clear whether such contents impose any constraints *on the temporal structure
of those experiences*. Indeed, the two main varieties of specious present views—
atomism and *molecularism*[11]—differ precisely on how experiences that have
temporally extended contents are themselves temporally structured.

2.4.1 Atomistic specious present

According to the *atomistic specious present view* (aka *retentionalism*), the temporal structure of the experience does *not* mirror the temporal structure of
what is presented in experience. While perception presents us with temporally

---

[11] As almost everyone who writes on this issue notices, we have to live with a bit of a terminological
jungle here. Perhaps the most common alternative labelling (which I mention in the main text here) is
extensionalism (for what I call here molecularism) and *retentionalism* (for what I call here atomism).
Notice that I use 'atomism' as short for 'atomistic specious present view', when there is no danger of
ambiguity; 'atomism' per se does well apply both to retentionalism and the various snapshot views.

extended successions, changes, and duration, the experiences themselves—through which we are aware of those durative contents—are punctate. I will come back to this aspect in Section 3.1.2, where I characterize them as *virtually instantaneous* (as opposed to *actually* instantaneous). For the purpose at issue in this chapter, what is important is that if the experiences are punctate, they do not have temporal parts, which are themselves experiences that mirror the parts of the extended content. And this can be either because they have no temporal extension, and hence no (proper) temporal parts at all, or because while extended they cannot be divided into parts. If experiences are punctate but they present us with extended contents, then the temporal extended entity with which we are in perceptual contact can be either *simply presented* to us, without any tensed mode of presentation, or they can be presented in a *tensed manner*; that is, with temporal parts of it presented as past (or with different degree of pastness) and a part presented as present (and possibly also with parts presented as future).[12] In both cases, we perceive movement or change because of the qualitative variation of the *moments* that compose the temporal *interval* (Section 1.1) that is presented within the boundaries of the specious present. Successions, with their different paces and rhythms, and durations are also presented in the same (or analogous) way, as metric or quasi-metric features of the content (see Figure 2.1).

E_0 E_0

e_0 e_0

MOLECULARISM   ATOMISM

Figure 2.1 Molecularism and atomism

Although not everybody agrees that atomism entails representationalism (for features such as change and movement at least), it clearly sits better with a representationalist understanding of the content strategy. For one thing, it is unclear how an instantaneous or short-lived mental event can be in some substantive relation with something that lags behind it *more* than the minimal time required to influence the mental processes underpinning its experience. But the parts of the presented interval that are farther away from the upper boundary are presumably in that situation. I said *substantive* relation because

---

[12] This is the distinction that Barry Dainton (2008b) makes between modal and nonmodal retentionalism. Geoffrey Lee (2015) is an example of non-modal atomism, Jan Almäng (2014) of a modal one. This distinction is not crucial in the context in this chapter, but I will come back to it in Chapters 4 and 5.

what we have called weak relationism (Section 1.3) is formulated in terms of the thesis that the relation with the external entity at least partially *explains* the what-is-like, the phenomenology of the experienced content. Of course, it may be that the relation is mediated by a causal chain that is longer than the minimum required to elaborate the stimulus. But then the contribution of the relation relies on a *retention* of the recent past. Although talking of 'retention' here does not entail that the information about the recent past that is integrated with the information about the present must be a form of second presentation as past of what was presented as present (for instance, this is not the case for atomists such as Grush and Lee, who indeed reject the label 'retentionalism' for their positions), it does entail that the intrinsic features of the punctate event in question crucially contribute to the explanation of the phenomenology. The best understanding of atomism is thus in terms of a temporally extended *representational* content, through which we are presented with an interval composed by moments (possibly qualitatively variated). There is definitely room both for an *internalist* understanding of the representational content in question, according to which the content is entirely constituted by the intrinsic feature of the punctate state, and for an *externalist* understanding of the content, in which the intrinsic features are relational nonetheless, or in which the content is constituted by elements that are not intrinsic (how and if this position is really distinguishable from weak relationism is debatable).

The representationalist understanding of the atomistic specious present helps us also to distinguish it from the snapshot memory theory, to which it bears certain similarities. According to the latter, the difference in phenomenology between observing a change and realizing, on the ground of observation, that a change happened is not entirely perceptual in itself. Although the retention of a short-lived iconic memory alters the phenomenology of perception, it does not *constitute* the content. The point can be made somehow more vivid by stating that in the memory theory case the content is punctate *since* it is not constituted by the retention (the retention just contributes a concurrent iconic memory), while in the atomist case the content *is* constituted by the retention and thus it is extended. However, it is not obvious how the atomist can explain the fact that the content is extended in terms of a representational feature of the punctate mental event. It could be, after all, that the stimulus in the recent past contributes to the representational content of the punctate event, but its contribution does not lead to the presentation of an *extended* interval, only to an enriched punctate content. This brings to the fore a problem for the specious present atomist, which I will discuss in more depth later (Section 2.6.2), while confronting the dynamic snapshot view with specious present atomism. The problem can be summarized in the following question: how can one be presented with non-instantaneous contents *during* an instantaneous experience?

Regardless of the exact way the atomist answers the question, what is important here to notice is that in order to use the presence of the temporal boundaries to explain the phenomenal contrast at issue (perceived change vs. inferred chance), they need to rely on the following principle.

Principle of Simultaneous Awareness (PSA). If one is aware of a succession or duration, one is necessarily aware of it at some one moment.[13]

The idea is that the phenomenological difference between the second hand and the hour hand experience is accounted for in terms of an extended content that presents us with a variation (through time in the position of the hand) vs. an extended content that presents us a 'monotonous' interval (no distinguishable variation in the positions of the hand) 'during' or 'in' a punctate mental event. The motivation behind PSA can be seen in a sort of *relational constraint*. Assuming that movement is a relation between the position of the entity that moves at a certain time and its position at another, the relational constraint says that we need both positions in the same experience to be aware of the relation between them. As much as in the spatial case, to be phenomenally aware of a spatial relation between two billiard balls, say, we need to have both in the same visual field. This sounds very close to requiring that it be *introspectively evident* both that certain mental events are instantaneous (since we conclude that the experiences' parts are simultaneous) and that through them we are presented with extended events (since we are aware of a relation between features instantiated at different times). It has to be evident to introspection because there are alternative explanations of how we can become aware of a succession, for instance by an overarching phenomenology intrinsic to a much shorter experience, or through a temporally extended experience whose content is in turn temporally extended. Of course, those explanations may be faulty for independent reasons, but if we assume that the retentional is the obvious account, this suggests that we are relying on some alleged introspective evidence. Setting aside the fact that this blatantly violates temporal transparency, the point is that it seems wrong to *require* such introspective evidence. Whether perceptions are temporally extended or punctate

---

[13] Locus classicus is Miller (1984: 107). This is Phillips's (2014a: 140) formulation.

is a theoretical dispute, one that has to be balanced in terms of overall evidence, including empirical evidence from neuroscience.

2.4.2 Molecular specious present

Let us move to the *molecular specious present view* (aka *extensionalism*). Also, according to the molecularist, the presence of upper and lower boundaries *of experiences* for the intake of information that characterize perception is crucial in explaining the specific phenomenology of movement and change. The crucial difference is that the explanation does not rely on the PSA, but rather on the rival principle below.

> **Principle of Presentational Concurrence (PPC).** If one is aware of a succession or duration (that happens in an interval *i*), one is necessarily aware of it during the same interval i.[14]

Usually, the PPC is understood as embodying a *mirroring* intuition. When it comes to their temporal locations, the content of experience and the experiences themselves go hand in hand (see molecularism in Figure 2.1 above). There are various degrees of closeness of the mirroring (Lee 2014a). Metric mirroring is the strictest. If I hear the following three notes (see Figure 2.2): a punctuated quaver la_4, a quaver do_5, and a semiquaver si_4, my experience will have the same temporal skeleton: during a first quite brief experience I am presented with a la_4, then an even shorter one presents me with a do_5, and then a much shorter one with a si_4. (If I am presented with a silence after that, I will probably also have the sensation of an interrupted tune.)

Figure 2.2 Notes

Less strict versions of mirroring require that only the relations between the qualitative parts of the content are reflected in the structure of the experience, but not the metric (topological mirroring), or that only the overall temporal

---

[14] This is my formulation, which mimics the structure of Phillips's formulation of the PSA that I gave above. The classic formulation is '[t]he time interval occupied by a content which is before the mind is the very same time interval which is occupied by the act of presenting that very content before the mind' (Miller 1984: 107).

interval is reflected (structural mirroring, which is the one that my formulation of PPC captures). Notice that at temporal scales that are larger than the specious present, mirroring, even the metric one (at least roughly), is very plausible. If I recall correctly that during the weekend I had brunch with my husband in the late morning, then we went for a stroll in the park, and then we met friends for a coffee in a bistro, I have good reasons to think that it is not only those experienced events that unfold through time as I just described, but also that my experiences of them unfolded through time in roughly the same way and for the same duration. However, this does not entail that the same is true at much shorter timescales.

The point of appealing to the PPC is to explain the experience of continuous motion in terms of succession of experiences somehow bonded together in a specious present. This way of putting things raises immediately the suspicion that the molecularist specious present is hardly distinguishable from the resemblance-theory-based version of the snapshot view (cf. Hoerl 2017). As I pointed out above, the cinematicist seems to have to take the relevance of the temporal boundaries of experience for explaining the difference between perceptual experience of change and 'static' experiences as a *brute* fact. Is then the difference between the cinematicist and the molecularist simply that the latter, but not the former, calls what goes on between such boundaries *one* experience? Now, one may think that even if the answer to this question is yes, it does not mean that the difference between the two positions is shallow or merely verbal. The molecularist can insist that her further tenet is explanatorily relevant: the reason why one experiences change while looking at the second hand of a clock or listening to the quick succession of notes in a sonata by Scarlatti, but not while realizing that it is late by looking at the display of a watch that contains only minutes and hours, is that enough (but not too much) qualitative variation is present within the borders of *that experience* (e.g. an experience of a quick movement or an auditory succession).

Let me spell out in some more detail how such a reply can be elaborated by the molecularist. I distinguish what may be called *glue-molecularism* from *no-glue-molecularism*. Glue-molecularism is the idea that the experiential parts of which an auditory experience of a triplet (say) is made of are linked by a relation of *phenomenal unity*. Crucially, such a relation links the experiences themselves, and it is not a relation between their contents. An obvious problem with the glue version of the view is what to say about the connection (if any) between the obtainment of the relation of phenomenal unity between experiential parts and the resemblance relation between their contents. If phenomenal unity is external to the content of the experiences that binds, that is, if it can obtain between experiences *regardless* of their intrinsic features (think, for an analogy, of the temporal relation of succession, which is independent from the contents that binds), then it is not clear how it could have explanatory import with respect to a phenomenal contrast such as that between perception of motion and awareness of stasis.

In other words, what exactly does the 'glue' contribute to the experience? If somehow it interacts with the intrinsic features of the experiences, then the theory would need to rely on the very same resemblance constraints that the atomist postulates. Therefore, if we understand molecularism in this bottom-up way, by starting from the parts and building up a whole out of them by some gluing operation, the charge of superficial difference with the cinematic view stands.[15] But that is not the only way to understand molecularism. The no-glue version of it goes top-down, as it were, beginning with the whole, that is, the experience that extends throughout the entire specious present (hearing a fast triplet in a sonata, say) and carving out the experiential parts.

Think of PCC and the mirroring intuitions. There are temporal boundaries within which our intake of perceptual information happens 'in one go', so as to explain the phenomenal difference between dynamic and static perceptions. And those boundaries are the boundaries of the temporally extended experiences through which we are presented with changes and successions. Now, the mirror intuition is not only ambiguous with respect to how detailed the mirroring is supposed to be, whether metric, topological, or merely structural, for instance. But, more importantly here, it is also neutral with respect to the direction of explanation (if any): has the experience temporal structure because it reflects the temporal structure of the content, or is it the other way around? The difference can be expressed by saying that the molecularist can either rely on the idea that the temporal profile of experience is *inherited* by that of the content (as for Inheritance below), or on the idea that the temporal profile of the experience is *projected* onto that of the content (as for Projection below).

> **Inheritance.** An experience E_C with content C_E has a certain temporal profile because its content C_E has a certain temporal profile.
>
> **Projection.** The content C_E of an experience E_C has a certain temporal profile because E_C has a certain temporal profile.

---

[15] To be fair, Barry Dainton, who is the author who comes closest to what I describe here as glue-molecularism, would not agree with this latter reconstruction of the view, since, in his view, experience is gunky, it always divides up into other temporally extended experiences, hence there are no 'building blocks' to be linked together (Dainton 2000). But the problems above are still something that those who agree with his view have to face.

Some may find my claim of the neutrality of molecularism here mistaken. Ian Phillips, for instance, clearly states that Projection characterizes atomism while Inheritance characterizes molecularism: 'According to the cinematic view [his name for Lee's atomism], experiential temporal content is possessed in virtue of the intrinsic temporal properties of experience. Naïvité [his name for molecularism here] reverses the order of explanation: in the absence of illusion, the temporal structure of experience is (in part) determined by the temporal properties of the objects and events that one confronts' (Phillips 2014b: 145). This claim is certainly false if we interpret 'determined' to entail that (i) there is sameness of temporal length, (ii) atomism is true, and by 'intrinsic temporal properties of experience' we mean the temporal features of the mental event in question—which (regardless of the details of the atomistic view) is supposed to be punctate and thus definitely *shorter* than the experienced content. It is true if atomism is true and by 'intrinsic temporal properties of experience' one means the temporal features that are presented in virtue of the fact that the punctate event has certain intrinsic properties. However, the fact that the claim is true in that reading does not exclude that an analogous claim applied to molecularism is true in either reading. It may be that we experience a content as temporally extended (and as having a certain structure) in virtue of our experience being temporally extended (and having the same structure).

As I have hinted at above, while discussing the resemblance-theory-based version of the snapshot view, there is a rarely noticed tension between the mirroring intuition and the idea that temporal experience is transparent.[16] I take the tension to be serious, and indeed it puts the molecularist at an impasse. On the one hand, if the molecularist uses Projection and explains the unit of the presented interval within the boundaries in terms of the unity of the extended experience (assuming that that would not be just a reformulation of the glue view), they seem compelled to accept that we have an introspective awareness of the temporal structure of our own experience that is independent of what we are presented with through them (i.e. their content). Unless, perhaps, one is independently committed to a sort of higher-order theory of consciousness that comes with such a stark violation of transparency, this horn is a no go.[17] On the other hand, relying on Inheritance also may be in tension

---

[16] Hoerl (2018) discusses in detail a tension in Soteriou's and Phillips's take on Inheritance and their adherence to transparency, which will be of the utmost importance in Chapter 4. The problem I am discussing here is different and pertains to the role of the boundaries of the specious present.

[17] I say 'perhaps' because I am not entirely convinced that even a higher-order theory of consciousness can save the day here. The reason is that it is not clear to me how *diachronic* higher-order

with transparency. No-glue-molecularism agrees that the phenomenology of change depends on what we experience within certain temporal boundaries—those of the fundamental units of experience. But do we need to be *aware* of the temporal boundaries of what is presented in perceiving motion to explain our phenomenology? If the answer is no, the molecularist agrees with the cinematicist that the brute fact that there are temporal boundaries accounts for the phenomenology of change and motion. If the answer is yes, then at least negative transparency[18] is violated. While this per se is not fatal, the requirement that we are aware of the boundaries of the specious present, even if only indirectly through our awareness of the temporal extension of the contents of our perception, is burdensome for the molecularist.

Let us see where embracing the second horn leads the molecularist. The temporal boundaries of the content of perception clearly depend on features of our own mental life. Indeed, how much intake of information there can be at a given pace is something that very likely crucially depends on our physiology, and this more or less settles the phenomenological width of the specious present. However, awareness of temporal boundaries of the interval the perception presents us with, and thereby of the temporal width of our own experience, is something that we can gather indirectly, by virtue of being aware of a temporally extended content. Although this 'nested' explanation seems twisted, it is actually quite plausible. Think of the spatial case. Michael Martin argues that we are aware of the spatial boundaries of our visual field (and other perceptual fields, although things get complicated quickly with other modalities) in virtue of being aware of the objects therein located (Martin 1992). If so, although negative transparency has to go, positive transparency, the thesis that we are always aware of features of the content of perception, is not violated. The same may hold for the temporal case. Take an auditory experience that presents us with a short period, composed of three moments so that the overall situation is that of listening to a fast triplet. Although we are not aware of the temporal boundaries of the interval *as if they were two further notes* at the ends of the interval, we are indirectly aware of them. And through such an awareness we become aware as well of the temporal boundaries of the experience that presents us with the interval.

consciousness would work. Cf. 'To actually perceive an object as enduring over time, the successive phases of consciousness must somehow be united experientially, and the decisive challenge is to account for this temporal binding without giving rise to an infinite regress, i.e. without having to posit yet another temporally extended consciousness whose task is to unify the first-order consciousness, and so forth ad *infinitum*' (Gallagher and Zahavi 2008: 73).

[18] Warning about Soteriou's use of the expression 'negative temporal transparency' as the thesis that we cannot distinguish our position in time from the position of the contents. I will discuss this point at length in the next chapter. Here I mean that we are never aware of the (temporal) features of our own experiences.

So far so good for the no-glue-molecularist. But how good? Notice that there is a bit of tension between the top-down strategy and the appeal to Inheritance. Consider this statement by Phillips: '[...] there are certain durations of experience that are explanatorily or metaphysically prior to their temporal subparts' (2014b: 149–50). Here the appeal is merely to the fact that the *durations* are prior. But it is clear from what follows that Phillips considers the explanatory priority a feature of the temporal structure of experience. For instance, when he says that the '[...] metaphysically fundamental units of experience are extended in time', and '[...] are of the order of half a second in length' (2014b: 150). And yet, given the indiscriminability of one's temporal location with the temporal location of one's perceptions, such a feature is given as a feature of the temporal field itself. If I am right (Section 4.3.2), we are presented with the temporal location of our own experiences, not with the temporal locations of the events around us, which appear to happen in the only temporal location we are presented with, namely our temporal location. In a sense then, the temporal features of experience that are inherited from the content are those that are (somewhat unconsciously) projected on it. There is clearly a circularity here: the temporal boundaries of the content are such *in virtue* of the temporal structure of the experience, but our awareness of the boundaries of the experience is inherited from our awareness of the content.

Maybe the situation is not so strange as it may sound, and the circularity is not vicious after all. But it still strikes me as if the only substantive explanatory work is done by *the fact that there are temporal boundaries* of the intake of perceptual information, and that information about the very recent past has to be integrated with information about the present, along with possibly information about expectations of what is about to come. And both facts are compatible with the dynamic version of the snapshot view that I will elaborate in the last two sections of this chapter. Before moving to that, let us have a look at another problem, possibly the most serious one, for no-glue-molecularism: that of temporal illusions.

2.5 Molecularism and postdictive illusions

Every view of temporal experience must say something about temporal illusions. However, molecularism is particularly problematic for certain perceptual temporal illusions, those involving so-called postdiction, because of its adherence to the PPC. Note that it is quite difficult to think of a counterexample to PPC *outside* the perceptual sphere. Cases of misremembering, for instance, only superficially pose a threat to the topological (or metric) reading of the principle. If on Sunday I experience the brunch with my husband, then the stroll in the park and then the coffee with a friend, but after one week I think that I had the brunch, followed by a coffee with a friend, and then a stroll in the park, this shows that I am mistaken about the order of my experiences (and of what I experienced too, incidentally), and *not* that it seemed to me that I had an experience of having a coffee with a friend while I was in fact having a stroll with my husband and vice versa.

Things are not so neat with perception at shorter timescales. Examples of illusion of postdiction, such as the cutaneous rabbit and apparent motion, are puzzling, regardless of the view one assumes of temporal perception (if any at all). Consider a classical setting for an illusion of apparent motion (see Figure 2.3).[19] You are shown in a window of 200 milliseconds three static images on a computer screen, separated by the same temporal interval. At t_1 you see a flash on the left of the screen (L). At t_2 you see a blank screen. At t_3 you see a flash on the right of the screen (R). The data is that *after t_3*, people prompted by asking what they saw tend to make the experience-based claim that a dot *moved* from L to R, passing through the centre (C) of the screen. Now, why is this puzzling? Consider the amount of time d that it takes for a visual stimulus—like the flash the subjects in the experiment see—to be elaborated and have an influence on central processing, such as verbal reports. If we take the verbal report as evidence that at $t_3 + d$ the experience e_3 is that of a dot that has just moved from L to R passing through C, then what is the experience e_2 at $t_2 + d$? We know that when no flash is shown at t_3, the report is that of a blank screen, and this seems good evidence to think that also in the experimental condition just described at $t_2 + d$ the experience e_2 is that of a blank screen. But how come then that at $t_3 + d$ we talk as if at t_2, just before we see the dot arriving at R, there was a dot moving through C, rather than a blank screen?

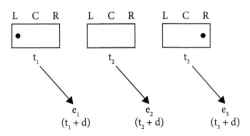

Figure 2.3 Apparent motion

---

[19] I am using a description that is based on the simplified view that Grush (2016) gives.

One way to explain the situation is in analogy with the 'unremarkable' case of bad memory that I presented before. Although at $t_2 + d$ we experience a blank screen, at $t_3 + d$ our brain has engaged in what is called *Orwellian rewriting*. That is to say, we have 'forgotten' the experience of the blank screen and quickly substituted for a fake 'memory' of a different past (one in which the dot is crossing the screen). The quotes around 'forgotten' and 'memory' are of course scare quotes since the idea is that the whole process is perceptual, or at least it involves fairly different psychological mechanisms than the trivial case of misremembering. As many have extensively noted, the Orwellian rewriting is not something in the toolbox of the molecularist, at least not in its crudest version. For one thing, it clashes with PPC in its topological reading. If PPC holds, our experience of the movement of the dot from L to R through C should be concurrent with the presentation of such a movement; that is, the experience should be constituted by the three parts e_1, e_2, e_3 that happen at $t_1 + d$, $t_2 + d$ and $t_3 + d$ respectively. But we have just seen that if one explains the illusion in terms of Orwellian rewriting, then *the experience of the movement of the dot at the centre of the screen* does not happen at $t_2 + d$ or later,[20] although we report that it did. It is not just that the information of what happened at t_2 and the information of what happened at t_3 have to be integrated to experience movement (something that also the molecularist can accept). Rather, the point is that if the experience is explained by the rewriting, then the experience that happens at $t_2 + d$ is not concurrent with the experienced movement of the dot through C. But this is in contrast to the central tenet of molecularism, according to which we are presented with a temporally extended content in virtue of having a temporally extended experience whose parts mirror the parts of the contents.

Orwellian rewriting is a natural harbour for the atomist, who can construe the integration of the information from the recent past in terms of a representation of an interval, and then accommodate the rewriting as a form of redrafting operated by the brain on the ground of certain heuristics that have independent evolutionary plausibility. The draft that contains a blank screen is quickly discarded and substituted by one that contains a fleeting dot. The more natural strategy for the molecularist to accommodate postdiction is a different one: the *Stalinesque delay*.[21] In its crude form, the idea is that the brain 'waits' a bit more than strictly necessary (that is, the interval d), before delivering a conscious output of what is going on. So, even if at t_2 the stimulus is a blank screen,

---

[20] The 'later' is there to rule out the Stalinesque delay. See below.
[21] The terms are from Dennett and Kinsbourne (1992).

given that at t_3 a dot has been detected in C, after $t_3 + d$, *when* we experience the sequence of events, we experience a dot moving from L to R, going through C. This view has been defended by Dainton (a molecularist). Here is a relevant quote:

> This processing makes for a delay—50–100 msec, say—but our brains put this to good use: they try to work out a single, coherent version of events on the bases of the fragmentary and (at times) conflicting data available to them. Only this 'final draft', as it were, reaches consciousness. (Dainton 2008: 382)

The Stalinesque delay strategy has been criticized on empirical grounds. However, Valtteri Arstila (2015a) argues that the delay in question may be not so 'Stalinesque' after all.[22] Considerations based on a careful reading of empirical data from recent neurosciences suggest that there are non-parallel processes that may explain the integration of the information of the just past stimulus with that concerning a present stimulus in a way that does not require a delay larger than the 'normal' delay d that is generally assumed. Arstila's considerations point towards a form of dynamic snapshot view, and I will come back to them later (Section 2.6). Here I put them to one side, and I consider two ways in which molecularists have tried to resist the idea that their position entails a Stalinesque delay.

2.5.1 Holistic molecularism

The first way is to construe molecularism as a form of *holism*. If we interpret the PPC in holistic terms, the fundamental units of experience are temporally extended events whose phenomenal character *determines* the phenomenal character of its parts. Applied to the example of apparent motion above (see Figure 2.3 again), this means the experience E_0, composed by the parts of experience e_1, e_2, and e_3, which happen respectively at $t_1 + d$, $t_2 + d$, and $t_3 + d$, is the experience of the movement of the dot (from L to R, passing through C), and the phenomenal character of e_1, e_2, and e_3 depends on that of E_0.

---

[22] For a defence of the empirical plausibility of the Stalinesque approach, see also Tim Bayne, who notes that in psychology '[. . .] the Stalinesque account is the received view of both apparent motion and meta-contrast masking' (Bayne 2010: 126). He also stresses that the relevance of consciousness for action guidance is not so straightforward as commonsense suggests and that the width of the Stalinesque delay is likely to depend on various factors. Cf. 'Given that certain types of perceptual features take longer to be processed than others, it is possible that the temporal window open for Stalinesque revision will depend on the features implicated in the particular perceptual state in question' (Bayne 2010: 130). See also Kiverstein and Arstila (2013).

The most basic facts about our experiential lives are facts about extended stretches of the stream of consciousness, and what is true at an instant is true only in virtue of that instant being an instant during such a period of experience. (Phillips 2014b: 150)

Understanding the parts as *dependent* on the whole experience raises two main problems. First, as Geoffrey Lee points out, holism entails the rejection of a very plausible principle that correlates the temporal location of the neural realizers with the temporal location of experience, the *Temporal Correlation Principle* (Lee 2014a; cf. Section 3.1.2), according to which experiences that are realized at the same time also happen at the same time. Trivially, if according to holism, experiences that happen at different times, such as e_1, e_2, and e_3, are realized by the same processes that realize E_0, then the temporal locations of experience realizers and experiences are not so correlated as the principle dictates. The molecularist could try and counter-object that the Temporal Correlation Principle holds for experiences, and experiential *parts*, such as e_1, e_2, and e_3, are not themselves experiences. However, it is unclear why the Temporal Correlation Principle should be so restricted, if experiential parts have distinctive phenomenal character as experiences do.

Second, as Richard Grush points out, holism entails that there are certain relations of dependence that point backwards in time, and the only plausible way to interpret that phenomenon makes such relations explanatorily irrelevant (Grush 2016). Consider e_2. Its phenomenal character is *not* an intrinsic feature of the mental life of the subject at the time at which e_2 happens, namely $t_2 + d$. Rather, it also depends on what happens at the future time $t_3 + d$. Grush distinguishes between future-oriented features of two kinds: the *game-winning* ones and the *McFly* ones. The first kind are ordinary. Think of a football match. The first half finishes with a tie, 0–0. During the second half one of the team scores a goal. Is this the winning goal? Well, it depends on what will happen later. If the match ends and no one else scores, then yes, otherwise no. *Game-winning* features are ordinary because they are causally inert; they do not have any causal influence on the events that happen *after* the event that instantiates them, but *before* the event on which they depend (see Figure 2.4). The fact that the goal is the game-winning one has no causal bearing on the subsequent events of the match before its end, namely before the event on which the fact that the goal is the game-winning one depends. After the end of the match, it can, of course, have causal effects, for instance causing a journalist to write an article about the game-winning goal. *McFly* features are such that they both depend on something in the future of the event that exemplifies them and are causally efficacious for the events that happen *before* the event on which they depend (see Figure 2.4). As the name suggests, those features are not ordinary, and require science-fiction scenarios involving time travel. Grush's example involves a time travel story that is incoherent in a linear time and requires a complicated 'changing the past' metaphysics (Iaquinto and Torrengo 2022a: Chap. 5), but also a simpler time travel scenario in a coherent linear time would do. Imagine that in this very moment someone touches your shoulder. You turn and see... yourself! As future-you explains to present-you, in one year from now you have managed to invent a time machine, and indeed future-you confirms that they remember that you were distracted by your future self while reading Torrengo's *Temporal Experience* (incidentally, precisely at this point of the book). The feature of the reading event of *being such that you were distracted while at it* clearly depends on something that happens in the future—it depends on you using the time machine one year from now—but it has causal efficacy even on the events that happen before you step in the time machine and activate it. For instance, it causes you tomorrow to remember that today you were distracted by someone tapping on your shoulders while reading.

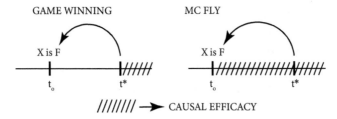

Figure 2.4 Game-winning features vs. McFly features

Now, the problem with holistic interpretation of postdiction is that unless we are prepared to construe the phenomenology of e_2 as a McFly feature, which is widely implausible, it follows that the phenomenology of e_2 is a game-winning feature, and as such causally inert with respect to what happens before $t_3 + d$. And this is puzzling. It is true that verbal reports on the content of E_0 come after $t_3 + d$, but it is also true that the holistic molecular understanding of post diction is supposed to be part of a *content* strategy. This means that the description of an experience as of motion is to be seen as cogent (Section 1.2), rather than just a later interpretation on what it was like to go through E_0. But then the relation going backward in time from $t_3 + d$ to $t_2 + d$ should be *irrelevant* for the cogency of the description, which should be given entirely by the intrinsic phenomenal characters of the successive parts.

There is a further, related, and perhaps deeper problem—which, to my knowledge, is not discussed in the literature. Roughly, it can be put as follows: what should we say of the phenomenal character of e_2 if we consider fundamental temporal units *distinct* from E_0 and yet *overlapping* with it? Consider, in Figure 2.5, experiences E_{-1} and E_{+1}, which both have e_2 as part.

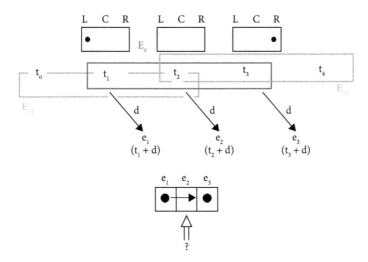

Figure 2.5 Overlapping experiences

Both E_{-1} and E_{+1} are experiences that begin with an empty screen as stimulus, followed by a dot on the left part and on the right part of the screen, respectively, and then finish again with an empty screen as stimulus. e_2 is the part of E_{-1} corresponding to the stimulation with an empty screen at the end of the experience, while it is the part of E_{+1} corresponding to the stimulation with an empty screen at the beginning of the experience. Experiences that are constituted by a sequence of stimuli such as those in E_{-1} and E_{+1} are *not* experiences of apparent motion. As long as e_2 is a part of either, there is no reason to attribute to it a phenomenological character of a dot crossing the screen (or moving in a certain direction). Why then does the phenomenological character due to e_2 being the part of E_0 'take over', as it were? The holistic account seems to be underdetermined here. On the one hand, the phenomenal character of a short experience depends on the fundamental temporal units of which it is part, as clearly stated by Phillips, discussing the 'cutaneous rabbit illusion':

> *Where was the tap felt to occur at t + δt?* is not a question that one can answer without settling facts about one's experience during the surrounding time. (Phillips 2014b: 151)

On the other hand, either fundamental temporal units can overlap, and the same short experiential part can be a part of distinct but overlapping experiential units, bringing thus in the question of which experience 'wins', or they cannot overlap (as Phillips explicitly claims), and we need a reason (independent from solving the postdictive illusion problem) to say that the experience begins at t_0 rather than t_2. Without further theoretical machinery, the holistic stops making sense.

2.5.2   Contextualist molecularism

The second way in which molecularism can be construed so as not to entail a Stalinesque delay is in terms of a *contextualist* understanding of the proper parts of whole experiences. An instance of this view is (or can be elaborated from) Hoerl's 'neutral' content interpretation of postdiction cases. The idea is that the content of e_2 remains neutral between an interpretation that leads to the description of a blank screen right after a flash on the left and one that leads to the description of a dot crossing the screen in the centre.

Grush criticizes this idea since he claims that if this neutrality is not a form of lack of content (if it were so, there would be a Stalinesque delay), and if it is not just another name for rewriting (which is incompatible with molecularism) then it is a form of implausible *ambiguity*. The phenomenal character of e_2 must support a plenitude of possible interpretations. And this is just very implausible, empirically speaking. According to this theory, the phenomenal character of e_2 is not ambiguous merely between a blank screen and a fleeting dot *towards the direction of R*, but also among many other directions and scenarios involving the dot mutating into a square, an oval, a star, a rainbow cat with a funny hat, or whatnot.

Now, Grush's criticism works if we take the hypothesis of neutrality of content to be part of a representational content strategy. If the description that we give of E_0 after t_3 is a cogent description of the representational content associated with the phenomenal character of the successive parts e_1, e_2, e_3, then the phenomenal character of e_2 must somehow contain *in its intrinsic features* a cornucopia of possible representational contents, which seems a bad result for the view. However, if Hoerl is endorsing a relational content strategy (Section 1.3), the criticism seems unfair. Remember that according to such a strategy the relation between the mental event and the stimulus is not representation, but rather *perceptual contact* or *acquaintance*. This means that the phenomenal character is not characterized in terms of satisfaction conditions. Crucially for the issue at stake here, what enters in relation with the stimulus is not a mental *state*, but rather a mental *event*, with temporal parts, and there is no representational relation linking the parts of the extended stimuli and the parts of the mental event, and a fortiori those latter are not individuated by satisfaction conditions. According to Hoerl (2017), the acquaintance relation unfolds through time, and this is what explains the unity of the experience. We need temporally extended processes of a certain kind to enter in an experiential relation with the world around us, and we are phenomenally aware of what enters in the content of our experience only through this unfolding of experience itself. I think that once we put it in those terms, it makes perfect sense to think of the phenomenal status of certain parts as undetermined or neutral *in themselves*. The phenomenology is given only by, and only relative to, the whole succession of experiences. As pointed out in Section 1.3, the relational content strategy is unstable between a weak reading or relationism, which, in certain contexts, risks being indistinguishable from representationalism, and a strong reading, which, in certain contexts, risks making sense only as a form of *interpretational error-theory*. I suspect that the weak reading is liable to Grush's objection as the representational strategy is. How bad would it be for molecularism to have to understand the phenomenology of movement in interpretational terms?

There are a few considerations to make here. Firstly, such interpretational molecularism ends up being an even more radical form of holism than the previous view. If the experiential parts—that is the elements out of which the 'molecule' is composed—do not have intrinsic phenomenological character, but they have it only in relation to the experiential whole that they compose, then the parts of the experience are *not* themselves experiences, since if they were, they would have an intrinsic determinate phenomenology.[23] Secondly, the interpretation that establishes, so to speak, the phenomenal character is largely *independent* from the intrinsic features of the experience to which the phenomenal character is attributed. It seems, then, in order to eschew Grush's too-many-interpretations problem (i.e. is the content indeterminate also with

---

[23] Cf. Hoerl (2013: 397, fn. 33). However, this seems to be in tension with what Hoerl maintains in other passages; cf. '[. . .] there is something like a limit to the period of time through which a perceptual relation with one's surroundings can be sustained, yielding individual experiences of movement or change within which we can individuate a succession of shorter *experiences* as parts, but which themselves are ultimately also fairly short-lived' (2013: 400; my emphasis) and see also (2013: 404).

respect to whether the dot will turn into a rainbow cat?), the molecularist has to embrace a flat-foot error-theoretic strategy, since the indirect description of the experience as an experience as of an object moving would be largely non-cogent. I do not have a strong argument against this. However, I fail to see what the theoretical reasons may be to endorse an error theory across the board here. There is a difference between the 'uneasy' cases, such as imperfect phi-movement or the waterfall case, and cases that are fully fledged apparent movement. And it seems reasonable to assume that the second cases have the same phenomenology of the cases of real movement experiences, at least when we are completely attentive. Other things being equal, I take it that an account that can account for the phenomenology of the 'normal' cases, when we are fully attentive, not as cases in which we merely interpret an amorphous phenomenal character (and thus we misdescribe the phenomenology), is preferable. It may be true that in certain cases in which the movement of change in question is not at the centre of our attention, or temporally extended stimulus is not optimal, that the indirect descriptions that we give of our experience talking about the world are interpretational and possibly not entirely cogent (more on this in Section 3.5.1). But lacking independent reasons to extend this explanation to the attentive optimal cases, I think it is at least worth a shot to look for an alternative content strategy.

2.6 Dynamic instantaneous contents

Versions of snapshot theories that we have seen before (cinematic view and memory theory) classify, in my general framework, as error theories of experience-based claims about movement and change. So does the *contextualist interpretational theory*, or at least I argued that the most coherent construal of the view does. However, a more recent variety of the snapshot view, the so-called 'dynamic snapshot view', qualifies as a representationalism strategy. The idea (defended by Artsila 2018 and explored in Prosser 2016) is that instantaneous contents can nonetheless represent movement and change. Roughly, we are not presented with temporally extended intervals, but rather with properties that encode information about the past and the future, and we have thereby past-directed and future-directed expectations. Suppose you see the actual movement of a dot through a screen from left to right. Although you are not presented with an object moving from left to right on a screen, the way in which you are presented with an object *o* at the centre of the screen requires that you expect that you were just presented with *o* at the left end of the screen and that you are about to be presented with *o* at the right end of the screen. I will explore this idea and then propose a variation of it, which I will use in a relational content strategy, rather than representationalism.

2.6.1 The problem from analyticity

An obvious problem that the content representationalist version of the dynamic snapshot theory faces is what I will call the *problem from analyticity*. In a nutshell, the problem is the following: how can instantaneous contents present us with movement and change, given that movement and change requires temporal extension? If every time movement or change happens, it is *analytically necessary* that some time has passed, then every time that we are presented with a movement or a change, we are presented with something that happens during an interval of time, rather than at an instant. Hence there is literally not enough time for information about movement to be presented to us in a non-temporally extended content.

How convincing is an objection to the dynamic snapshot view based on the problem of analyticity? It depends on what we ask of a *presentation* of change and movement in this context. Clearly, we can *conventionally associate* a static sign to a certain movement (e.g. if you see a red flag, it means that the crabs are crossing the garden), and clearly, we cannot *reproduce* change and movement (as we do in movies and video clips) without taking some time. Where does our experience of change and movement stand? The view is a content strategy; hence movement or change are supposed to be *phenomenally* presented in our experience. If the objection is sound, then our experience must unfold through the interval in which change or movement are phenomenally presented to us, and therefore cannot be punctate.

2.6.2 Dynamic state features

Let me tackle this objection in two ways, depending on whether it comes from an atomist or a molecularist form of the specious present view. As for the atomist, I begin with a *tu quoque* rejoinder. As I hinted at above (Section 2.4.1), the atomist has a hard time answering the following question: how can one be phenomenally presented with a non-instantaneous content *during* an instantaneous experience? The atomist theory tells us that punctate experiences present to us temporally extended contents, as they present us spatially extended contents, namely all at once. At this point, usually a diagram with a triangle is drawn (see for instance Figure 2.1), the upper vertex being the experience and the lower side its content. How does this help? The picture illustrates the distinction between the temporal structure of the experience itself, and the temporal structure with which we are presented, and aims to make it clear that being presented with a temporally extended content does not mean that our brain behaves like inspecting a short clip. Rather, for the atomist, neither the experience nor the content unfolds. Therefore, in order to make sense of the view, it is crucial to accept that temporally extended contents need not unfold, but can be presented all at once. I take this to mean that it is a brute fact that the phenomenology of perceiving change or motion (at the scale of the specious present) is captured by the PSA (or at least it is something that is motivated merely by the relational constraint I have discussed in Section 2.4.1). It being a brute fact does not mean that the view cannot avail of explanatory elements that come from the details of how the information about movement or change is processed in the atomic experience—e.g. the fact that information about the recent past or projected expectations gets integrated with information about what is happening now. However, these explanatory elements concern only the specificity of the contents (e.g. we are presented with the trajectory of a black dot from right to left vs. a red spot going upwards), and do not help with answering the more general question of how a temporally extended content can be phenomenally presented all at once to us. The more general question is answered *merely* by the assumption that PSA holds. It is something that the theory accepts as a brute fact. But then again, everybody has to accept brute facts sooner or later, and this one sits nicely with the proposal.

Now, regardless of how we consider atomistic specious present views, the dynamic snapshot view can avail of the same explanatory elements based on information about the recent past or projected expectations to explain the phenomenology of the temporally unextended content, even if it does not encompass PSA. The information, rather than being integrated in a representation of a temporally extended event, as for the atomist, is integrated in what can be called a *presentation of a dynamic state feature*. Dynamic state features come in simple and complex fashions. To understand what a simple dynamic state feature is, consider a vectorial magnitude such as *velocity*. Although velocity is defined over intervals of time, as the amount of space covered in a given amount of time, it makes sense to attribute instantaneous velocity to a persisting moving entity. In a sense, *what* is the instantaneous velocity of a moving body at a given instant depends on its location just before and after, but the *possession* of the property does not. Indeed, one can reconstruct the trajectory of a body by the vectorial quantity of velocity that it has at various instants.[24] Instantaneous velocity is an example of a simple dynamic state feature. Complex dynamic state features are constituted or made up of simple ones. For instance, consider cantering and galloping. Whether a horse is cantering or galloping at a given instant *t* depends on what is going on in the temporal surrounding of *t*. And yet it makes sense to attribute the property of *begin cantering* (or *galloping*) at *t*. Indeed, insofar as whether a horse is cantering or galloping depends on other dynamic state features that it has at *t*,[25] you can reconstruct the narrative of a horse switching several times from cantering to galloping over an interval by the attribution of dynamic state features to it at various instants. Begin cantering (or galloping) at an instant is a complex dynamic state feature. Information about both simple and complex dynamic state features can be encoded in temporally unextended contents.

Compare the idea of a dynamical state feature with one of the central ideas of holistic molecularism, namely that the fact that whether a mental event *e* can correctly be said to be φ at *t* depends on the fact that *e* is φ-ing over an interval *I* containing *t*. According to holistic molecularism, the basic experiential units are temporally extended experiences. Phillips, for instance, states that '[. . .] in virtue of having an experience *e* of an event Σ *over* some period δ*t*, S can be experiencing Σ at *t*' (Phillips 2014b: 150). The example is experiencing the ball's motion: we experience the motion of the ball at *t* in virtue of experiencing it over some interval containing *t*. The version of the dynamic snapshot view that I am exploring here reverses the order of dependence. It is in virtue of there being a succession of instantaneous experiences encoding a certain dynamic state feature, such as *directed velocity of a persistent object*, that the experience over a certain interval is an experience of an object moving along a certain trajectory. Each experience presents us with an object that— if nothing interferes—has come along a certain trajectory and will continue along it. In other words, it is a mistake to understand experienced motion as a relation between positions of entities at different times. The phenomenology of motion is intrinsic to virtually instantaneous experiences; the connection

---

[24] Dynamic state features bear similarity to Prosser's (2016: 123) idea of an instantaneous content that includes a vector rate of change, and Arstila's (2018) idea of *pure* temporal phenomenology. As in my picture, neither view interprets movement as a relation, nor require movement detection to be a detection of a relation.

[25] See Grush (2016), and his discussion of how the so-called Froude number is related to the distinction in bipedal walking vs. running. See also Young and Calabi (2018).

with its past and its future is merely in the fact that it comes with an expectation of both what just happened and what will soon happen. The relational constraint that specious present theorists endorse is thus unmotivated. We do not need to be presented with the position of an object at various times to experience its movement.

It is important to understand that dynamic state properties are properties of the *objects* that we are presented with, and what triggers the encoding of the information on the dynamic state feature can depend on how the object has been presented throughout a *temporally extended stimulus*. The hypothesis is that if the external stimulation, within a certain temporal interval, displays a certain configuration, for instance the displacement of a noticeable object through a certain trajectory, then a sequence of snapshots presenting dynamic state properties will be produced (assuming we are attentive). As we noted in Section 2.4.1, we just need the system to be sensitive to the variation of stimulation within certain temporal borders; we do not need to 'import' the temporal structure of the stimulation into the temporal structure of what we experience.

If this account is on the right track, both in the case of the apparent movement scenario, and in the case of a small object moving continuously in front of us, the stimuli will trigger a sequence of snapshots in which a persisting object is presented with dynamic state properties that determine the apparent (and possibly also actual) trajectory. The view entails that Stalinesque delays happen every time we detect motion, be it apparent or real. Although the plausibility of this hypothesis largely depends on the empirical details, there are three considerations that converge in corroborating it. First, Arstila-style delays seem to be empirically plausible. If so, the main empirical obstacle to the Stalinesque delays is overcome. It is true that Arstila's view concerns displacement only, and not change in general. But it may be that certain cases of qualitative change are treatable as cases of displacement, and others as discrete or smooth alteration (see Sections 2.7.1 and 2.7.2). Second, as I will argue in Chapter 3, I believe there are good reasons to think that our experiential flow has more 'gaps' than the way we usually talk about it suggests. If so, even if Arstila-style delays turned out to be implausible, we may not need to endorse an Orwellian strategy to account for the phenomenology of apparent motion, and it would not be a surprise that we report the phenomenology of apparent motion and that of actual motion in the same way. Third, as Daniel Dennett and Marcel Kinsbourne (1992) already noticed, it is an oversimplification to think of our conscious experience as coordinated in some Cartesian centre, in which the various parts of it get unified (cf. also Ismael 2016, and Prosser 2017). Indeed, in Section 3.3, I will argue that the description of our experience as unified should not be taken as cogent, and I will note that this factor contributes to the plausibility of the hypothesis of a dynamic snapshot account of the phenomenology of detection of movement and change.

2.6.3 Persistence feelings

As for molecularism, too, there is a *tu quoque* rejoinder, but concerning a different issue. When we move from the specious present scale to larger scales, but we still consider experiences that are phenomenally unified in some sense (see Section 3.5.1), we easily encounter phenomenal properties that distinguish certain experiences from others with different 'pasts'. To elaborate on an example presented in Sean Kelly (2005) and discussed in Alva Noë (2006), if you hear a soprano singing a note for two or three seconds, you may have a continuous auditory experience of the note and nothing else, as it were. But if you hear the same soprano sustaining the same note for a considerably long period, '[t]he note you hear *sounds* as if it has been going on for a while; it has that quality' (Noë 2006: 27). The problem that Noë is addressing is finding '[. . .] a way of accounting for the perceptible quality of temporal extent without supposing, incoherently, that the past is present now, or that we now have access to what has already happened' (p. 28). Notice that raising this problem is *not* question-begging with respect to specious present theorists. Unless one believes that the specious present is extended well behind the thresholds for movement perception, it is *in*coherent also for a specious present theorist (no matter whether it is of the molecularist or atomist sort) to suppose that what happened twenty seconds ago, say, is now *perceptually* affecting my experience.[26] More to the point, it is not obvious that the specious present theorist can apply what they say at the specious present scale to this larger timescale. Even if the specious present encompasses the recent past, which is thus perceptually presented to us, and successive specious presents somehow (by overlap? By a unity relation? By both?) present us with continuous changes of larger

---

[26] I am speaking loosely, since the point, of course, is not how long ago it happened, but where in space-time it is located. The so-called time lag problem is sometimes formulated in terms of a mismatch between something (the explosion of a star, say) being presented to us as happening now, while it actually happened in the past. But if one endorses an eternalist ontology (along possibly with a B-theoretic understanding of time) there is nothing weird to say that the event in the past (the explosion of the supernova, say) is perceptually related to my present perception, since it is in the past-light cone of my present experience, and *anything* that may affect my present experience *must be* in the past-light cone of it. Indeed, if that explosion, which is very distant in space, happened closer in time then it could not affect me (now) at all! What would be mysterious is for my present experience to be perceptually related to something that happened 100 milliseconds ago, but *outside* my past-light cone (on Alpha Centauri, say).

width, we still do not have an explanation of why '[w]hen you hear the singer's sustained note, you not only hear the way it sounds now, but you also hear it *as having temporal extent*' (Noë 2006: 27; my emphasis).

While the example just discussed is about a rather specific phenomenology, I think that it is generally true that perceptions come with *a sense of persistence* of the world around us (cf. Pelczar 2010). Plausibly, the feeling that the things we perceive have been around is part of the presentational phenomenology characteristic of perception, and possibly contributes to the phenomenal objectivity of its content (Sections 1.4, 4.3). Consider the following analogy with space. Imagine you follow with your sight a long hose that is in the garden (perhaps to check whether there are any leaks). You arrive at the end of the hose and stop. Now its last bit is almost at the periphery of your visual field, while you are focused on the nearby tree. The last bit of the hose is not presented to you as a detached piece of rubber, but as the last bit *of a longer hose*, which is now out of your sight. The same may be true even if you have not followed the hose by sight. Imagine you just came out in the garden and looked at the tree (perhaps to check whether there is already fruit on it). In this situation, too, you could be visually presented with the last bit of the hose not as a detached piece of rubber, but as the last bit of a longer object, which you do not see in its entirety right now (and perhaps you never had; the phenomenology is triggered by what goes on in the peripheral part of the stimulation in your retina). The same goes with the temporal aspect of temporally extended things. It is not just the sustained note that now sounds as if it went on for a while; when you move your head and new things enter your visual field, you do not take them to have come out of thin air, as though they did not exist before you turned your head. Indeed, they *do not look* as if they just began their worldly existence. When something *does* look like that, it usually scares the hell out of us. Things usually appear as if they have been around for a while, and as if they are not going to disappear very soon.[27] And this sense of persistence, this feeling from the recent past and the imminent future, is something that the specious present theorist cannot explain merely by appealing to the temporal structure of what we are presented with—even assuming their story about our perception of temporally extended changes, successions, and durations is correct. I will call these feelings as if the past and the future are somehow still around *persistence feelings*.

Both the problem of accounting for persistence feelings, and that of being presented with the recent past, require that we accommodate some feature of

---

[27] Cf. Casati and Torrengo (2011).

the present content of perception that somehow 'outstretches' it, or 'temporally points beyond it'. Thus, they are both varieties of the worry generated by the analyticity problem. However, the specious present theorists cannot solve the problem of the feeling of persistence simply by pointing out that their theory postulates temporally extended contents. Therefore, a molecularist should not insist that the analyticity problem cannot be overcome by the dynamic snapshot theorists, on pain of backfiring, since molecularists and atomists alike must admit of persistence feelings.

Now, I think that there is a connection between persistence feelings and the hypothesis that we are sometimes presented with dynamic state features. So far, the only examples of dynamic state features that I have given concern movement, and are what we may call *displacement dynamic state features*. Are there any *non-displacement dynamic state features*? The question is largely empirical.[28] The working hypothesis is that it is evolutionarily plausible to assume that human beings have several *detection systems* that are sensitive to temporally extended stimuli. Such systems may work either in some postdictive way, 'adjusting' the output, or they may work in a way that depends on projected expectations. That is to say, given a certain kind of stimulus, a default future stimulus is expected in the sense that the behaviour of the system is different if the stimulus is not the expected one. Given the general utility of detection systems like that, it is sensible to look for analogous mechanisms not just for the case of visual detection of motion, but more generally for detection of change across modalities. My proposal is to think of non-displacement dynamic state features as encoding information relative to *temporally extended gestalts*. It is important here to spell out carefully what is meant by 'encoding information relative to'. The stimulus is temporally extended, but the experience elicited is virtually instantaneous. Therefore, 'encoding information' is something different than being an experience in which we are *presented* with a gestalt. The phenomenology of *any* experience is interpreted in the context of the succession of the surrounding experiences. To encode information about a gestalt means precisely that the experience feels differently if previous experiences do not match the gestalt, and elicit an expectation of successive experiences having a certain matching phenomenal character. Whether the mechanism underpinning the experience is postdictive, and thus reconstructing the gestalt property after, or is predictive, and thus based on guesses about the future, depends on the case at issue, and there is no assumption that all

---

[28] As also Prosser (2017: 149) notices, it is not uncommon for cognitive scientists to label smooth qualitative change in general as 'motion'; cf. Rensink (2002).

mechanisms 'reach consciousness' at the same time or in a harmonic way (see Section 3.3).

To sum up: it is not incoherent to attribute dynamic features to temporally unextended contents, and indeed there are at least two families of features that can be plausibly attributed to instantaneous contents: (a) dynamic state features; and (b) persistence feelings, such as the feeling of having been around and of not going to disappear right after. I grant that it may still be difficult to grasp what exactly it means to *represent* such features *at an instant*, given that it cannot mean to present a trajectory or a temporally extended gestalt. But my version of the dynamic snapshot is not committed to this strong claim; only to the weaker claim that, sometimes, our temporally unextended experiences have a distinctive phenomenology of movement or change.

2.7 Change and succession

I come home after grocery shopping, and I stand in my living room. There is no noticeable noise and the smell, which I barely notice, is a familiar and invariant one. Nothing within my sight changes or moves. I feel the pressure of the grocery bag that I hold in my left hand, and I have a general sense of my body being in a standing position. Perhaps at some level I am conscious of breathing, and I feel my blood circulating. I stay put for a few seconds, and then I begin to walk towards the fireplace. Although there is nothing moving or changing that I can detect around me as I walk, my visual viewpoint shifts and reveals new sights of the room. I can hear the noise of my steps, and the rustle of the bag. I stop. Suddenly, Peaches, Petunia, Bimbo, and Beep Beep—guinea pigs—sneak out of their den and begin to make their typical food-request sound. I turn my head and see them moving nervously around the empty pellet bowl.

It is not uncommon over a relatively short period of time to undergo a variety of experiences that differ quite radically in their dynamic flavour, so to speak. There are moments in which nothing moves or changes around us, although our thoughts go on, and we possibly feel slight alterations in our body. There are moments in which nothing changes or moves, but *we* do, either by locomotion or by changing the orientation of our head, and there is a variation in the phenomenal character of our experiences, together with a feeling of action. And there are moments in which a movement or a change in sound or smell around us attracts our attention and we experience it directly. Those experiences are not only likely to be realized by quite different brain processes, but also have a different phenomenological structure. In the first case there is no dynamic element in what we are presented with, and indeed the only dynamic aspect seems to be the inner flow of our thoughts. In the second case, we are not presented with movement or change, but there is still clearly something distinctively dynamic in the way we are in contact with our environment through sight and the other senses. Even if we do not experience change, we go through a succession of different experiences (the room looks different from different visual perspectives). It is no longer just our thoughts or inner life that unfold, but we also experience a stream of sensations, while keeping on being presented with the same things (the objects in the room) through it. In the third case, we are aware of the movement of something not merely through the stream of sensations but in one go, as it were. We see Petunia making a small jump and we hear a high-pitched sound coming from Peaches. We are aware of those changes in sound and position in a way that seem distinctively different from the way those who loved it may be aware of the congruity of the landscape in the opening reference from Hardy.

In the next chapter, I will argue that we should understand awareness of succession in terms of having a succession of virtually instantaneous experiences, in a way that allows for the flow of experience to be more 'gappy' than suggested by the way in which we usually think of it. When a temporally extended stimulus is relevant for a detection system and shows certain characteristics, for instance it contains enough variety of information within the boundaries of what is differentiable for us, it triggers a dynamical state property phenomenology. Movement or change is presented to us, although briefly. This often calls for our attention and makes it the case that easily the sequence of experience is interpreted as the experience of an object that moves in a certain direction (say) *during a certain interval of time*. The indirect description of our phenomenology in sentences such as 'look, Petunia is trying to reach the bell pepper' is cogent in an important sense, since there is a directed movement that is presented to us in the experiences in which we are attentive towards Petunia. However, there is a sense in which it is not cogent since we are not presented with Petunia being at different locations throughout her small trip to her beloved vegetable. Imagine that Petunia is shy and insecure, and rather than running quickly at the bell pepper—as grumpy and bossy Peaches does— she goes slowly just a few steps towards it, then stops and looks around, turns, goes few steps back, then turns again and cautiously tries to nibble a piece, only to have Peaches pushing her away with her head... Surely the whole experience of looking at all this takes more than the minimal temporal distance required for noticing a movement, or even any plausible amount of time during which in some sense our experience 'feels' immediate. If I say, 'look, Petunia is trying to reach the bell pepper', there is a sense in which that experience-based claim is not a cogent description of my occurring phenomenology. I am presented with Petunia being at different places only through a sequence of experiences, although some of them have a directed movement phenomenology. What is true, and possibly makes me think of the indirect description as cogent also in the more stringent sense, is that when my attention is on Petunia, I am presented with her with a feeling of persistence. If Petunia were to disappear in a poof of nothing, or were to pop up out of thin air, I would be very surprised (and there would probably be something seriously wrong with my mental processing; or with Petunia).

Importantly, the case of the actual motion of Petunia and the case of apparent motion is treated in substantially the same way in this framework. The idea is that even if the temporally extended stimulus is *not* an actually moving entity (object or shadow), it can still display the feature that triggers the presentation of an object possessing dynamic state features. In many cases we do not distinguish apparent motion from real motion, precisely because of that. The stimulus is *optimal* and has all the required features. However, notice that—as Hoerl has pointed out—Whertheimer, in the original phi-movement experiment, *distinguishes* cases in which the phenomenology is reported to be as of actual motion, and those in which the subjects report to have a 'feeling' that the dot moved, without seeing it changing location (cf. Hoerl 2015: 11). I will not dwell too long on this here, but it seems that to make sense of those cases, even a specious present account must make space for something like dynamic state properties, or 'pure motion' phenomenology as it is sometimes called. Something analogous seems to happen in the so-called waterfall illusion case, which is usually taken as evidence in favour of the dynamic snapshot view (cf. Le Poidevin 2007; Arstila 2018). What I take all such cases to have in common is that the stimulus is *non-optimal* for a fully fledged experience of motion, namely one that goes hand in hand with an experience of displacement (veridical or not). The dynamic snapshot can account for the description of those experiences as unsettling or eerie in a straightforward way. The non-optimality of the stimulus triggers the presentation of the dynamic state feature but not the experience of displacement.

As accounts for the optimal cases (cashed out as forms of content relational strategy), the dynamic snapshot view and molecularism are in a sense close in spirit. For both the phenomenology of change is cogent, and for both at the level of virtually instantaneous experiences there is no presentation of displacement or qualitative variation across temporal positions. However, for the former the cogency of the phenomenology at issue is due to a feature of the content of virtually instantaneous experiences, whereas for the latter it can be recovered only at the level of extended experiences (which, in most varieties of the view, is the most explanatorily fundamental level).

However, I think that there are good reasons to take the dynamic snapshot as less prone to collapse onto an interpretational error-theoretic strategy. When we are attentive in experiencing change, our indirect descriptions can be cogent in the significant way I spell out above. There is an entity that *is* presented to us with a dynamic state property and a feeling of persistence. If everything goes well, we either have seen it moving before or we will (the 'or' here is, of course, inclusive). If something goes slightly wrong, as in the non-optimal cases, our experience is not of a smooth displacement, but it still seems to experientially encode movement information. To repeat the point, it is with respect to the *succession* of experiences that make sense to talk about an awareness of displacement, although each virtually instantaneous experience contributes to it by presenting to us directed motion. And in the non-optimal case, we may be unsure of whether we have been aware of displacement or not. It is thus important that the strategy here is a relational one. I do not claim that virtually instantaneous experiences somehow carry information about past and future locations of an entity that they represent at an instant. It is the external stimulus that is presented as possessing the dynamic state feature, precisely in the sense that it is cogent to describe the phenomenology as of a moving object in a certain direction, which is what we do in the optimal cases. However, as will become clear in the next chapter, there is a difference between the case in which we direct our attention to the moving object (and the experience-based claim is cogent) and the case in which movement is detected, but we do not pay attention to it, which I take to be cases in which more plausibly there is no definite phenomenal content, and we just interpret the overall sequence in a certain way.

Whether the relational dynamic snapshot account is to be construed as a content strategy, with definite phenomenology in the attentive case, and interpretational phenomenology in suboptimal cases, or is better construed as interpretational throughout, and thus a version of error theory, depends partly on whether Arstila-like delays are empirically plausible. If there is parallel processing such that the feedback from one process can influence the second processing (the one responsible for the phenomenology of pure movement or the encoding of dynamical state properties) without the delay being Stalinesque, then there is no reason to suppose that either we are rewriting the phenomenology in an Orwellian fashion, or we are merely interpreting an ambiguous phenomenology *post hoc*. When, and if, there are interpretational elements is something that must be settled case by case, depending on things like attention, and the (non-)optimality of the stimulus. But in optimal cases of apparent motion, and with our focus of attention on the dot (or whatever we are presented with as moving), the theory predicts that the phenomenology is indistinguishable from the case of real motion, since it is due to the activation of the same detection system.[29]

Now, one may wonder—even putting aside the issue of the empirical plausibility of Arstila's theory—whether this account is good enough as an account for the phenomenology of experience of *change* in general. Arstila-style delays are plausible for detection of motion, but they also seem to be very specific to it, and the explanation given does not seem to easily adapt to detection of variation in other properties, such as colour or shape, not to mention of variation within other modalities, such as haptic stimulation, audition, olfaction, taste, and also cross-modal cases, proprioception, and action phenomenology. As I said at the beginning of the chapter, the hypothesis that there is some genuine genus of phenomenology of change, that subsumes displacement, colour change, sound change, and so on, may be a sensible working hypothesis to start with, but there is no reason to take it as sacrosanct. After all, the theory fleshed out here is far from monolithic, given that it admits of cases in which interpretation explains the relation between experience-based claims and the experiences whose phenomenology the claims purport to indirectly describe, and cases in which the description is cogent.

Notice that in the visual modality there do not seem to be many cases of experience of qualitative smooth change that are not *also* experiences of motion detection. Going back to the example of experience of succession that I gave, when I am walking through a room in which no movement happens or no movement really catches my attention, I am aware of a change in the phenomenal character of the experiences I am having in succession, but I am not detecting anything changing. In other cases, I can say that I detect visually qualitative change, but I am likely also being presented with movement, and thus the phenomenology may be due to the activation of the movement detection mechanism. We can set apart the very slow cases, as when I notice that the light got dimmer towards the end of the afternoon in the park, which are clearly 'hour-hand' cases, in which a certain experience, which may very well be entirely static in its phenomenology, triggers a comparison with a memory

---

[29] According to Synofzik et al. (2008), something similar also happens in the case of the experience of agency. In optimal cases, the phenomenal content is taken at face value (they talk of a *feeling* of agency), but in non-optimal cases a reinterpretation takes place (they talk of a *judgement* of agency).

and the thought that something changed or moved. And we can set apart the very fast cases, which involve the sudden appearance of a coloured and shaped entity—an object, a light, a shadow—since they are either cases of movement, if they trigger the same or similar detection mechanism as ordinary cases of real or apparent motion, or are *discrete alteration* cases, which I will discuss shortly.

The ones that involve quick but smooth qualitative changes in a persisting entity are trickier, unless it is a change in shape which I take to be a case of displacement (we see the contours of an object or its parts moving). Consider a light that becomes dimmer, not as slowly as the sun during a lazy afternoon, but rather as the one in the living room when we move a regulator. If we are looking at the source, there is a case for saying that the borders of the halo around the light shrink, and thus there is a movement going on here too. However, even if that is true in terms of retinal proximal stimulus, it is unlikely that the borders of the halo around a light source are something that is processed as the change in shape of a solid object. Think of the phenomenological difference between watching someone rather quickly inflating a pink air balloon and looking at a lightbulb gradually becoming more luminous. The same goes for change in the position of shadows, which is likely to happen with a change in luminosity of a point-like source, but it is something our cognitive systems use for processing information about distances and depth, and it is rarely detected as a movement.[30] If we are not looking at the source, and the light dims rapidly enough for us to notice, my account compels us to either look for a detection mechanism which results in an experience of something (the room?) being presented as possessing non-displacement dynamic state features, or as a mere experience of succession. Similar is the case of change in colour of a persisting entity, although it is probably a somewhat rarer case, unless we live surrounded by chameleons. How is it plausible that in all cases in which motion detection is not triggered, there is either something like the detection of a qualitative change mechanism in place, and thus presentation of something as having a non-displacement dynamical state property, or we are simply aware of a succession of qualitatively distinct experiences?

---

[30] It is also rarely in the focus of our attention, unless it is seriously prominent (as when a big cloud covers the sun, and we see its sharp-edged shadow running across a half-empty piazza). Cf. Casati (2000).

2.7.1 Discrete alteration

I will not try to answer that question in any exhaustive way, but I will say some more by considering the non-visual cases, which are perhaps more instructive. It is easier to find cases in which movement detection and change detection part company in the haptic, auditory, olfactory, and taste cases. Notice that even when change and movement do *not* part company, as when we feel a spider crawling up our leg, hear the ambulance getting farther away, or smell the stinky dog getting closer, it is empirically implausible that the same detection mechanisms as in the visual case are exploited. So, it is not clear that even in those cases we can talk of a presentation of a dynamic state property. But I do not think that this is a serious problem for the view. Consider first what I call the *discrete alteration* cases. An organist plays a do_2 pedal note and a so_5 in a constant and sustained way for some time. Then, while the pedal note goes on unmutated, the right hand of the player moves slowly, pausing a fleeting moment, to a mi_5. I am aware of the change, and if I am attentive to the music, this change can well be phenomenologically prominent. However, it looks like the mere change in content of the two successive experiences has made me aware of the change. It is not implausible to think that there is some mechanism dedicated to bringing discrete alteration like this to our attention, since it seems something that may be useful evolutionarily. Think of a sudden loud clang in the silence, or a pungent smell invading a room quickly, or a flash of light lighting up the sky in the distance. Although in those cases it seems correct to say that we are *not* presented with a change, detection of motion and detection of discrete qualitative alteration may still share some elements of their phenomenology, probably linked to bottom-up attention mechanisms triggered by salience.

When I introduced the idea of dynamic state features, I characterized the sensitivity towards the temporally extended stimulus either as postdictive or as dependent on expectations. Perhaps basic detection mechanisms, such as the ones for motion that catch our attention, are more likely to work post dictively.[31] However, when detection of change involves higher, more central levels of cognition, it seems plausible to consider detection systems that are based on unconscious perceptual inferences in which predictive elements play a role. The framework that comes to mind here is that of a Bayesian theory of perception, according to which 'the perceptual process is [. . .] a matter of

---

[31] See Eagelman and Sejnowski (2000).

unconsciously keeping track of priors and of generating expected inputs (pre-dictions) given the best performing prior hypothesis' (Hohwy et al. 2016: 316). Since, as a matter of fact, the world around us constantly changes, the perceptual system expects change, and thus 'distrusts' the present. My working hypothesis is at least superficially in tension with their central thesis. The idea is that perceptual mechanics are often hardwired to the *expectation of non-variation*, and a breach in expectation is likely to be detected as a change in the surroundings.[32] This may be because if by default we expect no variation, when variation happens it becomes more salient (which may be evolutionarily advantageous). There is no reason to think that such mechanisms are encapsulated, so higher levels of cognition, such as beliefs and learned skills, can influence and integrate the capacity of detecting change and make what counts as non-variation contextual. If we are experiencing a continuous noise of rain falling, the noise of the rain does not count as a qualitative change, but a loud clang catches our attention and is detected as a change. However, if we are in the garden on a silent afternoon, the noise of the rain beginning to fall is likely to attract our attention and be detected as a qualitative change.

2.7.2 Smooth alteration

Smooth alteration cases are those in which we are aware that some qualities change smoothly but rapidly enough for us to notice. We see the colour of the chameleon mutating rapidly from yellow to green (the example of the visual case made above), we can tell that the smell of burned cheese is fading out quickly as soon as we open the window, we feel the cold air hitting our neck turning into a lukewarm and then hot blow when we activate the air con in the winter, we hear the viola playing the legato semiquaver triplet in the Allegretto, we feel the pleasure intensifying just before the orgasm. Changes in all such cases seem to be detected in a somewhat more direct way than in the cases of discrete alteration detection. But for those cases also we should keep in mind that detection can happen in virtue of an acquired perceptual skill, one that involves cognition at large and is context sensitive. Are there cases in which a non-displacement dynamic state property is detected, and it is

---

[32] I say that the tension is superficial because the idea that constancy is a perceptual default, and the idea of discounting the present as less likely, which is central to Hohwy et al.'s view, can be kept together at some level. The hypothesis that the Bayesian framework and expectation play a core role in the phenomenology of discrete alteration is compatible with the empirical evidence that it seems to be crucial that attention be activated by detection of transients, so that an input can be buffered in a short-term memory mechanism and can be compared with the incoming stimulus (cf. O'Regan 2002).

likely to encode implicit information about a fully fledged temporally extended gestalt? A case that seems to me a convincing example of being presented with a non-displacement dynamic state property is the experience of hearing words. There is a debate in philosophy of perception on whether we are phenomenally aware of meanings or not. A quite convincing argument from homophony goes against it. Very roughly, there is no *what it is like* to hear 'to' as opposed to *what it is like* to hear 'too' or 'two', so there is no reason to think that we are perceptually presented with a meaning property. However, even if we are not phenomenologically presented with meanings this does not mean that we do not have a capacity to detect language-specific diachronic units, phonemes, and the words that they compose. We can think of those as temporally extended gestalts which are encoded in the virtually instantaneous experiences that form a stream that we normally interpret as an experience of hearing what they are saying. In the literature, word recognition is often presented as the perceptual skill of detecting *articulatory gestures*.[33]

However, not all cases need to involve fully fledged gestalts and specific recognitional capacities. Consider the following example: I am at the kitchen sink and gently open the hot water faucet. The noise of the water hitting the metal base of the sink begins very softly and then intensifies until it reaches a stable intensity. I keep on hearing it while I am talking with my husband and attending to other things. It is just a noise, it is not qualitatively constant as a flute playing a sustained la_6 in the silence, but it goes on roughly as the same, and by moving the faucet I can experience smooth variation of it, or also quite abrupt change—for instance, if the water moves from hitting the aluminium base to hitting a cup full of water. Also, in this case there seems to be some expectation that the noise remains the same in play, unless we are aware of some alteration condition to be about to happen (for instance, we intend to move the faucet towards a cup full of water). My hypothesis is that the expectation of non-alteration in those non-discrete cases can be described as the presentation of what may be called a *gestalt sketch*, rather than a proper gestalt, as in the case of hearing words. And my hypothesis is that even if the expectation is not fully determined in its content, the experience still feels like one involving a dynamic state property. If the noise of the water falling were to stop abruptly, even if it was not in the focus of our attention, we would probably

---

[33] 'Such articulatory gestures, and the component configurations and movements they comprise, make the manner in which speech is perceptually experienced intelligible in a way that attention to the acoustic signal does not, since such gestures and their descriptions are less sensitive to context' (O'Callaghan 2015: 15).

interpret it as if our auditory experience just before has 'betrayed' us, leading us to expect more water noise when the future did not harbour any.

Finally, maybe I have made my life more difficult than I deserved. Psychologists are happy to classify many experiences of qualitative change as experience of motion, when at a quite early level of elaboration, the same mechanisms are activated (cf. Rensink 2002). If so, we may not need to drop our working hypothesis to put together change and motion at a phenomenological level.

2.8 Conclusions

The atomist dynamic model that I have defended in this chapter involves only the phenomenology of change and motion. However, the model can be expanded to other types of temporal experience, which cannot be explained by resorting exclusively to the conceptual tools elaborated so far, but whose account can be integrated in the story told here. In the next chapter, I tackle an obvious expansion, by investigating not the changes that we experience in the world outside, but our awareness of our own experiences being in flux.

3

The outer flow and the inner flow

Some—Work for Immortality—
The Chiefer part, for Time—
He—Compensates—immediately—
The former—Checks—on Fame
Emily Dickinson (1862)

Time appears both objective, distant, 'out there', and subjective, intimate, 'in here'. One way to understand such a duality is to claim that *phenomenological* time is constituted both by the outer flow of the world as it appears to us, and by the inner world of our private sensations.[1] In this chapter, I investigate the structure and essential features of that aspect of our experience that is constituted by the interaction and exchange between the outer flow and the inner flow.

In Section 3.1. *Awareness of succession*, I characterize the phenomenology of having one experience after another and distinguishing it from other phenomenal characters that are also temporal in nature, such as the experience of change and duration. In Section 3.2. *The continuity of experience*, I argue that even though the flow of experience is often described as smooth, we do not experience the temporal dimension as a continuous series of locations. In Section 3.3. *The disunity of experience*, I give reasons to believe that experience is not just discontinuous, but also constituted by disunified flows, and I resort to attention to explain how they interact. In Section 3.4. *Presentational phenomenology and phenomenal objectivity*, I distinguish between our outward-directed experience and our inward-directed experience and their respective specificity. In Section 3.5. *Narrative cognition*, I discuss the roles that thoughts play in our inner life.

---

[1] The question of the relationship between the outer flow of phenomenological time and physical time, namely time as studied by natural science (real time?), is an open issue, which will be touched upon in Chapter 6.

Temporal Experience. Giuliano Torrengo, Oxford University Press. © Giuliano Torrengo (2024).
DOI: 10.1093/9780191937804.003.0003

3.1 Awareness of succession

Imagine that for some reason (you lost a bet or something) you have to read one of those cheesy books on self-improvement full of over-explained moralistic short stories. A particularly dull one reads as follows.

> 'Every two weeks, a man buys a box of chocolates. Every day at 10:00 a.m. he opens it, takes a chocolate, eats it, and throws away the wrapper. When the box is empty, he piles it on the previous ones and buys a new one. Your days and the chocolates share the same fate. Make today the most precious time, today will never come again, but as an empty box'.

The author warns us against the inexorability of the unfolding of our life, but is there anything in this all but uneventful story that stands for, or symbolizes, *succession*? Obviously, the few lines above represent, in virtue of semantic conventions, a succession of events. But *in* the story, while each chocolate represents the day of its demise, nothing stands for the succession of the days of our life, apart from... the succession itself. The author here seems to have taken for granted that a succession can represent itself. Someone may complain that the author has thus confused the properties of the vehicle of the representation with those of its symbolic content.

When we talk about the phenomenology of succession, it is easy to fall into similar (but not quite the same) vehicle-content fallacies. Firstly, as we saw in the previous chapter, we need *more* than the unfolding of experience to account for the phenomenology of being presented with change and movement. Secondly, we should *not* infer that we are experiencing succession from the fact that we are having experiences one after the other. As James famously warned us, a succession of experience is not, in and of itself, an experience of succession (James 1890: Chap. XV). That warning, I suggest, should be taken with a grain of salt. It should not be read as the denial that it is phenomenologically apparent to us that our experience unfolds. Rather, it is to be read as the warning that our awareness of the unfolding of our own experience is distinct both from the phenomenology of change detection, and the cognitive awareness that we experienced different things in the past.

3.1.1 Overarching phenomenology

Consider the ordinary experience of change. We are aware of change not only through perception, but also through thought and memory. And we could not be aware of changes 'upon reflection' in this way, if we were not aware of the changes in our own experiences: I remember now that I *saw* the fork on the table, while now I *see* it on the floor. Remembering and thinking make me aware that my visual experience changed. But the changes we are aware of through perception are the same changes we are aware of upon reflection.[2] This can be the case only if the changes that we experience and the changes in our experiences share a 'common arena'. In other words, we are aware of both experiences and the things of which we have experiences as involving temporal successions in a *shared temporal dimension*. By navigating the world and experiencing it, we do not merely discover (more or less directly) that things happen one after another, but also that our own experiences happen one after another.

My hypothesis is that that could not be the case if the very unfolding of our own experience were not phenomenally palpable to us. It would indeed be difficult to imagine what an experience would be if it were *not* experienced as being a part of a succession of experiences, namely for which we are *not* aware that it was preceded by other experience and that it will be followed by other experiences. This suggests that awareness of succession is structurally necessary for having experiences in general, or at least for having experiences of the kind humans do. As far as I understand, pathological cases such as akinetopsia[3] are reported to have a 'staccato' phenomenology, but the subjects do not lack an immediate awareness of the succession of their own experiences. Subjects who lack a non-inferential awareness of their undergoing a succession of experiences would be persons with no memory whatsoever of the last twenty seconds (say), but only of having had experiences before that. Someone in this position would constantly have to realize that they are having a new experience by comparative reasoning with what they remember.

If the unfolding of our own experiences is phenomenally accessible to us, when we experience the world around us or we are lost in our thoughts we can always become aware of being in the middle of having a succession of experiences.[4] And in order for that to be possible, we need to appeal to a phenomenal character of the same type of what I have called feelings of persistence. A feeling of persistence is a sensation that what we are presented with has been around and it will continue to be around. But the same feeling can involve

---

[2] The assumption is that they are of the same *kind*. But in principle they could be the very same token, at least interpersonally. For instance, you may see the fork falling on the floor, while I see that it has fallen, because you were looking at it when it fell, whereas I heard the clang (and the meow), turned, saw it on the floor, remembered that it was on the table, and inferred that it fell.

[3] Cf. Heywood and Kentridge (2009). See also the case of schizophrenia in Stanghellini et al. (2016).

[4] I say, 'we can become aware', rather than 'we are aware' because, as I will argue in Section 3.3, experience is less continuous than we tend to think.

our own experiences: we are immediately aware of what we have experienced in the past and what we will experience in the future. I have already noted that while the phenomenology connected to hearing a soprano keeping a note for an unusually long time is uncommon, and the feeling of persistence is common, both share a certain temporal structure, namely they somehow connect us to things well in our past or future (see Section 2.6.3). Let us label the type of phenomenal characters that share this feature *overarching* (see Section 1.5). To make more examples of the uncommon variety, the feeling of eerie familiarity that one has when one comes back to the city where one has grown up after many years of having lived in other places; or the feeling of absence when we notice that a familiar sound is no longer around (didn't the elevator door make a clang at this point?). My working hypothesis is that awareness of succession is a common overarching phenomenology, which involves not what we experience but our experiences themselves. Tim Bayne seems to agree with the existence of such a phenomenological character when he writes 'There is something it is like to enjoy a typical stream of consciousness, but this "what it's likeness" is spread out—distributed across a number of distinct conscious states. It lacks the kind of unity that the phenomenal field possesses' (Bayne 2010: 25). Awareness of succession differs from the awareness of movement or change I discussed in the previous chapter precisely because it lacks the 'unity of the phenomenal field', and yet it is not to be identified merely with what it is like to have experiences over time. Rather, it is an immediate awareness that our occurring experience has been succeeded by others and it will be succeeded by others, that there is a connection between the experience that I am having now and the experience that I had in the past, and those that I will have in the future, in the sense that they constitute a flow, a smooth sequence.

One may think that by claiming that we have an intimate acquaintance with the fact that our experiences constitute a flow, I am covertly appealing to the extensionalist specious present model. This would be in tension with the dynamic snapshot account I defended (Section 2.6). According to the relational take on extensionalism, we are in relation with external events in a manner that involves temporally extended stretches of experience. We experience the world by virtue of the unfolding of our experience through time. But extensionalism is a theory that aims to account for successions that are presented to us, which is something that happens only when we consider temporal scales of half a second or so. What I am after here is an awareness of successions which span over longer intervals, but which at the same time is not mediated by explicit inferences. Even if we accept the idea that certain temporally extended experiences are glued together in a flow of overlapping specious presents, it is not very plausible to understand our awareness of succession in the same way, since it clearly spans over much longer intervals. As Christoph Hoerl correctly reminds us, we '[. . .] need to distinguish between the question as to what is involved in having experiences of succession, and the question as to what explains the unity of the stream of consciousness' (Hoerl 2013: 405).

An appeal to a retentional version of the specious present will not do either. Michael Tye, who defends such a view, notices that '[. . .] a feeling of succession is not a feeling of the succession of *feelings* [. . .]' (Tye 2003a: 102). The idea is that if, in order to be aware of a succession, let us say a fast triplet in a sonata, I must be simultaneously aware of the three notes, then in order to be aware of the succession of my experiences I should have a similar higher-order simultaneous awareness of my own experiences, which is empirically implausible. Tye here is appealing to the idea of temporal transparency and wants to derive our awareness of succession from our perceptual awareness of events in the world. However, notice that he distinguishes between the kind of awareness of succession that we can have within a specious present, and a more general form of awareness of succession, in terms of two different kinds of unity through time. Here is the relevant quote:

> What, then, is phenomenal unity through time? Let us distinguish between direct and indirect unity. Direct phenomenal unity through time is a relation between experientially represented qualities. It obtains if and only if the qualities experienced in one specious present are experienced as succeeding or continuing on from the qualities experienced in the immediately prior specious present. Indirect phenomenal unity through time is also a relation that obtains between experientially represented qualities. It obtains if and only if the qualities experienced in nonadjacent specious presents are linked by chains of direct phenomenal unity. Indirect unity is thus the ancestral of direct unity. (Tye 2003a: 100)

Now, how do we discover that *in*direct phenomenal unity holds between experientially represented qualities? Clearly, we often use memory and inferential reasoning to conclude that two specific experienced qualities are so related. For instance, the slight bitterness of the secret ingredient of your friend's salad reminds you of the taste of the tea you had this morning, and you realize that the two gustatory experiences are indirectly unified by a chain of other experiences. But does that mean that only *direct* phenomenal unity has immediate phenomenology? It seems to me that both retentionalists and extensionalists should give a negative reply to this question and recognize that, regardless of how one accounts for our direct awareness of extended events, we also are aware of the progressive nature of our experience, well beyond the temporal boundaries of the specious present.

3.1.2 Real and virtual instants

I will elaborate the idea of awareness of succession as an overarching phe-nomenology in the context of the atomist model that I began to outline in the previous chapter by expanding upon a dynamic snapshot account of expe-riencing change and movement. Roughly, given that in the snapshot view experiences are instantaneous and do not have temporally extended contents, having an experience with an overarching phenomenology means experienc-ing somehow a connection with what goes on during experiences that are not the one we are presently having. But what is it for an experience to be instantaneous, as the atomist model states? It is crucial to distinguish between being *virtually instantaneous* and being *strictly instantaneous*, and to distin-guish between those two notions when we attribute instantaneousness to experiences and to their contents. Even though mental events, being physical processes, are continuous, it is very likely to be false that *experiences* are strictly instantaneous, namely that they lack temporal extension altogether. This point has been stressed by atomist specious present theorists such as Geoffrey Lee and Richard Grush. The idea is that the neural *realizers* of experiences are temporally extended physical processes that are *pulse-like*. The neural activ-ity that realizes the various experiences that compose our alleged experiential flow are discrete: short, but temporally extended processes for which there are reasonably clear starting and finishing points. Our brain and sensory sys-tems 'sample' the external and internal environments at a certain rate, and those sampling activities are processes that extend over a brief lapse of time and succeed one another.

Here is a significant passage from Grush: '[. . .] let us say that every 20 msec a new estimate of the 200 msec interval is produced. And this state persists for 20 msec, at which point it is replaced by its successor' (Grush 2016: 11–12). This is a passage in which for ease of exposition few numbers are given, and it is formulated in the context of the temporal estimate model (a form of atom-istic specious present), but it is supposed to be empirically plausible, and as long as it is about the neural realizers of the experience, we can take it to be compatible with various accounts of the phenomenology. Now, there are plausible temporal correspondences between the realizers and the experiences that they realize. Geoffrey Lee (2014a) puts this in terms of the following two principles.

> **Temporal correlation principle**: if two experiences are realized over the same interval or moment, then they themselves occupy the same moment or interval.
> **Temporal identity principle**: experiences have the same timing as their realizers.

If the realizers are pulse-like, and the principles such as temporal correlation and temporal identity above hold, then we can say that the experiences in question are *virtually instantaneous*, and that they present us with virtual instants. Note, incidentally, that such virtually instantaneous experiences can encode dynamical state information, and feelings of persistence, by processing inputs from the recent past and imminent expectations, in line with what I have argued in the previous chapter. A virtually instantaneous mental event is such that it cannot be divided into shorter mental events that in turn are experience realizers. Each pulse is thus an *atom* and a virtual instant. Therefore, strictly speaking, even if the mental event is a continuous physical process, we can correctly attribute phenomenal character (and representational content, if any) only to those virtual instants, in a discrete manner.

Awareness of succession is a feature of virtually instantaneous experiences and *not* a property presented in a specious present. Even assuming that we need extended contents and experiences to experience change and motion, awareness of succession extends well beyond the specious present's borders. As with all overarching phenomenologies, awareness of succession involves a sensation that things *besides what we are experiencing* have been in a certain way and are going to be in a certain way. Having established that we can be phenomenally aware of the succession of our experiences, let us investigate if the way we describe such a succession, namely as continuous and smooth, is cogent.

3.2 The continuity of experience

It is sometimes pointed out that our experience is not only diachronically unified, but also *continuous* and *smooth*: each part of our experience flows into the next one (Dainton 2000). Although metaphors and images that aim directly to describe experiences as flowy or continuous abound,[5] such an aspect of our phenomenology is difficult to capture in terms of indirect characterization through experience-based claims (Section 1.3). The reason why[6] may partly be because it is a purported feature of our *experience itself*, rather than of what outward-directed experiences present to us. Sometimes it is put in terms of a feature of our own point of view on the temporal dimension: we experience the world while smoothly 'moving' from one present moment to the next (cf. Section 5.4.1). Such a feature is overt, or—at the very least—it seems very natural to conceptualize our experience in this way and give direct description of our experiences as succeeding each other in a smooth and continuous way.

It is important to keep separated the experience of change exemplified by the phenomenal contrast between seeing the fork falling and realizing that it fell not only from the awareness of succession, but also from the observation that our experience does not seem to have gaps. To see the point, consider the following two nominalizations involving awareness:

a) Being aware of a continuous motion
b) Being aware of having a continuous experience

There are reasons to think of these two awarenesses as distinct. Firstly, consider a very diachronically 'disunified' experience from a phenomenal point of view. Philippe Chuard gives the following example:

> [...F]irst, you experience the layout of my office (e_1), immediately followed by the crowd in a stadium (e_2), after which a uniform yellow surface is instantly presented (e_3), and then a kitten asleep on the sofa (e_4), all experienced within two or three seconds. (Chuard 2017: 128)

Chuard comments that 'such a succession should appear *discontinuous*' (p. 128; italics in the original),[7] and suggests, albeit tentatively, that the

---

[5] Cf. 'Consciousness, then does not appear to itself chopped up in bits. Such words as "chain" or "train" do not describe it fitly as it presents itself in the first instance. It is nothing jointed; if [sic!] flows. A "river" or a "stream" are the metaphors by which it is most naturally described' (James 1890: 526).

[6] Notice that insofar as this claim is true, it may be just contingently so, in the sense that maybe Indo-European languages are particularly bad at capturing the continuity of experience in terms of claims that indirectly involve perceptions, while other languages more naturally yield expressions that suggest a description of this aspect of the phenomenology.

[7] This is what happens according to the cinematic view, which is the one that makes the correct prediction according to Chuard; whereas according to an extensionalist such as Dainton (2014), who maintains that successions of experiences can be unified and 'made' continuous by some primitive relation, it is not clear why it should be so.

example is one in which we have neither experienced continuous change nor have a continuous experience.

Secondly, consider the experience of watching a dolphin emerging from and descending below the surface of a calm ocean at a roughly regular pace and at roughly equidistant places. You do *not* see a continuous motion (assume that the pace is above the 'tunnelling' effect, so that there is no experience of a continuous motion, not even in the sense of a-modal completion), but your *experience* is continuous. The 'staccato' element is in the movement of the dolphin; your experience of its gentle appearing and disappearing from the surface is continuous. To sum up, the disunified succession is an experience that lacks both (a) continuous motion and (b) continuous experiencing, but the dolphin staccato surfacing is an example in which (a) the experience of a continuous motion lacks, but which is (b) continuous as experience.

Although those two cases are prima facie different, we should not overstate their diversity. It may be possible to *reduce* the continuity of experience to the continuity of the *content* presented to us. If so, then we are wrong in taking the continuity of experience as a feature of experience itself rather than of its content, or that somehow it inherits from its content. Consider again the swimming dolphin example. Even if the *movement of the dolphin* is not presented to us as continuous, there are *smooth passages* from the stages in which we are presented with no dolphin (since it is under the water), and the stages in which we are presented with the dolphin surfac*ing*/disappear*ing*. The right kind of similarity in the *contents* of experience may account for our sensation of continuity of the experiences themselves. After all, what distinguishes the example of the dolphin from the example of the disunified succession provided by Chuard is precisely this lack of smoothness in the passages from one scene to the next.

The reductionist approach is promising, but we need to make some adjustments. The main problem with it is that we describe our experience as continuous not only when we are attending to what we perceive, but also when our attention is directed inward.[8] Indeed, the idea of *stream of consciousness* is primarily that of an inner flow, a smooth sequence of experiences that do not

---

[8] In what follows, I use a notion, akin to that of O'Shaughnessy, of attention as a *psychic space*, rather than as a specifically perceptual faculty. Cf. '[...] the psychic space that the attention provides for [...] a whole range of [...] mental phenomena, is a space of *awareness* or *consciousness*. [...] The attention, we say, is occupied or taken up by emotion, thought, intentional action, and perception. [...T]he items which occupy the attention are all *experiences* [...] they are that out of which the whatever-it-be that we describe as "the stream of consciousness" is constituted.' O'Shaughnessy (2000: 278).

necessarily involve what goes on around us. We are aware of our experience being continuous also (and perhaps primarily) when we are focused on our own thoughts, inner sensations, and mental imagery. If the continuity of our own experience were somehow reducible to the *perceptual* experience of continuous motion and change, when such clearly non-perceptual aspects of our phenomenology are prominent, we should be less aware of the continuity of experience, but allegedly this does not seem to be the case. There are two ways to overcome this worry: one is to adapt the explanation from the perceptual to the non-perceptual case, and the other is to argue that we overstate continuity both in the inner and the outer case.

As for the first way, it is plausible insofar as we are allowed to attribute to non-perceptual experiences (that have a phenomenal character) a content in the same sense in which we attribute to perceptual experiences a content. The idea is that also in the case of mind wandering and inward-directed attention we can be (and often are) in a situation in which there is enough similarity of the right kind between successive contents, and thus we have the sensation that our temporal viewpoint shifts smoothly from one thought to the next. This reply forces us to say that in inward-directed experiences we are *presented* with something. If that is our own experience, we may risk beginning a weird regress. But even if we are ready to bite the bullet, there is a more general worry. Reductionism is only as plausible as Chuard's example of discontinuity. At first the claim that the example is that of a discontinuous experience may seem convincing. Such a Dadaist, psychedelic experience would almost certainly feel 'eerie' to many if not all. But why think that it would fail to deliver a sense of having a temporal point of view that shifts *smoothly* from one experience to another? Someone jumping abruptly in front of us when we are slowly surveying a calm landscape, swiping our sight from left to right, makes what we see discontinuous; but they do not cause our own experiences to flow differently than usual; that is, they do not cause our experience to 'stagger', although they may very well cause *us* to stagger. My proposal is to take reductionism in a rather different direction. I will follow the second way to overcome the worry and give up the idea that our experience is as continuous as our indirect description of it purportedly suggests. When it is continuous, it is because we are experiencing smooth changes or persistent entities, but for the most part having an overarching phenomenology is all that it takes to account for the purported continuity of experience. I develop the strategy in the next sections, and at the end of Section 3.3.2, I shall draw the conclusions for the reductionist project.

3.2.1 The stream of consciousness

As I use the term, a *stream of consciousness* is a temporally extended mental event composed by a succession of conscious mental events belonging to one person. Streams of consciousness are individuated independently of their phenomenological properties apart from being in a conscious state. There are two main models of stream of consciousness. One can be called the *wake model*, and it is probably the more intuitive. According to it, every time we go into a deep dreamless sleep or faint, we terminate a stream of consciousness, and every time we wake up, or 'regain consciousness', we initiate one. Therefore, even if our life does not constitute one single stream of consciousness, each stream of consciousness, like our little life, is rounded with a sleep. According to the *life model*, sleep or non-life-ending situations—apart possibly from full anaesthesia and a few pathological cases—are not sufficient to end a stream of consciousness, since something like a potentiality for full consciousness is never lost, and this is enough to continue being in a conscious state.[9] According to both models, streams of consciousness are mental events and thus physical processes. Roughly, a physical process is *temporally continuous* if it can be divided into ever smaller intervals. We can describe a physical process as continuous by using the real numbers as parameters for temporal attribution of features to it. Various features can be attributed usually both at intervals d, and at instants t. If the process is continuous,[10] such attributions are to be taken at face value.

Mental events can be described as continuous in the same way. Although properties that I am assuming we can attribute to them such as representational content and phenomenal character are not obviously properties reducible to those in the physical sciences, there does not seem to be anything problematic in describing a mental event as continuous in this sense. However, for a mental event to be continuous in this sense it does *not* necessarily mean that it is phenomenologically continuous and smooth. After all,

---

[9] One reason to adopt the life model is that, when we wake up, we usually have a feeling of how long we have been sleeping. If this feeling is due to a merely comparative mechanism (e.g. our brain compares the level of a hormone or something), then this phenomenology is compatible with both models. However, if the feeling is due to some monitoring system that remains active during sleep, then there may be reasons to prefer the life model over the wake model. The phenomenology of the awakening is a surprisingly underexplored field, but see Windt (2015) and Crowther and Soteriou (2017) for some reflections and further references.

[10] It may be that continuity is a gauge feature due to our mathematical formalism. For instance, time may be discrete at the Planck scale, and thus physical processes are naturally divided into discrete temporal (tiny) chunks. If so, what I say here would require some adjustment, but nothing substantive would change for my point. I also do not consider the possibility that our experience is dense but not continuous (see Rashbrook-Cooper 2011).

it is unlikely that what realizes the experiences of persons that report having *discontinuous* phenomenology—such as people with akinetopsia—are physical processes that are not continuous. (Although it is possible that the activity of the brain is somehow 'halting' in those cases.) I will say that in virtue of exemplifying phenomenal characters, mental events are *experiential processes*. An experiential process is *smooth* as our ordinary description of it suggests when its phenomenal character satisfies the following definition.

> **(SM)** An experiential process is *smooth* if, and only if, in its phenomenal character (i) there are no salient temporal borders and (ii) there are no gaps.

While it may make sense to attribute phenomenal character at instants to a smooth experiential process, on the assumption that it is a physically continuous mental event, there is no reason to think that a smooth experiential process can be partitioned into ever smaller temporal intervals. There are limits to our sensorial processing such that under a certain temporal threshold we are unable to be phenomenally presented with anything. We must be careful to distinguish here the fact that it makes sense to attribute phenomenal character to an experiential process at an instant (since experiential processes, as mental events, are physically continuous), from the idea that the phenomenal character or our experience is smooth and continuous as our ordinary descriptions of it suggest. What I am trying to do in this section is to give reason to think that our experiential processes do not have the phenomenal character of smoothness; namely, (No-gap) below does not hold, even if experiential processes are continuous mental events.

> **(No-gap)** Experiential processes are smooth as our ordinary descriptions suggest.

If (No-gap) does not hold, then one of the two conditions for smoothness (SM) fails. Consider condition (i) first. We do not report, unless we are in a very peculiar situation, such as on the dance floor under a stroboscopic lighting, our experience as being constituted by clear-cut temporal units, with a staccato pace. Rather, we report that our experiences seem to flow one into the next, and that it seems to us arbitrary to fix temporal borders between them at all. Condition (ii) is ambiguous. What does it mean to say that there is a gap in the phenomenal character? There are at least two options. According to the first, (ii_A) there is a gap in experienc*ing*. An example would be losing consciousness entirely every second for a third of a second or so. According to the second, (ii$_B$) our experiencing is continuous, but there are 'blank', phenomenally amorphous moments in the phenomenal character, like the no-light moments on the stroboscopic dance floor. Notice that even if we interpret (any version of) the second condition in terms of there being some clear-cut temporal borders in our experience, the condition is still silent with respect to the saliency of such borders. If the moments of lack of consciousness (as for ii$_A$) are very short, we may not notice the borders between the experiences, and the same goes if the blank moments (as for ii$_B$) between the contentful ones are very short. Thus, if (No-gap) does not hold, it is possible that there are gaps in our experience both in the sense (ii$_A$) and in the sense (ii$_B$), and that there are temporal borders in the sense of (i), although the issue of their saliency requires closer inspection.

3.2.2 Synchronic and diachronic gaps

If we consider the temporal elements in a succession of phenomenally complex experiences, we should take into consideration not only the *diachronic* gaps I have introduced in the previous section, but also the possibility of *synchronic* gaps. Synchronic gaps are blank parts in what we are presented with. How plausible it is that there are gaps of either type in our ordinary experience depends on which gap source we consider, and in a sense also on the kind of explanatory enterprise we are after. In the literature on *consciousness*, we find discussion of (1), namely gaps that are due to an incomplete stimulus, and (2), namely gaps whose source is the fact that the elaboration of the stimulus does not happen at a conscious level. But here I am not concerned with the (otherwise interesting) question of what makes a mental state or event conscious, or more generally of what distinguishes the sphere of conscious elaboration of the stimulus and the unconscious one. My focus—my explanatory focus—is the experience of succession, what we ordinarily describe as flow of consciousness. For that reason, I think that we should discuss the hypothesis that also (3), lack of attention, is a source of gaps. The idea is that we cannot say that we are aware of the succession of our experiences when we are not attentive to what we are experiencing. Even though, when we become attentive, we may also become aware that we *were* experiencing something all along.

(1) Partial stimulus (e.g. foveal blind spot, darting saccadic movements)
(2) Unconscious perception/detection (e.g. change blindness)

(3) Inattentive perception/detection

I consider synchronic gaps first. Synchronic gaps can be thought of in two ways. Synchronic$_A$ gaps are total absences of phenomenal character, like missing spots in what we are presented with. That there are synchronic$_A$ gaps in our ordinary experience follows from certain interpretations of partial, incomplete stimulation such as the foveal blind spot, and of peripheral vision. Daniel Dennett, for instance, interprets the blind spot as a synchronic$_A$ gap:

> [t]he brain does not have to 'fill in' for the blind spot, since the region in which the blind spot falls is already labelled [...]. If the brain received contradictory evidence from some region, it would abandon and adjust its generalisation, but not getting any evidence from the blind spot region is not the same as getting contradictory evidence. (Dennett 1991: 355)

The region of the visual field, where the missing information lies, is interpreted ('labelled') as if the gap were not there. For that reason, gaps of this kind are often unnoticed.[11]

Synchronic$_B$ gaps are not characterized by a complete lack of phenomenology, but they are rather amorphous, out-of-focus, blank areas in what we are presented with. A synchronic$_B$ gap is an experience that has a merely interpretational phenomenology (Section 1.2). No description of it, *in isolation*, imposes on us. In the literature, certain cases of gaps that are assumed to be due to unconscious elaboration of the stimulus are described in these terms. Tye, who criticizes Dennett's idea of gaps, while discussing change blindness (*viz.* the inability to detect change even when we have all that it takes in the stimulus), writes: 'We do not see these things. Even so, our visual fields do not have gaps in them; however, they are somewhat sparser than we ordinarily suppose, in that some of the things we would ordinarily take to be represented at a conscious level are not' (Tye 2009: 167). In my interpretation, this is a case of a synchronic$_B$ gap, something that has a 'sparse' phenomenal character, indeed in the sense that what it is like to have such experiences is mostly a matter of interpretation.

We have already encountered diachronic gaps while speaking of the two readings (ii$_A$) and (ii$_B$) of the second condition in (No-gap) above. I will label

---

[11] When something unusual happens, we may notice the effect of the missing information on the experience as a whole. See the example that Tye makes (to criticize Dennett's interpretation, to be fair) of King Charles II, who used to 'decapitate' his guests by making them stay in a location of the room where, from where His Majesty was sitting, they looked headless (Tye 2009: 165–6).

the two varieties of diachronic gaps diachronic$_A$ gaps, which are periods of lack in consciousness, and diachronic$_B$ gaps, which are periods of blankness, respectively. Dennett (1991: 355) argues for the existence of diachronic$_A$ gaps. He notices that '[t]he blind spot is a spatial hole, but there can be temporal holes as well. The smallest are the gaps that occur while our eyes dart about during saccades. We don't notice these gaps, but they don't have to be filled in because we are designed not to notice them.' Again, the brain interprets the experience as if those gaps were not there, and thus the gaps are usually impossible to notice (Lee 2014b). For that reason, diachronic$_A$ gaps are compatible with smooth phenomenology. Indeed, this is one of the reasons why cinematic theorists can insist on the fact that there is nothing more to the similarity between the snapshots and their pace to the awareness of succession and continuity (Chuard 2011). If there is a short moment of inactivity between the snapshot, we fail to notice it, as we fail to notice the small differences in the changing contents. And small diachronic$_B$ gaps, too, would fail to be noticed. What I want to argue is that the presence of *non*-insignificant (namely detectable) diachronic$_B$ gaps in our experience is compatible with our tendency to describe experience as continuous and smooth.

But first, let me discuss the idea that the elements of our experience that are out of the focus of attention can be construed as synchronic$_B$ and diachronic$_B$ gaps. Begin with exploring the assumption that attention is sufficient for fully fledged, cogent phenomenology. If we are attending to a particular sound, a detail of a shape, or a smell in the kitchen, then we are presented with such things. This assumption may be a bit idealized, but I take the idealization to be innocuous in this context. Now let us ask: is attention also necessary for phenomenology? If there are no gaps, then the answer is a clear no. Maybe nature has no *horror vacui*, but experience does fear absences and blank areas. Like the façade of a baroque church, it leaves almost no naked space. But if there are gaps, then the answer could be yes, attention is necessary for phenomenology, at least non-merely interpretational phenomenology.

I think that if we are ready to accept synchronic$_A$ and diachronic$_A$ gaps with sources (1) and (2), then we should take seriously the idea that lack of attention can be a source of synchronic$_B$ and diachronic$_B$ gaps.[12] If being off the focus of attention is enough to have synchronic$_B$ gaps, then when we fail to see the gorilla, or we 'miss' the keys on the messy shelf, or we notice a component in

---

[12] My understanding of attention is similar to Nanay's (2010). My conception is in a sense more general than his, since it is characterized independently of whether one endorses a representationalist or relational view of content, but in a sense more restrictedly, since it is not just in terms of indeterminacy (determinable vs. determinate), but of gaps.

the smell of a perfume only after being asked 'can you spot the looming orange blossom?'; in all such cases, part of what we experience is like a background white noise, which turns into a proper phenomenal character only when, and if, we turn our attention to it. If being off the focus of attention is enough to have diachronic$_B$ gaps, then when we begin to notice the metallic clang in the distance that, according to our friend, 'has been going on for some time already, hasn't it?', or we are lost in our thoughts while walking in the corridor and do not notice the friend waving at us in the distance, in all such cases sections of our experience are phenomenologically amorphous, and their phenomenal character can be interpreted only if we turn our attention to them later.[13]

There is thus a distinction between the case of attending the smooth movement of a car passing by, in which an experience can be cogently described as a succession of experiences flowing one into the other, and the case of switching attention from the movement of the car to our friend talking, to a memory that pops up in our mind, then to a strong smell that comes from the garbage on the side of the street, and then back to the car which is now only a dot disappearing far away. Maybe, as long as we are directing our attention to *something*, our awareness of succession is smooth enough to justify the metaphor of the flow. However, switches of attention are not necessarily smooth passages and the parts of experience that are not attended to do qualify as diachronic$_B$ gaps in the purported stream. In the next section I will elaborate on these ideas. But before that, I need to make two related clarifications, which will be very important in what follows.[14]

While I think it is false that there are no synchronic gaps in our experience, the presence of synchronic gaps is compatible with what I call the *phenomenology of synchronic fullness*. Roughly, having a phenomenology of synchronic fullness means that it seems that *it seems* to us that every aspect of our experience has phenomenal character, that every part of our experience, apart from a few occasional exceptions, enjoys the same level of phenomenal vividness.[15] The phenomenology of synchronic fullness is akin to what

---

[13] For a similar point, made in terms of undetermined content, see Vosgerau et al. (2008).

[14] The distinction between diachronic gap$_A$ and diachronic gap$_B$ is similar to the distinction that James makes between interruptions in consciousness and interruptions in the content (James 1890: 521). It is different from the distinction between strong and weak continuity in Dainton (2014), which depends on the presence of a feeling of smoothly passing from one experience to another. It is more like the distinction between objective and subjective continuity in Arstila and Lloyd (2014).

[15] There is probably a sense of vividness that does not correlate with lack of determinacy in the phenomenology. One can have an intense experience of the *Temptation of Saint Antonius* by Hieronymus Bosch even before noticing the details in the picture (thanks to Gottfried Vosgerau for raising the point and giving the example). However, the lack of determinacy that is due to lack of attention is, in a sense, a lack of vividness. I do not want to enter a terminological battle here. My point here is only that we tend to describe our experience as if the non-attended parts of it and the ones in the focus of attention were phenomenologically on a par.

is sometimes called an *intellectual seeming* (Gow 2019). It is not the thesis that our brain fills in the details that cannot be elaborated from the stimulus, but rather the thesis that we tend to *not* notice the absence of certain details. What falls out of the focus of our attention can be characterized only in an interpretational way, and in most of the cases only after, in memory, or, if still available, upon re-examination. Consider the taste of violet in your cocktail that surfaces as having been there since the first sip as the bartender replies to your enquiry 'it's a violet–infused liqueur'. Or think of realizing that an earworm was playing in your head for a while. Therefore, if (No-gap) fails and yet we have a phenomenology of synchronic fullness, we will tend to misdescribe our experience as uniformly vivid although it is not.

Similarly, while I think that it is false that there are no diachronic gaps in our experience, there is a *phenomenology of diachronic fullness* (or *of continuity*). It seems that it seems to us that our experience never varies in the intensity of its phenomenal character; that is, we tend to think that it never significantly diminishes its phenomenal vividity across time. If (No-gap) fails but we have a phenomenology of diachronic fullness, there is no phenomenal smoothness, but our experiences are permeated by the sensation that there is. This is why (in part) we tend to use flow or stream metaphors in talking about what it is like to have experiences one after another. But the metaphors should *not* be taken as expressing more than the fact that we are aware of continuously undergoing a succession of experiences.

3.2.3 Experiential chunks

The presence of diachronic gaps in our experience, together with a reductionist approach to the continuity of experience, suggests that experience can come in *temporal chunks*. There are two related problems with this claim. The first is that there does not seem to be any non-arbitrary way to chop up experience. Tye argues that we should consider every stream of consciousness *one* experience (Tye 2003a: 96 and ff.). His reasoning is that if you take seriously the idea of temporal transparency, you should conclude that we cannot be aware of the temporal length *of our own experiences*, since in general we cannot be aware of the properties of our experiences per se. And it is of little use to look at the contents of our experiences (even assuming, in line with positive transparency, that we can read from the properties of the content those of the experience), because there are only arbitrary ways of cutting a stream of consciousness in experiential 'chunks'. If we adhere to the wake model of the stream of consciousness, as Tye does, the only bona fide borders of experiences are waking up and falling asleep. The second is that talking of the stream of consciousness as coming in experiential chunks is *wrong at a phenomenal level*. Consider an experience D of a longish arpeggio; an andante like that shown in Figure 3.1.

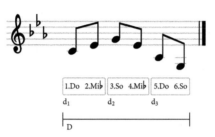

Figure 3.1 Andante 1

The objection is that there is something wrong with thinking of such an experience as being divided into temporal chunks. Let us frame the point in the language of the extensionalist specious present for simplicity. Let us say that a specious present cannot take on more than two notes in the succession in question. More specifically, we have a succession of three specious presents, that happen at the intervals d_1, d_2, and d_3 (composing the interval of the whole experience, D). During d_1 we are presented with the succession 1.*do*–2.*mib*; during d_2 we are presented with the succession 3.*so*–4.*mib*; and during d_3 we are presented with the succession 5.*do*–6.*so*. The objection is that during D, we are *also* presented with the succession 2.*mib*–3.*so* (and 4.*mib*–5.*do*). But if there is a hiatus between d_1 and d_2 (and d_2 and d_3), we should never be able to be aware of those successions in the same way we are of 1.*do*–2.*mib* (and 3.*so*–4.*mib*). And this is phenomenologically wrong. Or is it? Let us focus on what exactly is claimed here to be phenomenologically wrong. First, as the case is presented, with our attention beginning at 1.*do*, it is *not* obvious that we are aware of the passage from 2.*mib* to 3.*so* in the same way we are of the passage from 1.*do* to 2.*mib*. What is obvious is that we *can* be aware of the second passage in the same way in which, by assumption, we are of the first one. Why can we? Because we would if we change the context a bit. For instance, if we started paying attention to the melody just before 2.*mib*, it is very likely that we would be presented with the succession 2.*mib*–3.*so* in the same way we are presented with the succession 1.*do*–2.*mib* *when* we begin being attentive at

1.*do*. But given that we are *assuming* that we began to be attentive at 1.*do*, then we should not take for granted that 2.*mib* and 3.*so* sound as linked together as 1.*do* and 2.*mib* do.

Secondly, I agree that if we are not paying much attention, we can be aware of the arpeggio that goes on at D instinctively, and thus of the passage between 1.*do* and 2.*mib*, and the passage between 3.*so* and 4.*mib* in the same way. However, according to my hypothesis, in that case the whole phenomenology is largely interpretational, and thus it does not pose a threat to the idea that *attentive* experience can come in temporal chunks.[16] Thirdly, in a sequence that is rhythmically amorphous like that in the example, there may be interpretational elements also when we pay attention to it. The experience of the arpeggio in Figure 3.1 played by a machine, for instance, is likely to be undermined with respect to various ways of grouping notes together into possible 'musical objects'.[17] But that does not mean that our experience is essentially undetermined with respect to its temporal borders, it just means that how experience is organized diachronically sometimes depends on attention and other contextual and interpretational details. And this is compatible with the fact that other times it just *imposes* on us. Consider for instance an auditory experience with pronounced rhythmic elements, such as this other andante (see Figure 3.2).

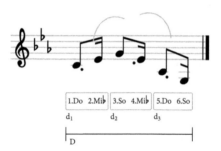

Figure 3.2 Andante 2

The first note, a *do*, lasts a bit more than half a second; the second, a *mib*, lasts only one third of the previous one and swiftly, in a legato manner, leaves room to the third one, a *so*, that lasts again less than half a second. In this case,

---

[16] Besides, if the hypothesis of disunified streams is correct (see Section 3.3), different chunks can be overlapping, or at least one of the effects of probing can be that we interpret the phenomenology as of overlapping chunks.

[17] Although other properties of the series may impose themselves phenomenologically, for instance its being a minor scale.

if we are paying at least a bit of attention, it would be very difficult *not* to group together 2.*mi♭* and 3.*so*, and leave 1.*do* on its own, as it were. If something as rhythmically pronounced as the second andante is in the focus of our attention, 'musical objects' are likely to be presented to us. That is to say, our experience is divided into experiential chunks that flow one after the other. Although I think that the possibility that our experience can be organized in temporal chunks is phenomenologically plausible, the picture that I have suggested in criticizing the arguments against it is too simplistic. In the next section I articulate it further.

3.3 The disunity of experience

The presence of both synchronic and diachronic gaps in our stream of consciousness suggests not only that our experience is not smooth as the metaphors of the flow and the stream suggest, but also that our experience is less unified than we may ordinarily think. I do not want to overstate this claim, since there are good reasons to take seriously the idea that at some level, and when we are attentive, our experience can be both synchronically and diachronically unified in something like a phenomenal field—at least in the minimal sense that our attention is divided towards several things at once. However, the fact that our experience is temporally unified in those circumstances does not mean that it has a *unique temporal structure*. Consider the synchronic case of experiences that appears unified across different modalities. When we say 'I was feeling the smell of the lilacs *while* I was listening to the music', we seem to give a cogent indirect description of our phenomenology, but this does not entail that our experience has a unified modal structure, namely that without such unifications *there would not be experience at all*. Rather, experience is structurally such that we can have attentive experiences that are synchronically unified across sensory modalities, but this does not rule out experiences that are *not* so unified. Let me dwell a bit more on this thought and expand it to the diachronic case.

3.3.1 The anarchic flow

Gerald Viera, while arguing for the disunity of temporal experience in an inspiring paper, notes that 'we perceive durations, temporal orderings, rhythms, etc., and while we perceive these properties across a range of timescales and through multiple sensory modalities, many scientists and philosophers nevertheless assume that a single mechanism or type of explanation will allow us to account for the human perception of time', and this is so because '[t]he various temporal properties we perceive are all integrated into a single temporal ordering in experience, and therefore, we should expect there to be some unity to the timekeeping mechanism in perception' (Viera 2019: 33). Interestingly, as he argues at length, our expectations are likely to be wrong.

I take it to be a datum that we are, *in some sense*, aware of at least some aspect of the temporal structure of our own experience when it comes to large timescales (hours or days, say). If we talk of parts without any commitment to what counts as a unity of experience or what is more fundamental, it is just trivial to say that we know that our experience, at large timescales, is made up of parts that come in temporal order. Indeed, it seems also trivial that we can appeal to such a temporal structure in explaining how we are aware of analogous properties of the things that we experience. If we are asked how do we know that Saturday night's dinner with friends *preceded* Sunday's oversleeping, a perfectly natural answer is that we experienced the former and then the latter. This does not mean that we are phenomenally presented with the temporal structure of our own experience, or that experience at much shorter temporal scales makes us aware of its own temporal structure (and of its mirroring the temporal structure of the events we are perceptually presented through it). If it is still utterly plausible to produce an answer similar to the one given above with respect to questions such as 'how do you know that the lightning seemed to precede the thunder?', it is doubtful that (unless one is committed to a specific philosophical view of perception) a similar answer is 'natural' in the case of questions such as: how do you know that the swift hand moved from the noon position to the one position? As Viera illustrates, depending on the different timescales and modalities, our brain uses different mechanisms to track the different temporal properties. Some of them respect mirroring—roughly, they represent the temporal properties by instantiating those very temporal properties—others do not.

The idea that sensitivity to difference in timescales challenges the thesis of a unique temporal structure of experience is not entirely new (although Viera's elaboration is original). In his criticism of the Cartesian theatre idea, Dennett suggests that the origin of its prima facie plausibility lies in an unwarranted extrapolation from what goes on at large timescales. Here is the relevant passage:

> The Cartesian Theatre is a metaphorical picture of how conscious experience must sit in the brain. It seems at first to be an innocent extrapolation of the familiar and undeniable fact that for everyday, *macroscopic time intervals,* we can indeed order events into the two categories 'not yet observed' and 'already observed.' We do this by locating the observer at a point and plotting the motions of the vehicles of information relative to that point. But when we try to extend this method to explain phenomena involving very short time intervals, we encounter a *logical* difficulty: If the 'point' of view of the observer must be smeared over a rather large volume in the observer's brain, the observer's own subjective sense of sequence and simultaneity must be determined by something other than 'order of arrival,' since order of arrival is incompletely defined until the relevant destination is specified. If A beats B to one finish line but B beats A to another, which result fixes the subjective sequence in consciousness? (Dennett 1991: 107)

Dennett's point is that there is not a single stream of consciousness, because temporal information does not, or does not always, get integrated in a single operating centre. I think we can make sense of this by resorting to the interplay of synchronic$_B$ and diachronic$_B$ gaps. Attention does not operate only synchronically, but also diachronically. We can follow with sight an annoying fly that we want to catch, and wandering with our gaze here and there after we lose it, we can indulge in feeling the taste of an old wine change in our mouth or follow for a while the bassoon part in a quintet. Yet on many occasions we do not attend to anything specifically. When it is so, it is likely that movements and changes around us, like someone beginning to talk to us, trigger our attention. If attention is necessary for cogent phenomenology, this means that there are more synchronic$_B$ *and* diachronic$_B$ gaps than we ordinarily suspect, and that they 'work together', thereby creating a disunified continuity. When we follow the annoying fly, its movement is presented to us in a cogent way, but many other things off the focus of attention are not determinately ordered along the movement of the fly in our experience. Imagine that when you move your gaze swiftly to the left after the fly has taken off again from its brief pause on the refrigerator door, you hear a loud squeak from Beep Beep, the guinea pig. She's hungry and has been whining for a while, trying to catch your attention. For a while, to be sure, but for how long? Before you started following the fly? When the fly made its first stop on the table? When it took off? Hard to tell. Indeed, there may have not been a unified phenomenal field in which the first audible whine from Beep Beep and some part of the flight of the insect were experienced together. It is only *now*, when you attend to both, that you are aware of them having appended together for some time.

I use Figure 3.3 below to give an idea of a succession of experiences that are not necessarily synchronized in a series of coherent frames, what I call an *anarchic flow*.

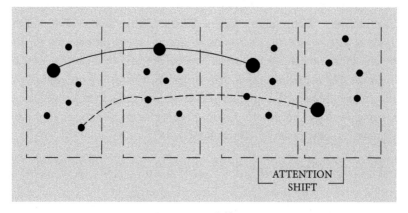

Figure 3.3 Disunified continuity

In Figure 3.3, the large dots connected by a thin line symbolize the experiences of the events in the focus of attention. If they constitute a sequence of experiences focused on a movement, a change, or something persisting, they will typically give rise to a smooth experience, which is cogently captured by the ordinary metaphor of the flow. But such a smooth experience, as in the example of the fly and the whining guinea pig, does not need to be unified with other sequences that are not in the focus of attention, and are phenomenologically undetermined. In the picture, the experiences 'off the focus of attention' are symbolized by the smaller dots. Switching attention to them has the effect of *probing* the stream of consciousness (more on this in Section 3.3.3) and enables us to retrospectively interpret their phenomenological character. For instance, the switch of attention depicted in the picture can be seen as reconstructing a sequence of a constant movement (the experiences connected with the dotted line) and rough 'fields of simultaneity' (the frames in dashed lines). However, there is no guarantee that we end up with a unified stream of coherent, continuous, and fully determined snapshots.

The psychologist Susan Blackmore, while arguing for the disunity of the stream of consciousness, writes:

> This [the fact that there is no requirement for there to be only one conscious stream at a time] is particularly helpful for thinking about the stream of sounds because sounds only make sense when information is integrated over appreciable lengths of time. As an example, imagine you are sitting in the garden and can hear a passing car, a bird singing, and some children shouting in the distance, and that you switch attention rapidly between them. If there were one stream of consciousness, then each time attention switched you would have to wait while enough information came into the stream to identify the sound—to hear it as a passing car. In fact, attention can switch much faster than this. A new backwards stream can be created very quickly and the information it uses may overlap with that used in another stream a moment later, and another, and so on. (Blackmore 2002: 27)

At large timescales, there is nothing wrong with thinking of the flow of our experiences as constituted by a synchronic grouping in successive snapshots of a stream. But for shorter timescales, the only phenomenology that imposes on us, and thus it is cogently captured by the continuity description, concerns the things that are presented to us in the focus of attention. Therefore, since roughly at the same time our experience can have parts that are in the focus of attention and parts that are not, an anarchic flow will not usually be unified. More precisely, it is such that it is usually undetermined *how* it is unified, since it is composed of overlapping chunks, some of which are under the focus of attention and have cogent phenomenology, while others are off the focus of attention and have only interpretational phenomenology.[18]

Finally, the anarchic flow is not a 'postmodernist' flow, for which *anything* goes. Firstly, there are constraints that come from the attentive elements of our experience. When I realize that Beep Beep is whining, I interpret what I was inattentively experiencing as a whine, and not as the neighbour annoyingly

---

[18] Cf. Bayne's talk of the imperial model of unity (for consciousness), in which every cognitive activity is somehow under the control of a directive centre, and of a federal model, in which consciousness is organized in a less centralized way. 'We should remain alive to the possibility that the correlation between consciousness and global availability seen in the context of the normal waking state is generated by "imperial" mechanisms of integration that are superimposed on top of the relatively more "federal" mechanisms responsible for the construction of consciousness itself' (Bayne 2010: 116). The anarchic flow is not to be confused with the federal model of consciousness. However, the fact that the anarchic flow does not require even a federal level of consciousness does not mean that it behaves erratically or rhapsodically. It behaves in an orderly way locally, but how the various parts connect globally is undetermined, and it becomes determined only as a consequence of the probing activity.

rehearsing with the trumpet, also because the loud whine that made me attentive towards what was going on around me was undoubtedly a guinea pig whine. However, if the neighbour was playing the trumpet, but I was sufficiently inattentive towards the trumpet, I may think that Beep Beep had been whining for a while even if she suddenly busted into a single loud whine. Especially if the neighbour stopped playing exactly when Beep Beep made herself salient (and if my neighbour on the trumpet does sound a bit like a guinea pig). Secondly, there are degrees of attention and thus degrees of phenomenological amorphousness. If the bartender asks me 'could you tell the violet in the cocktail?' once I am done with it, but they are mistaken and it was apricot liqueur that they put in it, I may be very reluctant to interpret my gustative experience as of violet ('are you sure you put violet liqueur in that? Wasn't it something fruitier?'). But if the bartender asks me the same question after I had only an absent-minded sip while talking with a friend, I may sincerely reply in the affirmative.

3.3.2 The phenomenology of diachronic fullness

I can now also give a more articulated explanation of the phenomenology of diachronic fullness that I mentioned before (Section 3.2.2) as something that comes with the awareness of succession. When I distinguish between uncommon and the common overarching phenomenology, my terminology may have suggested a reading of those notions in terms of frequency: common overarching phenomenology, such as awareness of succession, is something that we experience very often or virtually always, whereas an uncommon overarching phenomenology, such as a feeling of eerie familiarity, is something that we experience only rarely. This is *not* what I meant. That awareness of succession is common does not mean that we are aware of our own experiences succeeding one another all the time. Indeed, we are surprisingly unaware of this most of the time, when we are attentive to events in the environment around us, or follow the inner flow of our thoughts. However, we can *become aware* of the flow of our own experience in virtually every moment of our life. This is true both at a large scale, as when we think of what happened during last week or last year, and at much shorter scales, as when we ask ourselves whether it was one or two knocks at the door that we just heard. Awareness of succession is common because it does not require a specific context to happen, and not (necessarily) because it is frequent. The feeling of eerie familiarity, on the other hand, even if it may happen frequently in certain contexts (for instance, you walk around your old neighbourhood for one hour and at every corner a sensation of something new but old strikes you), requires a *specific* context (e.g. you are back after many years) and in that it is uncommon.

The same holds for awareness of succession and diachronic fullness. If it is possible to pass most of our daily life without having any awareness of succession of experiences, a fortiori it is possible to pass most of our daily life without being aware of the succession of our own experience with a phenomenology of diachronic fullness. It is only when we probe the anarchic flow and become aware of our experience being structured as a succession of experiences that we become aware of our experience in a way that suggests that the succession is smooth and continuous, as the metaphor of the flow suggests.

Others who, like me, argue for the discontinuous nature of consciousness have appealed to the phenomenology of diachronic fullness (without calling it that, and perhaps without fully realizing it) to explain the contrast between the claim that experience is *not* continuous and the presence of the metaphor of the stream in everyday thought. Consider this remark by Dennett: 'One of the most striking features of consciousness is its *dis*continuity [. . .]. The discontinuity of consciousness is striking because of the *apparent* continuity of consciousness' (1991: 356). The slightly paradoxical flavour of the remarks becomes almost a flat-footed contradiction if we think of Dennett's first-person operationalism, according to which it does not make sense to talk of experience as it is objectively speaking, and thus of experience as appearing continuous when in fact it is discontinuous.[19] A way to make sense of that passage, and smooth its contradictory flavour, is to take the talk of 'apparent' continuity as talk of the phenomenology of diachronic fullness that becomes prominent in certain occasions. There are parts of our experience that are indeed smooth, for instance when we are attentive to a continuous movement or a steady sound. There are others that can be interpreted as smooth in retrospect, but for which there was no smooth phenomenology while we were experiencing them. Therefore, the metaphor of the stream is largely a confabulation, albeit innocuous.

---

[19] Cf. 'We might classify the Multiple Drafts model, then, as first-person operationalism, for it brusquely denies the possibility in principle of consciousness of a stimulus in the absence of the subject's belief in that consciousness' (Dennett 1991: 132). And also: 'The Multiple Drafts model makes "writing it down" in memory criterial for consciousness; that is what it is for the "given" to be "taken"—to be taken one way rather than another' (p. 132).

3.3.3 Probing effects

We can say now that the reductionist picture (Section 3.2), according to which the continuity of experience is reduced to the continuity of the content, is more plausible once we consider factors that put in doubt that we are aware of the continuity of our own experience as much as we tend to think. If I am right and the awareness of succession is structurally necessary to have experience, then there is little reason to think of the experience of continuity as fundamentally distinct from the experience of continuous goings-on.

I have claimed that the phenomenology of diachronic fullness becomes prominent only on certain occasions, and I have labelled those occasions *probing effects*. But what are those exactly? The effects of probing are different if we consider large timescales and short timescales, and I think it is important to bring this difference to the fore. Dennett distinguishes the 'skein of content', very roughly what I call the anarchic flow, which is 'only rather like a narrative because of its multiplicity', from the narratives, which are the result of 'probing this stream at various intervals' (1991: 135). However, Dennett seems actually to put in the same boat probing with respect to long temporal scales and probing with respect to short temporal scales, since, in both cases, the result is a narrative, something akin to a belief concerning a certain sequence of events. Consider this quote:

> Probing this stream at different places and times produces different effects, precipitates different narratives from the subject. If one delays the probe too long (overnight, say), the result is apt to be no narrative left at all—or else a narrative that has been digested or 'rationally reconstructed' until it has no integrity. If one probes 'too early', one may gather data on how early a particular discrimination is achieved by the brain, but at the cost of diverting what would otherwise have been the normal progression of the multiple stream. (Dennett 1991: 113)

Here Dennett moves without signalling it from what is a long timescale probing (thinking the day after what happened the day before) to a short timescale probing (thinking of what just happened). This may be puzzling, since the outcome of becoming aware of the succession of our experiences at a large temporal scale is on the face of it something quite different from the outcome of becoming aware of the succession of our experiences at short timescales. When we become aware of the succession of our experiences at a large timescale, the result is what I call a *narrative thought*, roughly a belief about a succession of events in one's life (I will come back to this idea in Section 3.5.2). Regardless of the details, which may be controversial, it seems obvious that at different moments in our lives, the narrative that we construct about us and about what goes on in general may change. This 'changing the past' effect of probing at large timescales is hardly problematic. Indeed, we are not usually surprised to realize that we have incoherent memories. First of all, there may be a change in the availability, or relevance, of what we remember (regardless of how frustrating that may be). We forget things and neglect things, which maybe later, for the most various reasons, we retrieve and put back in place (not necessarily the same) in the succession of events that we care to remember. Secondly, we may even be fully aware of the changes; for instance, because we come to know new things. This is particularly evident in what may be called 'change of meaningfulness'. The very same succession of events may pass from being a funny weekend to the story of how you got tricked by a crook, and of course such a change of importance (meaningfulness) attached to the elements of a narrative may lead also to a change in the narrative itself. ('Wait! I thought they called after you told me that Joanna left, but given how they behaved, I realize now that they must have called me before'.)

What goes on with probing at a shorter timescale is much more controversial both among psychologists and philosophers. And it is quite natural to think that the nature of the controversy has to do with the fact that the effects of probing at short timescales are purportedly *phenomenological* and not merely cognitive. Becoming aware of the succession of our own experiences makes a difference for what it is, or rather *was*, like to have them. Consider for instance meta-contrast masking, a postdiction illusion (Section 2.5). A target visual stimulus, usually a full black circle, is shown briefly, and then a 'mask', usually a doughnut rounding it, is shown. If we ask the subjects to probe the experience right after, namely we ask for a verbal report of what they have seen, they will typically report that have seen both when the temporal distance between the two stimuli is either very short (around 20 ms) or very large (over 150 ms), while they report to have seen only the doughnut (which has thus successfully masked the circle) if it is somewhere in between. Interestingly, if instead of asking them to report the experience, we ask the subject to *react* to it, for instance in a non-verbal way—by pressing a button, say—the masking effect disappears, or more precisely becomes less and less pronounced the longer the temporal distance between target and mask. As Bayne (2010: 128) says by commenting on the experiment of Ansorge et al. (1998): '[s]ubjects appeared to be "aware" of the target when they were encouraged to treat it as an object of response but not when they were led to treat it as an object of report'.

It is clear that awareness of succession at short timescales is subject to much more 'dramatic' probing effects than what happens at larger timescales.[20] However, whether we are dealing with a divide between situations that have an effect on what the experience is like, and situations that merely affect the way we think or describe a certain succession of experience, or the two cases are indeed more similar than it seems, depends on what is the nature of the phenomenology at stake. In Dennett's construal, probing is strictly connected to a general antirealist view of phenomenology, the idea, in my terminology, that phenomenal characters are never cogent but always merely, and entirely, interpretational (Section 1.2). According to Dennett, '[j]ust what we are conscious of within any particular time duration is not defined independently of the probes we use to precipitate a narrative about that period' (1991: 136). The difference between the short timescale and the long timescale can be as dramatic as it gets, but it is not a difference between an effect on the phenomenological character and an effect on what we come to believe. Therefore, also in cases like apparent motion and meta-contrast masking, there is no seeming basis on which the belief that we come to form—for instance, that the dot has smoothly moved from one side of the screen to the other—is formed.[21] Others, like Bayne, have a realist interpretation of the probing effects at short timescales: '[t]he nature of the subject's experience is a function of probe-involving facts, but probe-involving facts are themselves perfectly determinate: given how a subject is (or expects to be) probed on a particular trial, there will be a corresponding fact about what they experienced on that trial' (Bayne 2010: 129).

My account allows for more flexibility than Dennett's or Bayne's. At a short timescale, one can probe what is *in* the focus of attention, or *by* shifting attention to what is going on in a sequence we were not paying attention to. In the first case, my account predicts that the phenomenology is cogent. For instance, let us say that the scenario is that of an apparent movement with an optimal stimulus, and we are fully attentive. We are presented with a dot that moves from the left to the right of a screen (and maybe changes colour along the way). The phenomenal character of the experience imposes on us,

---

[20] Another interesting probing effect in meta-contrast masking is given by whether the subjects are asked to provide a verbal report as soon as possible ('speeded trials') or are not put under pressure ('unspeeded trials'). In speeded trials the masking effect is diminished as in the reaction tasks; cf. Lachter and Durgin (1999).

[21] Cf. 'The trouble, one may think, with the Multiple Drafts model of colour phi, for instance, is that even if it includes the phenomenon of the subject's judging that there was intervening motion, it does not include—it explicitly denies the existence of—any event which might be called the seeming-to-be-intervening-motion, on which this judgement is "based"' (Dennett 1991: 133).

and the experience-based claim 'a dot just crossed the screen from left to right' is cogent. Many other streams may have been going on during the trial. Maybe there was a faint chatter in the background, or the buzz of an electronic device, or noises from the street. Suppose that after you have observed the dot moving and changing colour from red to green in the middle of the screen, you realize that you heard a klaxon sound, just a bit above the background noise from the street. The phenomenon of the sequence of experiences containing undertone street noises over which a louder klaxon abruptly emerges, according to my model, is radically different from the cogent phenomenology of the apparent movement of the dot in the focus of attention. Besides, as just pointed out, given that there was no unified experience in which the noises before the loud klaxon and some parts of the movement of the dot are presented together, the temporal relation between the two is phenomenologically indeterminate. What unifies them the moment I switch attention from the screen to the klaxon is the awareness of succession that becomes salient. In probing the anarchic flow about a series of experiences out of the focus of attention, we impose an interpretation on an undetermined phenomenology.

3.4 Presentational phenomenology and phenomenal objectivity

While the fact that we have a phenomenology of diachronic fullness may explain why we tend to describe experience as continuous and smooth, sometimes we do *not* describe our experience as smooth throughout. For instance, when we 'emerge' from a period in which we were engrossed in our thoughts, we may be surprised by the sounds, smells, and colours we find to have around us, and by how much time has passed. The 'switch' from inner attention to outward attention, as it were, can be perceived as a discontinuity factor in our experience. In other words, it does *not always* seem that our stream of consciousness appears smooth.

This remark allows us to illuminate a further sense in which the smoothness and continuity of our experience is often overstated, besides the one from gaps and lack of unity I have just discussed. We have described the inner flow and an outer flow of our experiences as often interwoven and overlapping. But is the talk of *two* flows to be taken seriously? I can think of two ways of taking this way of speaking seriously, and none seems particularly promising. One is to think of two entirely disconnected temporal successions. I have already noticed that our own experiences and the events that we are phenomenally aware of appear to happen in the same temporal dimension, and so do the events about which our cognitive states (e.g. beliefs) are. Intuitively, in the very same 'temporal arena' we find not only our perceptions and the things we perceive, but also our thoughts and the things we think of. It is indeed difficult to make sense of two disconnected temporal series, namely two series such that neither one comes wholly before or after the other, nor do they overlap partially or totally (cf. Quinton 1962). Notice that we cannot—as I have suggested arguing for the anarchic flow—appeal to the fact that there may be phenomenally disunified sequences of experiences, because for the inner flow and the outer flow to be disunified, they should be disconnected in principle, and not just as an effect of attention. And I fail to see how to make sense of two temporal sequences whatsoever being disconnected in some more robust sense than because we do not attend to them both. But if they are not really disconnected, then it may be more appropriate to talk about a succession of experiences that have outward and inward elements, which sometimes overlap.

One way to unpack this image is to distinguish elements in our phenomenology that come with either *phenomenal objectivity* or *outward-directed presentational phenomenology* and those that do not (Section 1.4). Certain experiences present us with entities that are out there; for others it is less clear what the status is of what is presented to us. For instance, after-images or other flickering visual experiences are usually considered as eerie not just because of their flimsiness, but also because they tend to behave not like things with phenomenal objectivity do: they follow the movement of our gaze, and cannot be inspected by moving around them. But at least some of them, even if they lack phenomenal objectivity, have outward-directed presentational phenomenology. An after-image of a flash from a camera is phenomenally different from a lightbulb, but like the lightbulb or the rainbow, it is out there. For others, such as the 'stars' that we see if we have low blood pressure and we stand up too quickly, it is less clear. Mental imagery (and perhaps moods) are also cases for which it is not always clear whether, even when they clearly lack phenomenal objectivity, they have outward or inward-directed presentational phenomenology, or lack presentational phenomenology at all.

I do not take this case-by-case vagueness to be problematic for the theory. Even if we assume that all such issues are settled, the idea that we are aware of a succession of experiences, some of them as part of an outer flow, others as part of an inner flow, is too simplistic. This is so because it clashes with the idea of disunity that I have explored and defended in Section 3.3. Only if there is a strong kind of phenomenological unity could we determine in principle whether an experience as a whole has phenomenal objectivity or outward-directed presentational phenomenology. A more articulated version constructs the two flows as *abstractions* out of various aspects of the disunified succession of experiences. In the next section I explore this more articulated version of the view.

3.4.1 The phenomenal time of the outer world

As I pointed out at the very beginning of this chapter, the time in which events around us happen and the time in which our experiences of them happen appears to be one and the same. However, the probing effect on our phenomenology at short timescales forces us to reconsider and possibly qualify that claim. When our attention is outward-directed the events of which we have experience will typically appear as happening at a certain time, which is also the time at which the experiences of them happen. For various reasons, we know that the events that appear in experience and the experience of them do *not* actually happen at the same time. Those reasons are: (i) the time lag due to the medium, and the time lag due to neural elaboration; and (ii) the presence of postdictive effects. Consider again the experience of apparent motion that we have in the colour-phi scenario. We can redescribe the situation in terms of *temporal locations* appearing to us in a certain way, namely containing this or that event. The temporal location t_1 appears to us as containing a red dot beginning to move towards the right. The temporal location t_2 appears to us as containing a red dot changing colour while crossing the screen. And the temporal location t_3 appears to us as containing a green dot arriving at the right end of the screen. If we put it that way, it becomes natural to ask whether we can take t_1, t_2, t_3 to be the temporal locations of the stimuli *as they appear* in experiencing them. That the answer is *yes* is not obvious, and indeed there are good reasons to think it is *no*.

I begin by noting that while saying that the *space* where the events that are contained in those temporal locations happen is 'out there' makes perfect sense, it is unclear to me whether we can really make sense of the idea of a time 'out there', which is not also the time in which our inner life happens (cf. also Section 4.3.2). An analogy with the spatial locations may help. In visual experience at least, it seems natural to say that various spatial locations appear to us as containing various instantiation of properties. Illusions and distortions are known to happen, of course. Things may appear to have depth when they do not have it, like in paintings; things can appear more or less distant from us than they actually are, and we can think of more contorted cases in which the right and left areas of a scene appear swapped. However, we experience spatial locations as 'out there', and in some important sense as independent from us. In other words, spatial locations have phenomenal objectivity, and this is why it makes perfect sense to say that it is the spatial locations *of the stimuli* that appear to us in certain (not always veridical) ways. Note also that the fact that those spatial locations can appear quite differently from how they are does not mean that our sensory systems affect or alter those locations in some way. The point is obvious, but it is important to stress it. In the temporal case, the idea of our sensory systems modifying the content of the temporal locations is even crazier, since, given the time lags, it would imply *backwards causation*, not to mention that postdiction may invite the contradictory thought that we can *modify the past*. But can we maintain, as in the spatial case, that it is nonetheless the temporal locations *of the stimuli* that appear to us?

If we consider large timescales, and the way we represent temporal locations in thought, it makes sense to take the temporal locations that we represent in thought as the ones in which the events that we remember happened, and those that we envisage will (possibly) happen. Even though there may be a lot of 'editing', so that reliving an experience may mean going through an experience with quite a different phenomenology, in any case of genuine remembering *what* we experience is the temporal location of the stimuli, namely the moment in which the things that we have experienced happened. And also, in cases of imagining the future, the temporal locations that we have 'in mind' are those of the future events we envisage, and that (if we are right) we will experience. However, we are not phenomenologically aware of those temporal locations. Things can look, feel, smell, or taste *like* the past (or the future), but they do not look, feel, smell, or taste past (or future). Those past and future times are *believed times* represented in thought; they are not *lived times* presented in the occurring experience. The represented past and the represented future in thought may have a distinguishing cognitive phenomenology, but it is the phenomenology of the presently occurring mental event. Those temporal locations do not appear to us as such and so; we are not presented with them, rather we think about them. Although the believed times are the temporal locations of the stimuli, we are not phenomenally presented with them.

With respect to shorter timescales, it equally makes no sense to say that we are phenomenally presented with the temporal locations of the stimuli, but the reasons why it is so vary depending on the details of the approach one adopts. In the Dennettian multiple draft view, as we saw, the large timescale and the short timescale are strictly analogous. When probing our experience of an apparent movement with an optimal stimulus, we end up with the belief of having seen the dot moving across the screen (and changing colour). The brain has not filled in any missing experience, although we may report otherwise. The only time that is involved in the experience of being aware of t_1, t_2, t_3 as containing the phases of the movement of a fleeting dot is believed time, or time represented in logical space: a conceptual representation that we use to interpret the phenomenological character in question.

For the atomist specious present theorist, there is a more substantive difference between the long timescale and the short timescale case. There is a determined, cogent what it is like to be aware of t_1, t_2, t_3 as containing the phases of the movement of a fleeting dot. But it is not what it is like being presented with the three temporal locations in succession, since according to the atomist we are aware of the apparent motion in virtue of an Orwellian rewriting (Section 2.5). The time in which we find t_1, t_2, t_3 does not constitute merely a logical space, such as the time of our memories and expectation, in which the temporal locations of the stimuli can be represented, but it is rather *retained* and *protended time*. The temporal locations t_1, t_2, t_3 are presented to us in retained and protended time, but retained and protended time appears to us in our *occurring* mental event. Husserl struggled through continuous writing and rewriting to make sense of the idea of a temporal location that appears as not present, but it is not merely remembered or expected; rather, it appears now as just past or as about to come.[22] It is, however, difficult to understand how such a temporal location can be the location of the stimulus. The location of the stimulus is the one that happened (or that will happen), and in the current experience *it* cannot appear, we cannot be presented with it. To think otherwise is to confuse the fact that we can represent in thought the temporal location of the stimuli, as when we remember *that* so-and-so happened, with the fact that what appears to us in experience seems to have a temporal location.

For the molecularist, and for my version of dynamic snapshot (Section 2.6), the difference between the long timescale and the short timescale case is even more radical. What appears to us when probing the anarchic flow in the context of short timescales is lived time. We are phenomenally aware *not* of the temporal location of the stimuli, for the same reason that I pointed out discussing the atomist case, but rather of the temporal locations *of the experiences*. We are presented, one after another, with the temporal locations in which our life happens. I have already explained that in my account there is a difference

---

[22] Cf. 'The problem with Husserl's account, as I see it, is that it seems only to name the phenomenon instead of to explain it. We have no interesting account of what it is now to experience something as just-having-been, except to say that it is the phenomenon involved in the experience of the passage of time. But this is the phenomenon we are trying to explain. It does no good just to give a name to its various parts' (Kelly 2005: 16).

between the case of full attention and optimality of the stimulus, in which the phenomenology is cogent, and the case in which we probe a stream that was off the focus of attention, and we interpret our experience of a gap (which we did not realize was a gap) in a certain way. In both cases the temporal locations that appear in our experience are lived time, namely the temporal locations of our own experiences, which appear as containing various *external* goings-on. But in the first case the way in which they appear imposes on us; it is cogent and fully determined. In the second case, probing brings about the interpretation of the temporal structure of an undetermined phenomenological character.

It is important to understand that although it is the temporal locations of our own experiences that appear to us, their content is—or at least typically is in perceptual situations—events happening in space 'out there'. It is perfectly coherent to say that we are presented with things that happen around us and have phenomenal objectivity, while happening at the time that our experience is happening. In this sense, there is a deep difference between experiencing spatial locations, and experiencing temporal locations. We experience a *system* of spatial locations, although presumably always partially and from a given perspective. The temporal locations that appear in the phenomenal time of the *outer* world are the temporal locations of our own experiences, namely the temporal location of the *inner* flow. Crucially, as I will argue more extensively in the next chapter, we do not have phenomenal awareness of the connection between temporal locations, because we do not have a (phenomenal) perspective on them. We think of them as temporally connected, and we can think of their sequence from our temporal standpoint. But the way temporal locations are phenomenally presented to us is as isolated realities, detached from their past and future counterparts. And even if molecularism is true, and what we are phenomenally presented with is temporally extended, each specious present is *all* what we are presented with in each experience. As I will explain later, this is a crucial aspect of our experience of passage as well (Section 6.3.1). To sum up, the phenomenal time in which the outer world appears is the phenomenal time of the inner world insofar as external spatial locations appear to us—namely, insofar as the content of the temporal location of our experience has either phenomenal objectivity or presentational phenomenology.

3.4.2 The phenomenal time of the inner world

We can individuate the outer flows in terms of those aspects of our experience that are cogently captured by experience-based claims about the world, and the inner flow in terms of the phenomenal aspects that are not so captured, namely that fail to have phenomenal objectivity or outward-directed presentational phenomenology. One may be worried that this merely negative individuation of the inner flow does not sufficiently catch the intense inner life that we sometimes seem to undergo. About this I have two remarks. First, lack of phenomenal objectivity or outward presentational phenomenology means that every inner experience is in a certain sense an experience of an absence. We experience our inner world as what is *not* outside. Although there is a phenomenology of our inner awareness, we are not presented with an internal 'space' inhabited by mental objects of some sort. I am aware that I am stretching the terminology a bit here, since I want to say that we are presented with the temporal location of our own experiences, and yet I am denying that those temporal locations have presentational phenomenology at all (more on this in Section 4.3). But this opposition between an outer flow in which things are somehow given to us in experience and an inner flow in which quite literally nothing appears is crucial to make sense of the idea that when we shift from experiences that are mainly outwardly directed to ones that are mainly inwardly directed, or vice versa, we experience a discontinuity of some sort.

Second, I am not taking a stance here on whether there is a cognitive phenomenology or not. My model predicts that if there is a cognitive phenomenology it lacks phenomenal objectivity and outward-directed presentational phenomenology, but that is true also of any mental imagery of an inner speech or whatever inner phenomenology accompanies our thoughts. The only difference is that while cognitive phenomenology may lack presentational phenomenology altogether, an inner speech may have an inward-directed presentational phenomenology. But again, inward-directed presentational phenomenology, if there is something like that, is not being presented with an inner space.

Note also that my model is compatible with proprioception, and feelings like pain, heat, and cold, and even certain instances of emotions and moods to be part of the outer flow; that is, to have either phenomenal objectivity or outward-directed presentational phenomenology. Moreover, anything that is not in the centre of attention requires a supplement of interpretation to be characterized phenomenologically, and thus in general there will be a wide range of indeterminacy with respect to what counts as inner and what counts as outer flow in our experience.

The issue of whether there are presentational aspects in our inner phenomenology is traditionally cased out in terms of the question whether there are non-perceptual representational contents. I have treated the issue of attribution of representational content as one of the strategies to explain the connection between indirect description of our experiences and the phenomenal character of our experiences. So, it should be clear by now that I am not committed to accounting for the representational content of our experiences in general. However, if the inner flow is at least in part a stream of *thoughts*, and thoughts are endowed with representational content of some sort, I need to say something more on whether by entertaining a thought I take our experience to present us with something, and how.

Note that even if the inner flow is entirely void of presentational aspects, this does not mean that our inner awareness does not possess representational content. There is a long-standing debate on whether thought, or the more cognitive aspect of our mental life in general, has, or is intimately connected to, a sensory phenomenology. If cognition is not essentially linked to phenomenology, then it may be that we are not *phenomenally* presented with the objects of our thoughts, even though our thoughts have representational contents, namely they are about this and that.

One current of this debate is Geach's criticism of James's idea of a stream of thoughts. Roughly, according to Geach it is mistaken to characterize thought as a phenomenal stream. Having a thought is not something processual, as is drinking, dancing, or swimming—something that we do over a stretch of time. Rather, it is like an achievement or an accomplishment, like finding a banknote on the street or reaching the top of a mountain.[23] As Soteriou (2013) convincingly argues, Geach's predicament should not be overestimated. Firstly, one can analyse mental life 'in terms of mental states and events/processes that are changes to/in those mental states [. . .]' (2013: 38). The phenomenal properties of the mental states can be understood as specified by veridicality conditions. But the parts of the veridicality conditions, let us say that it is an experience of a reddish guinea pig, are not 'spread' through the interval during which the mental state obtains. In line with what I said before (Section 3.1.2) about the possibility of attributing phenomenal character and representational content at an instant to a temporally extended process, the property of being an experience of a reddish guinea pig is possessed by an experiential process at an instant in its entirety.[24]

---

[23] On the distinction, see Vendler (1957); see also Varzi and Torrengo (2006).

[24] Cf. 'Contents with veridicality conditions may be used to specify the kind of conscious experience undergone by a subject over an interval of time, but such intervals are not to be thought of as intervals that can be broken down into sub-intervals in each of which there occurs a conscious experience that is to be specified in terms of some part of the content experienced, where such parts lack veridicality conditions' (Soteriou 2013: 39). Surprisingly, this does *not* seem miles away from what James thinks: 'It takes time to utter the phrase [The pack of cards is on the table] [. . .] Of course the thought has

Such an analysis is compatible with understanding the explanatory relation between representational content and phenomenal character either as *intentional representationalism* does, according to which the nature of the representational content determines the nature of the phenomenal character, or as *phenomenal representationalism* does, according to which the nature of the phenomenal character determines the nature of the representational content (Section 1.3). Soteriou seems to think that neither way would respect the deep temporal structure of experience, which, like a process, necessarily unfolds through time. The idea is that once we accept that mental states can have phenomenal properties and representational content, the intrinsic properties that constitute the stream of consciousness—even if they are something upon which the states and their properties supervene—are explanatorily idle with respect to experiential dimensions of the process. The reason why the process is experiential—namely, has a phenomenal character—is that it is constituted by phenomenal states, and not that those states supervene on a mental event. His solution is to understand the underlying process and the mental states, with their phenomenal and representational properties, as mutually interdependent. Let me quote extensively one of the most significant passages:

On this view, although there are such things as phenomenally conscious perceptual states [. . .], a subject's psychological perceptual life is not analysable in terms of mental states and events/processes that are simply changes to/in those perceptual states. This is due to the intimate way in which phenomenally conscious mental states and phenomenally conscious mental events/processes are related. The latter cannot occur without the obtaining of the former, and the former cannot obtain without the occurrence of the latter. (Soteriou 2013: 47)

Now, one problem with this account is that it seems to characterize the outer flow rather than the inner flow. (Go back to the quote; Soteriou talks of 'a subject's psychological *perceptual* life'; italics mine.) And it is unclear how the story could be adapted to the inner flow. One possibility is to make Soteriou more Jamesian than I depicted him. What he is suggesting is that any cognitive

---

time-parts. The part [is on] of it, though continuous with [of cards], is yet a different part from [of cards]. Now I say of these time-parts that we cannot take any one of them so short that it will not after some fashion or other be a thought of the whole object "the pack of cards is on the table." They melt into each other like dissolving views, and not two of them feel the object just alike, but each feels the total object in a unitary undivided way. This is what I mean by denying that in the thought any parts can be found corresponding to the object's part. Time-parts are not such parts' (James 1890: 116).

mental activity is accompanied by a sensorial phenomenology, a perception-like awareness. If so, there is no crucial difference between the outer flow and the inner flow. This is compatible with my suggestion that the only difference between inner and outer flow is the presence of either phenomenal objectivity or outward-directed phenomenology. However, it is still fair to ask what phenomenal elements are specific to the inner flow—specific to those successions of mental events that do not have phenomenal objectivity, and have at most inward-directed presentational phenomenology.

Imagine you are engrossed in your thoughts. It all begins with an episodic memory, say, then you entertain several abstract considerations and ponder what is the best. One of these abstract considerations happens to engage you intensely, and indeed a certain emotional state, let us say a mixture of anger and uneasiness, perhaps fear, begins to arise in the background. Now the images of what would follow from that decision are definitely more vivid. You imagine the voices, even the emotions of the persons who are involved (someone would be angry and shout at you, others would be saddened?). Still other abstract considerations enter the picture. Then at a certain point the waiter arrives at the table and captures your attention by asking what you would like to drink. Earl grey, piping hot, please.

Part, perhaps a lot, of the phenomenology of what goes on in such a temporally extended and variegated experience can be characterized in terms of some *propositional content*, intuitively speaking the propositions that somehow describe *what* the protagonist—you—were thinking. How exactly such attributions capture the phenomenology of the experience is a theoretical issue. Is there cognitive phenomenology connected to those propositions? Is there an inner speech mixed with several visual mental images with inward-directed presentational phenomenology? Here, I do not care how to answer these otherwise interesting questions. My point is that attributions of such propositional content are cogent descriptions of the phenomenology of the experience, which is a preponderantly inward-directed experience. Cogent, but also partial; and partial in three different ways. First, it is partial because even though your experience is preponderantly inward-directed it also encompasses perceptual elements. If what I have said before (Section 3.3.2) is along the correct lines, as long as those perceptual elements are out of focus, their contribution to the overall phenomenology is somewhat indeterminate. An experience-based claim such as 'the other customers are chattering' would probably be an interpretational, not fully cogent, description of the experience, but it would still say something about what it is like to be lost in one's thoughts in those specific circumstances. However, concurrent perceptual ingredients of the experience are clearly not meant to be captured by the attribution of propositional content, since they do not represent (if they represent anything at all) what the thoughts are about.

Second, it is partial because there are, at least in certain phases of the temporally extended experience, emotional aspects that are not captured by the mere attribution of propositional content. Those aspects can be in the focus of attention and lack phenomenal objectivity. However, also those aspects are not eminently cognitive, and thus they should not be expected to be captured by the attribution of propositional content either. Therefore, I left them on the side as well. Third, and more interestingly, it is partial because there are cognitive aspects of the experience that are not captured by the propositional content. Traditionally, philosophers and psychologists have talked about *modes* or *attitudes* attached to contents. Is the protagonist *believing* that giving the promotion to John is the best option? Are they *hoping* that nobody gets too upset? Are they *afraid* that almost certainly somebody will? I take that such attributions as well are, or can be, cogent descriptions of the phenomenology in question. Also in this case, I will set aside the otherwise interesting question concerning cognitive phenomenology: is there some specific phenomenal character attached to experiences like the one just mentioned, or by attributing them do we individuate some cluster of phenomenal elements, which are not as such specific to attitudes or modes? What is important is that the aspect of the phenomenal character that typically enters the inner flow can be captured by descriptions that involve not only propositional contents, but also modes or attitudes attached to it—such as desiring, feeling disgusted by, being intrigued by, and so on.[25] It may be that sometimes it is not clear whether any of those would be a cogent description of a given experience, and other times it is undetermined which attitude is involved. For instance, I have a thought that can be perhaps described as thinking about a doctor walking on a street downtown, but am I remembering this, is it just something that I am imagining, or is it a fear that I have (the doctor, is she going towards my dear friend's house?). This is partly a shortcoming of our linguistic and conceptual limitations, and partly a consequence of the phenomenology being not fully determined. In the case of the inner flow as well, not all its ingredients 'impose' on us, and large parts of it may happen to have a merely interpretational phenomenology.[26]

---

[25] Note that those attitudes can sometimes be emotionally charged.

[26] Another interesting question, which has occupied early phenomenologists, is whether there is something like a 'neutral' attitude that is entailed by all the others. Perhaps 'entertaining', or 'presupposing'. But note that one thing is to ask if it is possible to remain neutral with respect to various

3.5 Narrative cognition

The propositional content that characterizes our inner flow and our cognition more generally can be about things in time. Although the phenomenology of having such experience lacks phenomenal objectivity, they are experiences that often represent in thought the outer world. Experiences of this sort are the effect of long time probing of the anarchic flow, what—as anticipated—I label *narrative thoughts*. Although over time the narrative thoughts can change (we misremember, we 'project', etc.), we have, in general, an awareness of succession that keeps together one overall narrative. As Jenann Ismael points out, 'When we move beyond perception, it is even more obvious that we have representational states whose contents span a series of successive observations' (Ismael 2016: 54). I will not go into the details of my account of narrative cognition.

3.5.1 Narrative units

We saw in Section 2.4 that on some conceptions of the structure of experience there is unification of more than one experienced moment within a specious present. Traditionally, the term 'specious present' has been used as the duration of an experience that does not require an explicit use of memory or other non-perceptual capacities to be embraced all at once. Recently, in psychology and empirically informed philosophy of mind, the term has been used in a somewhat stricter sense to mean a minimal threshold duration that allows us to perceive a movement or a qualitative change, which is how I used it in the previous chapters. Although James talks of a specious present that may cover up to around twelve seconds, while contemporary psychologists talk of a threshold of less than a second,[27] both conceptions are entirely perceptual ones. But perception is not the only means through which stretches of experience can be unified: there are experiences that outstretch even the longer Jamesonian specious present, but are still *unified* in some obvious sense. The examples are easy to find. A dinner with friends is a complex experience with different temporal phases that cannot be apprehended all at once, but which can be thought of (and often is remembered as) an experiential unit. A walk

commitments (reality being like that, wishing reality to be like that, as others take reality to be, etc.), and another to ask whether there is something like the mere entertaining of a representational content.

[27] James (1890: Chap. XV): 'The specious present has, in addition, a vaguely vanishing backward and forward fringe; but its nucleus is probably the dozen seconds or less that have just elapsed.' For the operational notion exploited in empirical psychology, see Artsila (2018).

with your partner in the park, in which you discuss your plans for the future and point out your worries, and listen to their suggestions and criticisms, is also an experience that, while having several qualitatively different parts, is unified. Even a whole day can come to be seen as a unit revolving around, for instance, the endeavour to solve a problem.

The unity of an extended experience in this sense does not need to rest on features that are intrinsic to its phenomenal nature, and where its temporal boundaries can be not only vague but fairly arbitrary. I will refer to these sorts of complex extended experiences as *narrative units*. The *principle* on which the unity of such experiences rests may vary substantially from case to case. Sometimes phenomenology is relevant: there is a *phenomenal harmony* between the various phases, as if the experiences could be naturally understood as a sequence of phenomenal presents collectively exemplifying a distributional property. Although we can attribute a temporal distributional property to any temporally extended entity (cf. Parsons 2004), from a phenomenal point of view certain distributional properties are less gerrymandered than others. Think of the spatial case. A tablecloth displaying a drawing of a starship battle, to the left of a countryside picnic, and right below a large Mondrian-style configuration counts as less unified (if unified at all) than one displaying at its centre a drawing of a big pheasant about to take off the ground, surrounded by sumptuous cornucopias of autumn vegetables, all in the same pastel colours.

Other times the principle of unity is (at least partially) extrinsic to phenomenology, and it is given by cultural defaults that work as 'scripts'. Consider the sequence of experiences that someone has had yesterday while going out for dinner and then walking home. It is more natural to parse the sequence in a unit encompassing the dinner events, followed by another unit encompassing the walk home events, than in one unit encompassing the first half of the dinner, followed by another unit encompassing the second half of the dinner and the walk home. This way of unifying is more natural not on the basis of the intrinsic phenomenological features of the dinner and the walk home (although there may be situations that phenomenally justify the unusual parsing mentioned above, for instance a change in mood in the middle of the dinner that carries over to the walk home), but on the basis of how our social life is organized. Experience can constitute narrative units also in virtue of subjective, interest-driven principles. The second half of a work meeting and the following talk with a client can be a unified experience given our interest in getting a certain business done. And pure conventional unifications are possible, too. Someone can think of the experiences she had between five o'clock and six o'clock on a certain day as unified, merely on the basis of the conventional way of dividing up the hours of the day.

Depending on the way an experience is unified, the unification can be judged as more or less strong or weak *from a phenomenal point of view*. However, what principle of unification is the relevant one is *always a context-dependent matter*. No matter whether the unification is strongly 'suggested' by the phenomenal properties of a sequence of phenomenal presents, or it just reflects an extrinsic criterion, a narrative unit always requires the contextually driven *selection* of a unifying principle. Notice that this does not mean that narrative units are *abstract entities*. As unified experiences, they are series of mental events, successions of possibly overlapping phenomenal presents (see Section 4.1.2.1). They are *concrete* entities,[28] even though they have *fiat* temporal borders—that is, the way we pick them up depends on some (potentially arbitrary) decision concerning a unifying principle.[29]

Narrative units can cover a whole *stream of consciousness*, which again are concrete entities. Consider the wake model for simplicity (Section 3.2.1). Every time we lose consciousness, we terminate a stream of consciousness, and every time we wake up or otherwise gain consciousness, we initiate one. Thus, streams of consciousness have *bona fide* borders. But the fact that a whole stream of consciousness has non-arbitrary boundaries does not make it more apt to be a narrative unit than some of its parts. Narrative units are 'cheap to get', and it only takes the possibility of thinking of a certain sequence of events as a unit to pick up one.

That is why sequences of streams of consciousness can also constitute narrative units, as when we think of the events that happened during last weekend. A complete succession of streams of consciousness and the pauses between them is an individual *world-line*, the succession of events that begins with our birth and ends with our death and has us as protagonists. The whole of our world-line can thus be conceived as an alternation of streams of consciousness and events of lack of consciousness between them.[30] Yet another concrete entity that potentially constitutes a narrative unit.

---

[28] The notion of concreteness I am using here does not rule out that mental properties belong to the concreteness sphere. See Iaquinto and Torrengo (2022b).

[29] On *fiat* and *bona fide* boundaries see Smith and Varzi (2000). Many concrete entities that are temporally extended have *fiat* rather than *bona fide* temporal boundaries.

[30] Of course, if we use the life model of the stream of consciousness, world-lines and streams of consciousness would generally coincide.

3.5.2 Narrative thoughts

Thanks to memory and other non-perceptual cognitive capacities, we can have *narrative thoughts*; that is, thoughts about narrative units, regardless of their length. Certain aspects of those thoughts can be modelled by reference to *narratives*. As I use the term here, a narrative is a *representational entity*, namely an *abstract entity* that we can use to model what thoughts about sequences of experiences or events in general are about.

For a theory of narratives in this sense, it is important to distinguish three elements. Firstly, *narrative thoughts*, which are non-perceptual mental episodes (thinking of something, remembering something, imagining something, and the like) about sequences of events. Secondly, *narratives*, which are abstract representations of sequences of events, typically involving individual experiences and facts relevant to one's own life, that model *what narrative thoughts are about*. Thirdly, the *narrative target*, which is the concrete entity which the narrative thought is typically about. Narrative units can be, and often are, narrative targets, and if so, they are represented by narratives (see Figure 3.4).

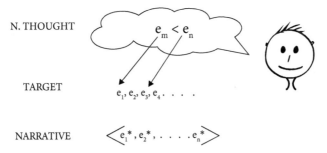

Figure 3.4 Narrative thoughts and narratives

A narrative does not have a psychological reality (it is an abstract representation), but it is used to characterize narrative thoughts, which are mental events that have psychological reality. As for what models the target of narrative thoughts, a narrative is not necessarily a detailed or accurate representation of a narrative unit or some other sequence of events. The psychological processes involved in narrative thoughts are plausibly based on elements of simplification and 'editing'. A narrative about yesterday's dinner party, for instance, may represent just a few episodes among the ones actually lived by whoever entertains a narrative thought about it the day after (and there may be indeterminacy with respect to what comes first). A narrative about future plans may contain many indeterminate passages, and more generally a narrative can be updated as one's train of thought unfolds. Besides, a narrative can also be about events that do not involve consciousness, or it can fail to have a target, when it is about an utterly imagined reality. The narrative target is thus an optional element in the theory.

Note that it may be undetermined, or arbitrary to a certain extent, whether a narrative thought has a target or not. Indeed, it is not easy to establish what amount of inaccuracy is sufficient for a narrative to be about an imagined reality, rather than about something that happened in the actual world. Imagine a situation in which someone takes a drug that slowly disrupts her memories. She starts thinking of yesterday's night, and little by little her thoughts change from being about a dinner with friends (a roughly accurate memory) to a ball in which all participants (including herself) are giant lizards (an utterly inaccurate memory). When did her narrative thoughts stop having a target? When she first 'remembered' the person at her left on the table to look like a giant lizard? When everybody around the table was a lizard? When the lizards began to dance? Besides, it is unclear whether a narrative that is (partly, at least) about the future can have a target. Maybe it will have a target if accurate. All these questions are interesting, but we can leave them on the side for the purpose of this chapter. Note also that I am here stipulating that a narrative thought about an imagined reality does not have a target. I believe that a coherent (alternative) theory can be elaborated where the targets of imaginative narrative thought are platonic entities, or abstract entities dependent on the activity of a creator. Again, those are interesting issues, but not ones that need concern us here.

The role of narratives in my theory is partially analogous to that of propositions in theories of formal semantics for natural languages. It is an abstract representational entity that the theorist uses to capture some aspects of our psychology—in the case of proposition and formal semantics, the intended or understood meaning of linguistic expressions, in the case of narratives and theory of narratives, thoughts about sequences of events. However, narratives are not meant to capture the *representational content* of narrative thoughts, what is presented to us in a non-perceptual phenomenal present by having a narrative thought.[31] It is unlikely that we can grasp a narrative all at

---

[31] I leave it open that narratives capture some other kind of mental content, one that is not phenomenally present, like a mnemonic structure or a mental file. I do not intend to speculate on this. At any rate, I do not need to be committed to such a claim either. Surely, I do not need to maintain that there is a 'narrative box' in our heads like someone thinks there is a belief or a desire box.

once in a mental episode of thinking or imagining; there is simply too much information represented for that to be the case. Narratives capture something about narrative thoughts in the sense that when a narrative N is a model of the target of a narrative thought T, all the information contained in N is easily *available* or *retrivable* through different mental episodes to someone to whom we (correctly) attribute T.

The idea of a narrative as an abstract representational entity is, to my knowledge, novel. However, the idea that the notion of narrative can capture some aspect of our psychological reality is old and relatively uncontroversial. There are differences in opinions about the role and importance of narratives for our individuality, personality, moral value, and meaningful existence.[32] Some, like Strawson (2020) and Zahavi (2007), are highly sceptical about the notion playing *any* significant explanatory role concerning our psychological profile, mainly because they do not take memory to be an essential ingredient of one's psychology. Although I am sympathetic towards such scepticism, I do not need to take a stance here. No matter how bad our memory is, both in the sense that we realize we cannot remember something, or we are tricked into false memories, or how irrelevant is remembering for one's personality, we still can (and sometimes explicitly do) think of our life or parts of it as a succession of events, and so we do more generally for events we remember or imagine. This is all that it takes to make sense of the idea of a narrative used here. The existence of narrative thoughts may be irrelevant and trivial for elucidating the concept of personality, or for capturing the moral implication of personal responsibility, but it is interesting and crucial in providing a complete picture, together with awareness of succession and the phenomenology of diachronic fullness of our inner flow.

Narrative thoughts are cognitive structures that show up when we probe our internal states. The centrality of narrative cognition in our life may even suggest that awareness of succession and the phenomenology of diachronic fullness are actually projections, whose nature is captured by the metaphor of a continuous flow. They are a projection not in the sense that we attribute a feature of our own experience to the things outside us, as in certain accounts of our experience of colours, but in the sense that they are a consequence of how narrative thoughts suggest us to describe our phenomenology (Section 1.5). From the perspective of wide narratives, experiences are structured as

---

[32] For narrative enthusiasts, see for instance Schechtman (1996); Hutto (2008); McAdams (2019). The notion of narrative is also widely used in an important part of the hermeneutic tradition (cf. Ricoeur 1984), in which it is exploited to elucidate the dimension of meaning. For a more realist take on internal and external memory, see Ferraris (2012).

successions of events with no gaps between them. Since we are aware of this, we infer that this wide-scale picture on the small scale *should* feel like a smooth flow of mental events.[33] And this is why we tend to describe an occurring mental episode as if we were constantly presented with a smooth succession of cogent phenomenological characters. I will come back to this hypothesis in discussing the experience of passage (Section 6.3.1).

3.6 Conclusions

Humans are, in a sense, identical to time.[34] Such a bold claim means not only that temporal elements are central both to our sensorial and to our cognitive life, but also that even though we are able to think of time as something outside of us, and we can even take perceptual experience to suggest that the events around us succeed one another, we are only aware of the time of our inner life. There is where everything happens, including the external world, which does not stop to look (and be) external because of that. We construct in our mind narratives of our lives and of the world around us that can be as diverse as those envisaged by Emily Dickinson in the quartet I quoted at the beginning of the chapter. Some people see themselves only in the moment; others often take a bird's-eye view on their whole existence and beyond.

[33] Narrative thoughts also suggest the wake model over the life model of the stream of consciousness, because falling asleep and waking up are moments that from the general perspective seem clear-cut, even though it is not obvious that when we live them, they actually are so.

[34] This is not just an exaggeration of the dawn of postmodernism. Cf. 'L'homme [. . .] est identique au temps' (Debord 1967: Chap. 5).

4

Presentness

Reflect upon your present blessings—of which every man has many
—not on your past misfortunes, of which all men have some.

Charles Dickens, *Sketches by Boz*
—Characters, Chap. 2 (1836)

The past and the future are important to our lives in many respects. We learn
from our past mistakes, and much of our emotional life relies on past experiences, as when we regret something, or we cheerfully indulge in reliving an
experience in imagination. We plan for the future, and we consider how our
actions may influence it, as when we make sacrifices for our career. However,
both the past and the future seem ultimately to derive their importance from
the present. The lesson that the past teaches us is a lesson for our present
perusal, and we care about the emotional connection with the past because
emotions are the salt of our present life. Future plans have their roots in present
desires and moods, and considerations about the consequences of our actions
are grist to the mill of our present decisions. The reason for the paramount
importance of the present is, in a sense, obvious. The present is now, where
we, the *things we have experience of*, and the *things we act upon* also are.
The past and the future are somewhere else, and they *cannot* be important
to us unless they carry some connection with us, with the present. But is this
sheer 'locational fact' what makes up for the whole specialness of presentness? In this chapter, I will argue that it is. There is nothing metaphysically
or phenomenologically deep in presentness.

In Section 4.1. *More than one present*, I investigate various notions of presentness, focusing on the ones that are relevant for our temporal experience,
and I present the red thread of the whole chapter: how do we explain the
fact that we often *talk and think* as if both our experiences and the things we
have experience of are present? Is the source of this implicit belief that both
of them are presented as present in our *perceptual* experience? In Section 4.2.
The phenomenal prominence of the present, I explore various accounts of the
fact that the present seems to be prominent in our experience, and I argue that
there is a distinction between the perceptual dimension of this prominence,

Temporal Experience. Giuliano Torrengo, Oxford University Press. © Giuliano Torrengo (2024).
DOI: 10.1093/9780191937804.003.0004

towards which I have an eliminativist attitude, and its conceptual dimension, which I think can be explained in terms of certain structural features of what I have called *narrative thoughts* (Section 3.5.2). In Section 4.3. *Presentness and phenomenal objectivity*, I tackle the issue of the transparency of temporal experience. We are aware of certain temporal features, such as presentness, in a way that seems to violate the idea that we are never directly aware of the features of our own experiences. Discussing this point will allow me to complete my hypotheses on the origin of the narrative present, the feature of our cognition that explains our ordinary talk and thought about events and experiences thereof being present, as I will elaborate in Section 4.4. *From locational awareness to the narrative present.*

4.1 More than one present

In ordinary communication we make experience-based claims concerning what happens *now*, what will be the case *right after this moment*, or what has caused something to be the case *at present*. In line with the general project of this book, my guiding question in this chapter will be what the ground of such claims is. Why do we talk and think in terms of things being present and being more or less 'temporally far away' from the present? I will begin by distinguishing two notions connected with the term 'present' and its cognates. The *indexical* notion, roughly synonymous with 'this time', and the notion of *experiential* present, that is the 'temporal niche' where our phenomenal awareness takes place, and whose different interpretations will occupy most of the discussion to come.[1]

4.1.1 The indexical present

Temporal reference is realized grammatically in very different ways in different natural languages—by means of morphological tenses (as when verbs are inflected), adverbs, clitics, particles, and other syntactic elements (cf. Comrie 1985). Besides, different languages embody different defaults about how the temporal dimension and the speaker relate (is it the self of the speaker that crawls through time, or time that streams through her? Cf. Gentner 2001)

---

[1] There is at least a third notion relevant for temporal phenomenology, namely the *objective* present, the idea that there is a fact of the matter with respect to which things (events, states-of-affairs) are located in the present. I will come back to it in Chapter 6.

and about the mutual orientation of speaker and temporal dimension (is the speaker facing the future or the past? Cf. Boroditsky 2000; Núñez et al. 2009).

However, in the philosophical literature it is for the most part agreed that indexicality is an essential feature of our language and thought.[2] In the temporal case, indexicals are required to motivate the (intended) timeliness of our actions. Only the fact that we possess and use the conceptual and representational resources to think that *now* is the time to go to the station (as opposed to thinking that 11:45 is the time to go to the station) can explain why I go to the station when I do. More precisely, we need the capacity to represent in a non-perceptual way (in our beliefs, for instance) things that happen in time in a *tensed format*, that is from a temporal standpoint, along with an indexical mechanism of reference that allows us to pick up the moment that we happen to occupy, in order to explain certain features of behaviour.

It is important to notice that temporal indexicals are essential in an analogous sense also to *communicate* when certain actions take place. The need for interpersonal communication in an environment in which our *own actions* are also spatio-temporally located makes the individuation of the temporal location of our objects of discourse *from the temporal point of view* which we occupy often mandatory. The very idea of mutual *coordination* of behaviour, which is at the base of collective actions, seems to require referential mechanism of the sort captured by the indexical notion of the present. And since we are aware that our temporal location gets *updated* as time goes by, in a way that in a sense is independent of us, it is important to have a linguistic device that allows us to pinpoint the temporal location we occupy *when we use* language and thought.

Being present in the indexical sense thus is *being located at the centre of one's temporal perspective*; it is being exactly where in the temporal dimension your perceptions and actions take place. Note that I do not claim that terms such as 'present' or 'now' necessarily pick up an instant, or the minimal temporal interval containing the centre of your perspective. This empirical claim is false for English, and analogous ones are false for other natural languages. When we talk about 'the present', we may have in mind a span of several years (or even millennia, if we are among geologists), and '*now* we make things differently' may mean that we make things differently since 1883 (for instance, because we are talking about the invention of toilet paper). But this is irrelevant to my point. It is the theoretical rather than the reference of ordinary language

---

[2] *Loci classici*: Castañeda (1967); Perry (1979); and Lewis (1979). For a voice out of the chorus see Cappelen and Dever (2014).

terms, such as 'present' or 'now', that is exhausted by the point in time where the perspective of the speaker's, or thinker's, experience is centred. And it is only this notion that interests us here.

What is philosophically interesting about indexical presentness is that it is *phenomenally and metaphysically lightweight*. The present, in this sense, neither targets a phenomenal aspect of our experience, as perceptual predicates like terms such as 'red' and 'square' do, nor does it target features that we attribute to reality on the ground of our categorizations and conceptualizations, such as ordinary terms like 'cousin' and 'carburettor' do. The notion of indexical presentness neither characterizes our experiences from a subjective point of view, nor what we experience from an objective point of view. Rather, it characterizes the relation between mental states and their contents from a *functional* point of view. There is no robust property of indexical presentness, but only the role of *index* that a time can play with respect to a cognitive system. When one time passes from non-being present in this sense to be present in the indexical sense, what changes is the role it plays with respect to us. And this role can be played not because of the representational capacities of the system, but because the system itself is located at that time.[3]

There are two ideas here that we have to be careful enough to distinguish while appreciating their connection. The first is that human psychological motivation for action and communication thereof involves referential mechanisms that rely on the time at which we *use* them. The second is that by *being* the centre of the temporal perspective in which one's perceptions and actions take place, a temporal index has an important experiential role. And whether this role is entirely exhausted by the role it has in motivating action and in communicating the motivation or not, it is not a trivial question.

The reason why the indexical notion of presentness is metaphysically lightweight makes it the case that it is also an unproblematic notion. Everybody agrees that we use embodied cognitive mechanisms of this sort, and possibly also other, less cognitively sophisticated animals do too. Also spatial reference, for instance, seems to rely on an analogous indexical mechanism.

However, spatial and temporal indexicals work on different assumptions about their field of applicability, that is the spatial and temporal dimensions respectively. An utterance of 'here' in a communicative exchange *can* refer to a shared space, for instance the room or apartment in which we happen to be, but the centre of the spatial perspective of *each* of the participants to the communicative exchange is assumed to be different. That is why (i) utterances of

---

[3] On the notion of index as role, cf. Perry (2013: 497–8). Cf. also Ismael (2007: Chap. 6).

'here' by other members of the communicative exchange will usually refer to *different* locations within the shared space (and thanks to long-distance communication devices there may not be a relevant shared space), (ii) there is no fact of the matter about what place *really* 'here' refers to—whether it is the place where I am, rather than where you or Petunia the guinea pig are, or the apartment we all are in. The width of 'here' is not only context-sensitive, it is also essentially relative to each of the participants of the linguistic exchange.

This is not the case for 'now'. Canonical uses of temporal indexicals presuppose that the centre of the temporal perspective expressed by the use of the indexical is *shared* by all participants to the communication. Different utterances of 'now' will typically refer to different times, because the common temporal perspective continues to update as time goes by, but the centre of the temporal perspective of *each* of the participants to the communicative exchange is assumed to be the same. That is why (i) if you and me are involved in a communicative exchange, I will take an utterance of 'now' by you as picking up the centre of what is also *my* temporal perspective, and (ii) there *is* a fact of the matter about what time 'now' refers to in a given context; regardless of who is speaking, it is the centre of the temporal perspective which we assume to be shared.[4] We can *imagine* a shift of temporal perspective in the past and in the future, and (at least in English) we can use temporal indexical in shifted ways in certain context,[5] but there is a non-imagined shared temporal perspective.

4.1.2 The experiential present

From a third-person perspective, the experiential present is, very roughly, the time at which our experiences happen. If one aims to capture this time from a first-person perspective, there are various versions of it that are relevant. I begin with two that are linked to the perceptual dimension of experience: the phenomenal present and the represented present, and then move to the narrative present, which pertains to the experiential sphere in a wider sense of the term.

---

[4] The fact that we assumed that there is a shared temporal perspective when we communicate with each other is likely to be a consequence of certain 'robust' regularities that are relevant for how our cognitive systems work; in particular, the fact that we usually communicate with people that are not at some significant fraction of a light year away from us.

[5] For instance, in 'mental time travel' cases (cf. Michaelian 2016) and in 'shift of context of utterance' generated by pragmatic or rhetorical artifices (cf. Predelli 2009). Imagine a pompous history teacher lecturing about the Waterloo battle: 'Sunday, 18 June 1815. Napoleon looks at the battlefield in front of him. Nelson's troops are advancing. *Now* he knows that his future will be decided today.'

4.1.2.1 The phenomenal present and the represented present

What I call the *phenomenal present* is the content of experience that is presented to us 'all at once' at a given time, like the peaceful view of the street below that you admire from the balcony, the jump of Peaches towards the newly delivered lettuce, the first half of the arpeggio played by the neighbour in her self-taught trumpet lesson, and the quick change in the smell that pervades the kitchen when the delicious crust on the baked potatoes turns into an inedible black veneer.[6] Non-perceptual experiences also have contents that are phenomenally present. Consider the phenomenology of episodic memory, for instance. We cannot apprehend in a visual memory all at once the very long dinner we had with friends yesterday, say (although we may have in some sense the whole event 'in mind', as when we remember a certain mood or emotion that we connect to the whole night). But we can recall visually (and sensorially more generally) parts of the dinner and have a succession of more focused episodic memories in which the various events (the look we exchanged with someone, the indulging in a second piece of camembert, etc.) are grasped at once in a sequence of non-perceptual phenomenal presents.[7] In this section, I will take into consideration only the perceptual case.

As we have seen by discussing the experience of change and movement (Chapter 2), philosophers and psychologists disagree on the temporal structure of the content of perception, and hence of the phenomenal present, in particular whether it is (virtually) instantaneous or temporally extended: for the *snapshot* theorists it has no extension, and thus all that is presented to us at once is a moment, whereas for the *specious present* theorists it has extension, and thus a short interval is presented all at once. Some philosophers talk of a 'temporal field' to denote an extended temporal location where things in various sensory modalities (sight, smell, touch, hearing, etc.) are presented to us. I will come back to the idea below (Sections 4.2 and 4.3); for now, unless otherwise specified, in what follows when I talk of 'what is presented to us' I mean the content of the phenomenal present, the things or events that we perceive all at once, regardless of whether such a content is temporally extended or virtually instantaneous.

---

[6] Cf. 'Whatever I experience is, in one sense, "present" to me at the time when I experience it, but in the temporal sense it need not be present—for example—if it is something remembered' (Russell 1913/1992: 38); and 'Experiences, as I am interested in them here, are states that can be enjoyed "all at once"' (Bayne 2010: 23).

[7] Note that I am not assuming here that those sensorial experiences are somehow reproductions of the event we are recalling from the first-personal perspective in which we experienced them (if we are not misremembering). It may be that the mental image is from a completely different perspective, or it is somehow without perspective (e.g. like in an axonometric projection). I am only assuming that those mental episodes come with some form of sensorial phenomenology. This is compatible with there being people unable to have them (people affected by a strong form of aphantasia, for instance).

Disagreement arises also with respect to the phenomenal import of the phenomenal present, although it is difficult to find an explicit and clear discussion of the issue in the literature. The phenomenal present may be phenomenal merely in the sense of being a phenomenal content of some sort, or in the sense of being a content displaying a specific phenomenology. Whatever this phenomenology is exactly, it is not necessarily temporal—as should be clear from the fact that episodic memories have phenomenally present contents. In contrast, what I call the *represented present in perception* is the moment that is singled out as present, in a temporal sense, by being *felt as privileged*. As for the phenomenal present, differences in the way one thinks of the temporal structure of the content of perception, when change and movement are involved, reflect different conceptions of the represented present. Snapshot theorists maintain that we are always presented with *one* moment (what we perceptually apprehend all at once is a 'snapshot' of the world around us). Therefore, according to the snapshot view, *if* perception somehow singles out a moment as temporally special, then we are presented *only* with the represented present. Specious present theorists maintain that we are presented with a *succession* of moments (what we perceptually apprehend all at once is the material of a very short 'clip' of the world around us). Therefore, according to the specious present view, *if* there is a moment that is perceptually privileged, then we are presented with the represented present and the interval just before or around it. (The two italicized 'ifs' are important, because, as we will see, a lot of disagreement turns around them.)

Although the distinction between the phenomenal present and the represented present is in principle intelligible, its substantiveness can be questioned. We can make sense of it if we consider a specious present that spans for a whole phenomenal present which includes a represented present (see Figure 4.1). This is roughly what, in the literature, is called the modal version of the specious present (cf. Dainton 2008b). However, there are at least two ways to dispute the legitimacy of this picture. According to the *elimination view*, nothing is felt as privileged in perception. Thus, eliminativists[8] consider the notion of a phenomenal present as the only acceptable one. There is no represented present in perception, because no felt sense of privilege is delivered by our perceptual phenomenal states. The elimination view is somehow more natural for specious present theorists, and the conjunction of the two theses is roughly what is sometimes called, in the literature, the non-modal specious present (see Figure 4.1). According to the *conflation view*, being felt as privileged *is*

---

[8] Cf. Mellor (1998); Braddon-Mitchell (2013); Cameron (2015); Callender (2017); and Hoerl (2018).

being presented all at once. Thus, conflationists[9] maintain that the two notions are acceptable, but in order to acknowledge that our perception delivers phenomenally a sense of privilege, we do not need to accept something over and above the phenomenal present. The conflation view goes well with the snapshot conception of the content of perception (see Figure 4.1); after all, if there is only 'space for one moment' in perception, *and* we believe that perception represents a moment as present, there is no reason to think that being presented in perception and being presented as present signal two distinct phenomenal characters. However, nothing prevents a snapshot theorist from denying that perception has anything to do with representing a moment as present, and thus to combine the snapshot thesis with the elimination view (see Figure 4.1); indeed, I will defend a version of this idea.[10]

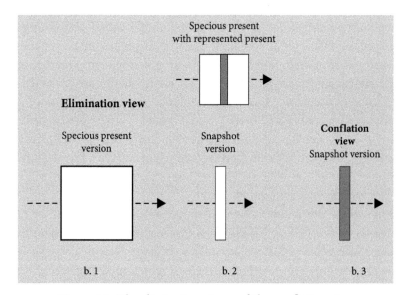

Figure 4.1 The elimination view and the conflation view

For our purposes, the important opposition is between the defenders of the idea that there is a phenomenal property of presentness of which we are aware in perceptual experience[11] and those who deny this idea; which

---

[9] Cf. Hestevold (1990); Dainton (2000); Paul (2010); Lee (2014a); Skow (2015: 192); and Solomyak (2019: 250).

[10] Lepoidevin, who defends a version of the snapshot view, is ambiguous with respect to his take on the represented present. See Torrengo and Cassaghi (2021).

[11] Note that the issue here is not whether there is a property *of experience* of which I am aware (an issue which will be relevant shortly). Here I am just distinguishing between who thinks that perception makes us aware of things as located in the present time and who does not. The *kind* of 'phenomenal property' I am talking about is uncontroversial (as a kind). Even someone like Alex Byrne, who argues

versions of the conflation view in the contemporary landscape count as one or the other is a question that does not concern me here. I will return in greater detail to the idea of presentness as felt privileged in Section 4.2; here let me just point out that denying that there is a represented present in perception does not entail that we are not in a position to *think* of a moment as temporally privileged, i.e. present. Indeed, many critics of a sense of privilege in perception admit that we ordinarily believe that there is a present moment.[12] In other words, the notion of represented present can be relaxed to encompass not only the represented present in perception, which is problematic, and towards which an eliminativist attitude is not unheard of, but also the represented present *in thought*, which is a relatively uncontroversial notion. To avoid confusion, I will call the represented present in thought the *narrative present*, which I will discuss more carefully in the next section.[13]

4.1.2.2 The narrative present

The thesis that we have a *commonsensical belief* in the existence of a present moment is often considered trivially true. Insofar as this claim is obvious, it should *not* be confused with the stronger claim that humans, as 'naive metaphysicians', are realists about an objective present. Whether experience suggests that *reality* contains an ever-changing present is controversial.[14] What is obvious is that, regardless of one's pre-theoretical beliefs about the 'nature' of the present (if any), and independently of how culture-permeated they may be, one believes *of any time at which one is having an experience, that it is present*. The present is where one's occurrent experiences take place and one's actions have an immediate effect.

Such a belief requires only the conceptual resources of the *narrative present*, that is the resources to entertain the thought of a temporally ordered sequence of events with a *focus*, namely a moment presented as somehow distinguished

against the idea that there are properties of experience of which we can be aware, acknowledges that there are phenomenal properties in the sense that, for instance, one may be in a position of being aware that something looks red to her (Byrne 2009: 235). What *is* controversial is whether presentness is one of them.

[12] Cf. 'We may well have *beliefs* concerning the presentness of events in the external world, but that doesn't mean we *observe* the tense of events' (Callender 2008: 342).

[13] For perception, I use the terminology that I have used in Torrengo and Cassaghi (2022). What I call 'the represented present in perception' is called 'the temporal present' in Valberg (1992) and Hoerl (2018).

[14] Latham et al. (2020b) have argued that empirical evidence points towards the contrary, or at least that philosophers tend to overestimate the 'proximity' to common sense of the A-theory (on the A-theory and B-theory see Section 6.1). For criticism of those empirical results see Shardlow et al. (2020). Nothing of what I claim in this chapter (indeed, in this book) goes against this empirical evidence. More on this in Chapter 5.

from the others. That those resources are ordinary and minimal is suggested by the facility with which we can find examples of mental episodes involving them: we think of what happens yesterday during a dinner with friends and we 'zoom in' on the moment in which an argument started, we think of what we will do next after buying groceries and before passing by the office, we think that after we have arrived at the crossroad, the light has turned green and we can keep on walking, and so on.

In order to pin down the notion of narrative present, we need to move from experience in a strict sense—that is, experience of our own *occurring* mental episodes, in the teeming fullness of their phenomenal nature—to experience in a wider, more liberal way, as the sum of thoughts, credence, emotional attitudes, and stances, which are not necessarily phenomenally present, but constitute our lives over a given period of time (Section 1.1). This aspect of our temporal experience was highlighted in Section 3.5 with reference to narrative thoughts and the theory of narratives as abstract objects modelling our cognitive life. To recap, I call a *target* a certain narrative unit, namely a series of (concrete) events that involve a person or are somehow relevant for a person. A *narrative thought* is a mental event that is about some of the events in a target, and a *narrative* is an abstract construct that models the capacity of the person to 'move along' the target with narrative thoughts about the various events in it.

Narratives have certain structural elements, that is elements that are not due to any specific content of a narrative. First and foremost, the relation of *temporal succession* of events. I take this relation to be part of the minimal structure of a narrative, since it is a necessary condition for its existence: without represented succession, there is no narrative.[15] Possibly also some causal element must be part of a sequence of events to qualify as a narrative. An utterly Dadaist succession of snapshots can qualify at best as a limiting case of a narrative.

---

[15] This is true of narratives as I specified in the previous section. However, one may object that it is perfectly natural to talk of narratives even when the sequence at issue is not a temporal one, but— for instance—one that encodes explanatory links. Think of someone having a thought, in a seminar on quantum mechanics, about the connection between two entangled systems and how the instantaneous collapse in one system affects the other one. One can think of the connection as in an explanatory sequence, even if the two events are not one after the other in any temporal sense. Another example could be someone thinking of a globe on a pillow and linking in her mind the shape of the globe and the shape of the pillow. I think a generalized theory of narratives should also encompass non-temporal cases like those. However, for the purpose of the book, I focus only on narrative thoughts that are about sequences of events in a temporal sense, and thereby on narratives that have temporal structure. A distinct issue is whether a narrative that contains only one (instantaneous) event counts as having temporal structure. I think one can think of that as a limiting case (both of a narrative and of temporal structure).

However, I will not dwell on causal constraints here, because they are not central to my point.[16]

What is more interesting is that a narrative needs to have what we may call— for want of a better term—a *transcendental narrator*. The narrator is not the *protagonist* of a narrative. Sometimes it may be difficult to pin down who or what is the protagonist of a narrative, if there is indeed any at all, and some- times different parts of the same narrative will have different protagonists. But *if* there is a protagonist, it is explicitly represented in the narrative. Contrari- wise, the transcendental narrator is not explicitly represented in the narrative. It is tempting to think that the transcendental narrator is the person who is entertaining the narrative thought, who is implicitly referred to in the narra- tive. But that is not the idea of a transcendental narrator I am using in the theory, and indeed I think that it is misleading to think of the transcenden- tal narrator in personal terms whatsoever. The transcendental narrator is a structural element of a narrative; it is what allows the narrative to have a *focus*.

Given that a narrative is a representation of a *sequence* of events, it does *not* contain a moment that is singled out as present. Yet we often focus on a moment, for instance, and typically, because it is the moment *when perception takes place and action initiates* for the protagonist of (that part of) a narra- tive. We can model this aspect of our thoughts by including in the narrative a dividing point between what came before and what will come according to the way things are presented in a *centred* narrative (a narrative with a focus). This dividing point is the *narrative present*, the moment that enjoys a rep- resentational privilege that is temporal in nature, by virtue of the fact that it is signalled out in a temporal sequence. Note that the narrative present is an optional element of a narrative. Narrative can also be entertained from a point of view outside time, as it were, since surely we can think of sequences of events without considering any of them as present. Hence a narrative present can be a structural element of a narrative only in the sense that it does not depend on any specific feature of the narrative content; any part of the narra- tive can be in the narrative present, that is, can be considered as representing the present moment. However, the possibility of having a narrative present, that is the existence of a transcendental narrator, is both a structural and non- optional element of a narrative.[17] I take it to be non-optional because given

---

[16] More specifically, I do not intend to overplay the role of causality. Even if causality has a structural role, surely it does not impose constraints as strong as nomic or historical plausibility on the content of the narrative.

[17] One may think that a narrative present is required for a narrative to be complete. However, unless one is a realist about the objective present, it is doubtful that a description of reality that does not

any narrative thought about a sequence of events without a centre, it is always possible to consider one of its parts as present.

Neither streams of consciousness (Section 3.2.1) nor unified experiences (Section 3.5.1) are phenomenally present, since they typically outstrip what can be perceived at once.[18] A fortiori, the same goes for larger partitions of one's world-line (e.g. the experiences I had during last weekend). However, precisely because they are not abstractions, but sequences of phenomenally present experiences, they are composed by parts each of which is phenomenally present *when* it happens. A narrative thought has a phenomenally present content (although not perceptually so), being a concrete event, and although the narrative that models its target is an abstract entity, it may contain as a part a moment that (as a matter of fact) is, or has just been, phenomenally present. Consider cases in which certain events are in the focus of a narrative that models my thoughts and are described as present in my communicative exchange, because they are (or they just have been) in my phenomenal present. In those cases we can say that the phenomenal present is the centre of the temporal perspective that I occupy. The temporal perspective itself is *not* phenomenal. The temporal dimension does not appear to us (from a perspective or otherwise), it is represented in our thoughts. But what is at the centre of the perspective *is* phenomenally presented to whomever is having the thought. For instance, suppose my husband and I plan to go to the theatre with two friends, meet at the exit of a metro station, go for a drink before the show, and then wait in the foyer. There, at a certain point, I notice the lights going on and off; I therefore realize that the beginning of the play is imminent and communicate this thought to my friends who are distractedly chattering by saying 'we should move, the play is starting now.'

This is the *embodied* case of use of a narrative to model a thought. The narrative present here represents the moment that is phenomenally present for the subject having the narrative thought that is modelled by the narrative. In such cases, the represented present in the narrative is the index (in the

---

contain a present moment should be seen as metaphysically incomplete; cf. Dummett (1969). Maybe one could still cling to the idea that such a description would be *informationally* incomplete. This is, for instance, 'a tenseless description of the history of the world (including the description of people's tensed statements and their truth values) is fundamentally incomplete, because it cannot tell us which time is the present' (Nagel 1986: 59). However, also incomplete thoughts can be useful. If I ask you at what time the movie begins, I may find more useful the information that it begins at 20:30, rather than 'in six and a quarter hours' (for instance, because at the moment I have not a watch, but I know that later on I will have access to one). For those reasons I do not think that the notion of completeness here plays any significant role.

[18] It is possible that someone faints, regains consciousness, and then faints again right after, so that their stream of consciousness is entirely contained in a phenomenal present, which is also a unified experience, but this is a limiting case. (I am assuming the wake model.)

sense specified in Section 4.1.1) of the moment that is phenomenally present
when we entertain the thought modelled by the narrative or we use it (the
thought) in communication. In other terms, being represented as privileged,
in those cases, is being represented as the content of a concurrent phenomenal present that is experienced (or has just been experienced). I take this fact
to be quite uncontroversial. What *is* controversial is whether this functional
connection between the narrative present and the content of an occurrent perceptual activity is *all there is* to the experiential present in general and if it can,
per se, explain the origin of our belief that our experiences and the events we
have experiences of are present, and our ordinary way of talking in terms of
experience-based claims involving presentness.

Surely narrative thoughts can go beyond embodied cases. I can remember,
imagine, suppose, desire, hope that a moment is present, and regardless of
whether the sequence of events I am considering contains sentient beings or
not. Those are the *detached* cases of use of a narrative to model a thought.
Although it is tempting to think of the narrative present as the 'narrative
counterpart' of a phenomenal present, the narrative present is not always the
moment for perception and action in the narrative. This is why I stressed that
the notion of a transcendental narrator is to be identified *neither* with that of
a protagonist, *nor* with that of the subject that is having a narrative thought. A
narrative present requires a transcendental narrator, but the relation between
the transcendental narrator and the phenomenal present of the person who is
having the narrative thought at issue is not trivial. What we should ask then
is what is the *origin* of the narrative present; how does it connect (if it does at
all) with the other experiential aspects of presentness, in particular those that
are more phenomenal and perceptual?

4.2 The phenomenal prominence of the present

There are several hypotheses that could explain the origin of the narrative
present from the phenomenal present. Presentness may be a *perceptual content property*, a feature of the phenomenology of perception that 'tells' us that
what we perceive is present, as there are features of our visual phenomenology
that 'tell' us that the rose we see in the vase is red. Or it may be a *perceptual
vehicle property*, an intrinsic feature of our experiences themselves of which we
are aware, the temporal analogous of a bright spot on the 'lens' of our visual
field. Although I will argue against both solutions in favour of an *eliminativist*
position, I maintain that there is a datum of prominence of the present, in the

sense that the idea of a narrative present *imposes on us* in virtue of certain structural features of the phenomenology of our experience. Without such a prominence we could not explain how the narrative present originates from the experiential present, namely how we form the belief that our experiences are present, and in the case of perception, so appears to be what we have experience of. Before expanding my take on eliminativism and explaining how I reconcile eliminativism with the idea that a narrative present is a core element of our temporal cognition, I briefly consider the main alternatives.

4.2.1 Presentness as perceptual content property

The more obvious way in which the narrative present could impose on us is because it is grounded in a perceptually represented present—be it identical with the phenomenal present (if the phenomenal present is instantaneous, and thus the conflation view is true), or with a part of it (if the phenomenal present is extended, and thus the conflation view is false; see Section 4.1.2.1). According to this view, while past and future are determinations that have only, or mainly, a conceptual nature, in the sense that we are not presented with them in perception,[19] presentness is a property of perceptual content, one that we come to understand through direct perceptual acquaintance. Schlesinger suggests this when he writes:[20] 'The property of "presentness" may be too basic to lend itself to a strict definition. However, our attitude to the present may be described regarding it as distinct from every other temporal position, for while the future is yet to be born and the past is rapidly fading, the present is palpably real' (Schlesinger 1991: 427).

If this hypothesis is correct, presentness is a phenomenal property that has outward-directed presentational phenomenology, like *being red* or having *an A_8 pitch* and other so-called secondary qualities. We can use a narrative present to model thoughts because we perceive things *as* present (or as in the present), as we perceive objects as having a colour and notes as having a pitch. As narrative thoughts are about things that have colours and have pitches, they are also about things that are present. The mechanism behind the formation of a

---

[19] I said 'mainly' because if the specious present hypothesis is correct, then there can also be a perceptual dimension to being past (in retention) and possibly to being future (in protention).

[20] See also Michael Tye: 'Presentness is part of the content of perceptual experiences in all modalities' (Tye 2003a: 86) and Alva Noë: '[. . .] as a phenomenological matter, there is a difference between *thinking* that something out of view is present (e.g. that there is money in the purse), and its *looking* as if something out of view is present (e.g. that the tomato is not a mere tomato-façade). What we want is an account of the *perceptual* presence [. . .]' (Noë 2006: 26).

narrative present is (or is analogous to) that of perceptual belief formation. As we form the belief that the apple in front of us is red, because we see it as red, we come to think of the events around us as present because we perceive them as present. William Lane Craig resorts to the notion of *basic belief*, roughly a perceptual belief non-inferentially generated, to elaborate a position that goes in this direction.

> [. . . O]ur vantage point in the present is not a self-conscious inference drawn from experience, but is just the way we experience events happening. [. . .] Our belief that they are happening presently is really no different than our belief that they are happening—and that they are happening is a basic belief grounded in part in the circumstances that we are appeared to in just that way. (Craig 2000: 139–40)

Famously, Hugh Mellor (1998) criticizes the thesis that presentness is a content property on the basis that we cannot *detect* presentness in what we see. Observing a distant star that has been dead for millions of years and the light of a nearby descending plane may be phenomenally very similar experiences. And even when the experiences differ qualitatively, the different temporal locations of what we perceive are not given through this difference.[21] An obvious reply to Mellor's observation is that the fact that a visual experience of a present aeroplane can have the same content of a visual experience of a past star can equally well be explained by the hypothesis that *both* present us with their object as present, rather than neither do. If anything, Mellor's example speaks against the possibility of perceiving pastness, rather than presentness.

I will not revise the debate around Mellor's point here. I will just note that *if* presentness is a perceptual content property, then it is a sui generis one— and one for which it is doubtful that, *as phenomenal property*, could do the job of grounding the narrative present, or a perceptual belief about presentness. Note also that if presentness is a perceptual property then it should be the temporal locations of the stimuli that are presented to us, contrary to what I have argued in Section 3.4. Consider the phenomenal property of redness involved in our visual experience of red roses. Assuming certain normal environmental circumstances hold, our experience presents us with red objects when we stand in the appropriate relation with surfaces that possess certain

---

[21] I do not deny that an experienced eye can 'see' the difference, and that the difference can amount to a difference in perceptual content, and not just in what an expert can infer from what she sees; cf. Siegel (2010). However, this would not be the notion of *being presented with something as present* that we are after here, since I do not see how we could use this perceptual content property to explain the origin of the narrative present.

physical properties and *not others*. If they had possessed other properties, we would have been presented with differently coloured objects (yellow sunflowers, say).[22] This is why the phenomenal property of redness can be said to *track* or *signal* certain physical properties—more specifically, reflectance properties of surfaces.[23] Contrariwise, if presentness is a phenomenal property, it is *not* one that can signal our responsiveness to a property rather than another. All that is required for us to be presented with things around us as present is: (i) us being conscious; and (ii) the entities around us impinging—*some way or another*—on our sensory receptors. There is no property that phenomenal presentness can be said to track, or to be responsive to in normal circumstances. In other words, as content property presentness lacks *discriminating potential*, and since discriminating potential is a key feature of prototypical content properties, it can be at best a sui generis content property.

In a sense, Craig seems to concede that much when he claims that '[. . . o]ur belief that they are happening presently is really no different than our belief that they are happening'. However, he also maintains that we believe so because 'we are appeared to in just *that way*' (italics mine), and it is not clear what way 'that way' could be, given the lack of discriminating potential just noted.[24] Maybe the conflation view is false and there is a represented present *within* the specious present, and so presentness *does* distinguish certain perceived entities from others. The moment perceived as present in the interval presented to us is more 'palpable', it has a phenomenological *oomph*—as it were—that the others lack. However, the represented present is differentiated from its retention tail (and its protention front) *entirely* in virtue of its position within the phenomenal present. There is no *qualitative* aspect that is connected to its palpability or oomph: literally any phenomenal character can end up in the represented present (Torrengo and Cassaghi 2022). Think of a spatial analogue; imagine that your visual field does not present you things all with the

---

[22] This is a simplification, because of many 'colour illusions' and because of the existence of the so-called colour metameres, namely different reflectance surface spectra that give rise to the same colour experience.

[23] I am putting the example in terms of tracking a physical property for ease of exposition, but I am not relying here on the theory according to which colours *are* those reflectance properties of surfaces, indeed not even on the weaker position that the 'tracking' here is an epistemically reliable relation. What I am relying on is the weaker point that red experiences signal the reaction to a *specific* stimulus situation; this situation could be entirely proximal (the receptor cells reaction) and have no distal physical significance. Cf. Prosser (2016: Chap. 2) where he makes an analogous point with respect to the experience of the passage of time.

[24] Cf. Le Poidevin (2019): 'To perceive something as present is simply to perceive it: we do not need to postulate any extra item in our experience that is "the experience of presentness".' I think that Craig is trying to defend something like the conflation view (Section 4.1.2.1), whereas Le Poidevin, if I read him correctly, assumes the conflation view for the purpose of a *reductio*.

same vividness, but that things visually presented at its centre look more vivid (in a sense, this is what is actually the case, if with vividness we mean accuracy; cf. the famous example of the card in Dennett and Kinsbourne 1992). There is no specific content property that comes with extra-vividness. Now a red thing is at the centre of the visual field, but you move your head and a moment after a yellow thing is. If presentness is a phenomenal property linked to a part of the phenomenal present, then it is not a content property.

4.2.2 Presentness as perceptual vehicle property

In criticizing the idea that presentness is a property of things around us that we perceptually 'pick up', Mellor does not deny that the commonsensical belief that the time at which our perception happens and our actions initiate is the present, and has an experiential base. However, he maintains that this base is not in the phenomenal character of our outward-directed perceptions, but rather in the awareness that accompanies every experiencing itself. Even when we do *not* introspect on our own experiences, 'being present must itself be an aspect of experience, something of which we are directly aware' (Mellor 1998: 43). When we have a visual experience of a red rose, we attribute redness to the rose, but we do not usually attribute redness to our own experiences. Yet there is a certain 'what it is like' to have a visual experience with such a phenomenal character. We can say that phenomenal redness is *constitutive* of certain experiences. That our experience is so constituted is one of those facts of which we are usually thought of as having *infallible* first-personal knowledge. We may be mistaken in taking the rose as red (it's white, and we have not noticed the red light shining on it), but the fact that our visual experience is constituted by redness (that *feels* like there is a red thing in front of us) is something about which we cannot have a false belief.

When we have experiences that are constituted by phenomenal redness, we are *aware* of this fact. But we are *not* aware of this fact *in the same sense* in which we are aware that the rose in front of us is red. Being aware of the fact that redness is constitutive of our experience is *not* being presented with *our own experiences* as being red.[25] Let us assume there is such a mode of awareness, and let's call it vehicle-awareness (where vehicle stands for the vehicle of experience as opposed to its content). If there is vehicle-awareness,

---

[25] I will stay neutral here on whether, *in addition*, we can, when we experience perceptually red roses, introspect, and thereby be presented with our own experiences as constituted by phenomenal redness.

maybe there are phenomenal properties of which we may be aware *only* through vehicle-awareness; let us call such properties *perceptual vehicle properties*. An example of those may be pain. On the one hand, we do not tend to attribute the property of *being in pain* to the bed corner into which we bumped our pinkie toe.[26] On the other hand, neither do we typically come to know that we are in pain through introspection. Rather, we are aware of our pain as something that constitutes our experience, even when we do not focus on our experiencing it, or on the part of the body that has been hurt (the pinkie toe), or on what caused it. In order for us to be vehicle-aware of pain, it's enough to be in pain *and* be conscious.

Assuming this account of how we became aware that we are in pain is correct, maybe the same goes for presentness. To be vehicle-aware of presentness, it's enough that our experiences are constituted by phenomenal presentness and we are conscious. That is, we are aware of phenomenal presentness as something that constitutes our experiences, even when we do not focus on our experiences, or on what we experience. But what is it, then, for an experience to be constituted by phenomenal presentness, given that it is *not* to present us with something (not even the experience itself) as present? The only available reply in this context seems to be that to be constituted by phenomenal presentness for an experience is just *to be an experience*. After all, we are never in a position to say that one experience feels more present than some other, or that it feels present *as opposed* to others that do not feel present at all. If so, also as vehicle-property presentness lacks distinguishing potential, and we are not better off than with the hypothesis that it is a content property to explain how the narrative present arises.[27]

4.2.3 Presentness as perceptual mode property

The negative conclusion of our discussion of presentness as perceptual content, and perceptual vehicle property as source of the narrative present, should not prevent us from noticing two positive take-home messages. First, we are

---

[26] Cf. 'In the case of the experience of a located bodily sensation, you seem to be presented with a phenomenal event whose phenomenal properties you can attend directly [. . .]' (Soteriou 2013: 83). In the following pages, Soteriou argues that we are introspectively aware of pain. I am presenting an account which is not so demanding, but what I say can be adjusted to his view. Note that vehicle-awareness, though, is *not* in contrast with the thesis that we are not presented with the temporal locations of the stimuli, but rather of our own experiences as occupied by external stimuli.

[27] Cf. '[. . . P]henomenal properties serve as a means of distinguishing some experiences from others. [. . .] *Being present*, however, serves no such discriminatory function. Since all of my (present) experiences *are* present, the property *being present* does not allow me to distinguish certain of my present experiences from other present experiences' (Hestevold 1990: 542–3).

not presented, either in an outward-directed way or in an inward-directed way, with presentness. Whatever the way presentness appears to us, it has no presentational phenomenology whatsoever. Second, the phenomenal prominence of the present cannot be grounded in presentness being a feature specific to *perceptual* experience. If in some sense (to be specified in Section 4.3 below) we are aware of our experiences as located in the present, then such an awareness is based on a phenomenal aspect that pertains to non-perceptual mental episodes too; memory of the past, imagining of future paths, emotional reactions, moods, and abstract reflections are all experiences that, too, happen in the present along with perceptions, and of whose temporal location we are aware too.

Before moving on to elaborate this idea into a form of phenomenal eliminativism, I will consider what may be taken to be an objection to this a-specificity of presentness with respect to the modes or attitudes of experience. A respectable tradition in phenomenology dating back to Franz Brentano considers the various modes or attitudes a conscious subject can have towards a mental content (perception, episodic memory, imagination, etc.) as characterized by specific ways in which the contents are represented. When we are afraid of a growling dog approaching us, for instance, we represent-as-dangerous the dog. Dangerous is not a property represented in the content of the attitude, but it is rather a property that *characterizes* our fear-attitude (it is what in this tradition is often called its *formal object*). Although fearing the dog does not require that we mentally represent the dog as dangerous, we may form the belief that the dog is dangerous, on the grounds of the emotional state of fear in which we are. Whether such a belief is correct depends of course on whether our emotional state was justified, that is, whether we have not misinterpreted the behaviour or intentions of the dog (maybe she was just happy to meet us).

Uriah Kriegel argues that presentness may play a similar role to perception than that of dangerousness to fear: 'it is built into the very nature of perceiving, as a type of mental state, that it represents-as-present its object' (Kriegel 2015: 409). If so, we are aware of certain events being present in virtue of being aware of our temporal orientation in *perception*. Other mental attitudes may differ precisely because they are characterized by a different temporal orientation; episodic memory, for instance, is characterized by representing-as-past an event. The fact that it is a matter of temporal *orientation*, that is a relational feature sensitive to the relative positions in time of both the subject and the content—rather than a qualitatively intrinsic feature that characterizes the mode of perception—is important, since it is supposed to help explain how perceptual states may be the experiential basis for self-locating judgements

(Recanati 2007; Torre 2009; Kriegel 2015). The idea is that perceptual experiences present us as located in the same moment at which we find what we experience. On their ground we can thus conclude (correctly if nothing has gone awry) that both our experience and what we are experiencing are happening now.

I think this position captures something important about the role of perception in our way of thinking and talking about the present, since it is substantially correct to maintain that perception is characterized by a specific way to locate temporally what is experienced. However, it forces us to adopt a double-origin thesis that is unnecessary. According to this view, when we think of our perceptions and their contents as happening in the present, we do so in virtue of the temporal orientation of the perceptual attitude, while when we think of our non-perceptual mental life as occurring in the present we do so on some other basis, presumably on having an experience *of some sort*, that is not specifically on the basis of the kind of attitude (since we are talking about non-perceptual experiences). It may be that we become aware that non-perceptual mental episodes are present in virtue of them always being 'anchored' to some concurrent perceptual mental episodes. But also if this hypothesis is correct, extra complications concerning the details of such an anchoring arise. It is difficult to make sense of the idea of us being aware of a relation between these two mental episodes, or two temporal properties of mental episodes, without resorting to some higher-order form of cognition. As I will argue (Section 4.4.2), the perceptual specificity of presentness can be captured in terms of the embodied uses of narrative thoughts, while its phenomenal prominence is captured in terms of certain structural features of experience, and it is compatible with an eliminativist stance towards its purported perceptual aspect.

Besides, as will become clear while discussing transparency and perspectival features of perception (Section 4.3), temporal orientation cannot be entirely captured in terms of perceptual phenomenology only. To conclude, although I do not have knock-down arguments against the Brentanian take on presentness, I maintain that the specificity of the perceptual component to presentness talk and thought is better explained by the distinction between embodied and detached narratives that I elaborate later on (Section 4.4.2).

4.2.4 Presentness eliminativism

If the phenomenal prominence of the present cannot be identified with either presentness as a perceptual content property or as a perceptual vehicle or mode property, then maybe it entirely resides in the fact that we are presented with a temporal location in the phenomenal present, namely that we apprehend what we are presented with all at once. This means that the phenomenal prominence of presentness should not be construed as a phenomenal specificity of any sort. It is not just that presentness is not specifically perceptual, it does not have its specific phenomenal character at all. And when we talk about things happening now or in the present, those experience-based claims are mischaracterizations of the phenomenology that prompts them. The thesis that those claims are true is what I call *phenomenal eliminativism with respect to presentness*, or *presentness eliminativism* for short. A full defence of this position will have to wait for Chapter 6, where I discuss and discard the possibility that the phenomenal prominence of the present (and of passage) is explained by the assumption that there is a shifting objective present. Here I take it as a working hypothesis that, given the unavailability of the main alternatives, the best explanation of the phenomenal prominence of the present is eliminativism. The question of how the narrative present originates from the phenomenal prominence of the present becomes thus more difficult to answer, since I am now working with a deflated notion of phenomenal prominence. How exactly can the phenomenal present together with some non-perceptual mental event single out a moment as present in the narrative, given that it is not phenomenally prominent neither in the sense of a content property, nor in the sense of a vehicle or mode property? In other words, how can we be in a special cognitive relation of accessibility to the present, as O'Shaughnessy (2000: 50) puts it? In order to carry out my explanation, I need to turn to phenomenal objectivity and see whether it can function as a link between the phenomenal present and the narrative present.

4.3 Presentness and phenomenal objectivity

Phenomenal transparency, namely the thesis that it seems to us to be perceptually presented only with features of the external world, captures an aspect of the idea that perception, as opposed to other sensorial mental episodes, such as imagination and abstract thought, comes with what I have called *phenomenal objectivity*. Through different and possibly integrated modalities (sight, smell, touch, etc.) the 'external world' is revealed to us *as the external world*. Experience prominently presents us with things that inhabit the same *space* and *time* we also inhabit, but which are located—quite literally—outside our heads. If full transparency holds, then even *ephemeral experiences* such as after-images and phosphenes present us (illusorily) with things of the external world, although we *misjudge* them to be pure sensations. And we make that mistake because of the presence of *phenomenal defeaters* of their phenomenal objectivity: after-images tend to flicker and flutter as objects around us do not, they 'move' in relation to where we move and direct our gaze, they do not appear constant in size, and they cannot be inspected from different perspectives. If full transparency does not hold, certain aspects of our experience may lack presentational phenomenology and thus it would not be misjudging to take ephemeral experiences to be pure sensations. How is presentness related to phenomenal objectivity? On the one hand, perception seems to have a special connection with presentness, and thus we may be inclined to see the two as strictly connected. On the other hand, we tend to describe all experiences, even the ones that do *not* involve phenomenal objectivity, as happening in the present. Let us investigate such a quandary more closely.

4.3.1 Space: structural and locational properties

What have been called *structural* aspects of perceptual experience (cf. Martin 1992; Richardson 2014; and Hoerl 2018) play an ambiguous role with respect to phenomenal objectivity. To my knowledge, the ambiguity has not been appreciated in full. Considerations come both from temporal and spatial elements of experience, although there are core differences between the two. Consider the spatial case first. Visual experiences, for instance, seem not only to reveal properties of the objects in our visual field (such as colour and shape), but they also come with an awareness of the *perspectival way* in which we are presented with such objects (cf. Green and Schellenberg 2018). We are aware of the *circular* shape of the coin on the table *and* of its looking *elliptical from our spatial standpoint.* There are good reasons to take the latter as a property of the visual field itself. Why so? Because perceptually we cannot be aware of the shape of something but from our standpoint in space. This holds not only for shape but for any property whose experience is sensitive to spatial location, and not only for the visual field, but also for the other sensorial fields. The spatial aspect of the visual and other sensory fields *is* perspectival, it comes with a centre and an orientation, which is given by our position in the space that it presents to us. And this seems to be a feature of the field itself, and not of what we are presented with within the field, as is apparent if we think that the way something looks from a certain standpoint changes with our position in space.

Now, on the one hand the things we visually experience have phenomenal objectivity *in virtue of* (or, at least, partially in virtue of) being presented as at a distance from us. They look *out there* because they are presented to us as not being *here*. Therefore, awareness of the perspectival features is an important element of visual experience being an experience of an external world. On the other hand, they bear all the signs of mind-dependency: they change as we move around, they do not remain stable so that we can inspect them, and so on. Hence, they violate full phenomenal transparency, which is the thesis behind phenomenal objectivity, and thus there are prima facie good reasons to take them as features of the visual field.

One way to solve the tension is to bite the bullet, after all full phenomenal transparency is prima facie plausible, but not sacrosanct, and weaker forms of transparency may as well capture the phenomenal objectivity of perception. In particular, it may be enough to have positive transparency. It may be that we are aware of the perspectival features of the visual field (and in general of the structural features of the various sensory fields) only *through* being aware of the objects that inhabit it. We are perceptually aware of the perspectival features of the visual field, but not as a further object that can be subject to visual inspection and at the centre of the focus of attention.[28] If so, full transparency fails, because negative transparency fails, yet positive transparency holds. We can*not* be directly aware of the perspectival features themselves, not even in introspection, we can only be aware of them indirectly, by attending to the objects out there and their properties. The *elliptical way* in which the coin looks from our standpoint is a way in which a coin is presented to us *as round*. Indeed, it seems impossible to attend to the elliptical shape *without* being aware of the round shape. If we manage to do so, as soon as we lose the awareness of roundness, *being elliptical* stops being *merely* a way something looks (from where we are) and becomes a property of what is presented to us. When we look at a trompe l'oeil of a coin without realizing it, the reverse seems to happen. The property of being elliptical that the paint exemplifies is seen as the way a round object appears to us from a certain perspective.

An alternative route to solving the tension is to retain full transparency but explain our tendency to talk otherwise in terms of phenomenal defeaters. Think of the analogous move in the case of ephemeral experiences, for instance after-images. One may argue that after-images (illusorily) present us with entities out there (cf. Philipps 2012). If this claim strikes us as phenomenally dubious, it is because their behaviour (we cannot inspect them since they

---

[28] Cf. 'Rather than thinking of the boundaries of the visual field as boundaries of some thing one is sensing, we should think of the boundaries of the visual field in terms of one's sensory limitations' (Soteriou 2011: 193).

move 'with us', and so forth) indeed suggests that they are features of our own experience. However, those defeaters lead us to *misjudge* them to be such.

To understand what a defeater would be like in the case of structural properties, compare location and shape of visible material objects. In a sense, we are directly aware of both the location and the shape of an object in the visual field: we are presented with the coin being at a certain location (on the table) and having a certain shape (round). But being directly aware of them is not in tension with the fact that both are presented to us from the standpoint we occupy: I see the coin *over there*, which is the position things on the table looks to be in from where I am, and I see the coin *elliptical*, which is the shape *round* things look to have from where I am. But since the *ways* in which I am presented with the locational and shape properties change as I move around, I tend *not* to take *them* as properties of things in the external world.

As it stands, there is something weird in this reply. The problem is that phenomenal defeaters make sense when we are talking about what we judge about *objects* rather than *ways objects appear*. I do *not* take the coin that looks elliptical from where I am to *be* elliptical, but that does not mean that I tend to think that there is a mind-dependent elliptical object with which I am perceptually presented. If I come to believe that (wrongly, methinks), it is because of philosophical reflection that has led me to embrace some form of sense data theory. Therefore, there is nothing to explain by appealing to phenomenal defeaters to begin with. Being aware that a way in which something in the external world appears is *subjective*, because it depends on my spatial position and it changes accordingly, is not being aware of something over and above the external world. This is why positive transparency is all it takes to capture phenomenal objectivity.

Maybe the question whether we are aware of perspectival features of perceptual experience as a property of the sensory field, or as subjective ways in which things appear to us, cannot be settled unless a 'god of introspection' descends and tells us what direct and indirect descriptions of the phenomenal character of our experience are true. If so, it is probably an issue of little philosophical significance. What seems clear is that spatial perspectival features of perception do not have the eerie appearance of after-images and phosphenes, even if they bear the mark of mind-dependency or subjectivity, in particular they change as we move around.

More importantly, *spatial locational properties* are not structural properties as perspectival ways of appearing are, they are rather just further properties of the entities we are presented perceptually with. Regardless of the phenomenal and metaphysical status of the *ways* in which properties that are sensitive to spatial location such as shape for vision appear from different standpoints, we are aware of the *locations themselves* of the objects that we see and smell and hear around us in the same perspectival way. Locational properties of the objects in the visual fields are presented to us as properties that are sensitive to spatial location and thus 'look differently' depending on where we are. They are presented to us as *directly* as a round shape of a coin is directly presented to us by looking elliptical from where we stand. The same does *not* hold for *our own* location. We are only *indirectly* (in the same sense of directness) aware of our own position: there is no way in which our own position 'looks like' from where we are, because nothing that is here, where we are, perceptually looks like anything *at all*.[29] The only way in which we can be aware of our own location is *through* having an experience of the positions of other things. This is trivial if you think that clearly, we do not perceive where we ourselves are as we perceive where the apple in front of us is. But both cases of awareness entail that locations are presented in a perspectival way: we are directly aware of the position of the apple insofar as it appears to us *from this standpoint*, and we are indirectly aware of our position through how 'things out there' *appear from the standpoint that we occupy*.

4.3.2 Time: lack of phenomenal discriminability

The temporal case is only partially analogous. Full temporal transparency in its phenomenal reading is the thesis that introspection of our perceptions does not reveal the temporal properties of our own perceptions, we are only aware of temporal properties of the content of our perceptions, *viz.* the external events we perceive. This seems to be in tension with what I have claimed in the previous chapter, namely that it is the temporal locations of our own experiences, and not of the stimuli, that appear to us. And it appears as containing the external stimuli: things in space 'out there', which are thus and so. How can we settle the tension? Do we need to jettison full transparency? One reason to think that we do is that, as a matter of phenomenological datum, experiences seem to

[29] Note that nothing changes if one maintains that the *locations* in the sensory fields of the objects we see, hear, and smell are perceived in a more indirect way than other properties that are sensitive to spatial location, but have a more definite qualitative nature, such as their shape. Cf. Taylor Burge: 'Representation as of temporal relations [. . .] gets its representational role derivatively, through its association with perception of other things' (Burge 2010: 521). It may be that the location of a coin in the visual field is presented to us only through the ways in which its shape looks like from the position it has relative to us. Call this way of appearing a direct* way of appearing (as opposed to the direct way of appearing of shapes and other qualitative properties). The point is that *our own location* in any of the sensory field appears neither directly nor directly*.

somehow contain information about their own temporal location (and duration), along with information about the temporal location of their object. We tend to describe not only what we perceive as located in the present (even when it is thunder in the recent past or a dying star in the distant past), but also our own experiences as occurring *now*. And those descriptions are purportedly based on perceptual phenomenology. More precisely, they are based on what appears to be a datum: we are not in a position, phenomenally, to distinguish between our position in time and the position in time of what we experience. As Louise Richardson puts it: 'It is tempting—and I will suppose, true—to say that there does not seem to be any distinction, in experience, between the apparent temporal location of the objects of experience [. . .] and the temporal location of the experience itself [. . .]' (Richardson 2014: 12*).

The difference between the spatial case and the temporal case can be put down as follows. In the spatial case, being aware of features that have a subjective, mind-dependent nature—for instance how the round coin *looks elliptical from here*—is essential for being (indirectly) aware of your own position. And this makes it also the case that there is a *felt difference* between the spatial location of the perceiver and that of the perceived content. Whereas in the temporal case, we do not experience any differentiation between the location of our perception and the location of the perceived content, and it is not clear that subjective, perspectival, or otherwise structural features play any role in the awareness of our own temporal location.

Does this mean that the temporal case is not problematic for full transparency after all? No, because explaining this lack of *phenomenal discriminability* between the perceiver's temporal location and the temporal location of the content *without* appealing to introspective access to the property of our own experiences (in particular, without appealing to phenomenal awareness of one's temporal locational) is not a trivial deed. And of course, one may wonder how to do it while keeping the account of awareness of succession that I have given, which explicitly relies on being in contact with our own temporal location. In the literature, there are at least three ways to account for the fact that it does not seem to us that we can differentiate the temporal location of our own perceptual experience and that of what we perceive. I list them below under the labels 'Jungle', 'Maquis', and 'Desert'. The terms suggest the amount of perceptual phenomenal information about temporal position that they require to account for the lack of discriminability—from large to none.

> **Jungle.** We are aware both of the temporal location of our occurring perceptions and of the temporal position of their content, *and* of their being *one and the same*.

Maquis. We are aware of the temporal location of our occurring perceptions *through* our awareness of the temporal location of their content.

Desert. We are aware *neither* of the temporal position of our occurring perceptions, nor of that of their content.

Christopher Peacocke seems to endorse a form of Jungle strategy, when he claims that both the time of the event and the time of the experience that represents it are represented to the perceiver: 'perceptual experience itself has a present-tense content. It represents to the perceiver the event as occurring then—at the time of the experience' (Peacocke 1999: 280). On the face of it, the Jungle strategy violates full phenomenal transparency, and possibly even positive phenomenal transparency, insofar as it is distinct from Maquis, and thus requires that the perceptual awareness of our own temporal location is not gained through attending to the temporal location of what we perceive. What is worse, there are three ways to implement it, and they all are dead ends. Either: (i) we are presented with the same location in two distinct ways (two perceptual modes of presentation); (ii) we are presented with two entities sharing a location; or (iii) we are presented with our own location and we project it onto what we are perceiving.

If (i), we are aware of the *relation* between *two distinct modes of presentation* of locations, and somehow 'see' that they present to us the same location. This fails to capture the lack of discriminability in the purported phenomenology, even if it succeeded in explaining our judgements about sharing temporal location with the content of our perceptions.[30] Think of the spatial case. It does not make sense to say that something may look in different ways (with respect to how it looks relative to our spatial location) with respect to the same spatial location. If the same holds for temporal location, and my experiences and their content appear as in the same temporal location, we cannot be aware of this fact in virtue of comparing two distinct modes of presentation, since the location being the same, the mode of presentation should be the same. Maybe the same location, from the same perspective, can be presented twice over. The closest to this would be, in the spatial case, looking at an object through

---

[30] Think of the spatial case, it does not make sense to say that something may look in *different* ways (with respect to how it looks relative to our spatial location) with respect to the *same* spatial location. If the same holds for temporal location, and my experiences and their content appear as in the same temporal location, we cannot be aware of this fact in virtue of comparing two distinct modes of presentation, since the location being the same, the mode of presentation should be the same. Maybe, the same location, from the same perspective, can be presented twice over. The closest to this would be, in the spatial case, looking at an object through a two-faced corner of a large crystal that shows us two images of the object, and us being aware that the object's position is presented to us twice (alternatively, and a bit more loosely, think of a Cubist portrait). Again, this does not capture the phenomenology: even if we are aware perceptually that it is the same position presented to us twice, it would be not because we are unable to phenomenally distinguish the ways in which it is presented to us.

a two-faced corner of a large crystal that shows us two images of the object, and us being aware that the object's position is presented to us twice (alternatively, and a bit more loosely, think of a Cubist portrait). Again, this does not capture the phenomenology: even if we are aware perceptually that it is the same position presented to us twice, it would be not because we are unable to phenomenally distinguish the ways in which it is presented to us.

If (ii), ourselves and the content of our experiences are perceived to be in the same location, as we can be perceptually aware of a hammock and the thick thread of which it is made to occupy the same spatial location. This would capture the phenomenology of lack of discriminability, but it clashes with the phenomenological datum that we are never in a position to directly perceive where *ourselves* are located in our sensory fields.

If (iii), one can resort to the *Projection Principle* (see Section 2.4.2) and claim that it seems to us that what we perceive happens in the present, because we project on it the temporal location of our own perceptions, of which we are directly aware. Therefore, we are aware of the temporal relation between our location and the location of the events that we perceive not because we perceive the relation, but because we 'create' it.[31] This manoeuvre does not provide any explanation of how we can be aware of the temporal position of our own perceptions, and ultimately suffers from the same problems I have highlighted in Section 4.2.2 about the possibility that presentness be a vehicle property.

The Maquis strategy is compatible at least with positive transparency.[32] One could think of an analogy with the spatial case and defend the idea that we are indirectly aware of the temporal location of our own perceptions by being aware, in a perspectival manner, of the temporal relation between them and their content. The problem with this take on the strategy is that the temporal relation in question is *simultaneity*, and it is not clear that a relation of simultaneity can appear in a perspectival way from the point of view of one of its relata. Notice that here the point is not that, the location being the same, the two relata cannot look different from the point of view of one another—as for (ii). The point is: how can the simultaneity relation appear to us in *any* perspectival manner to begin with? The phenomenological datum of the lack of discriminability we aim at explaining is precisely that what we are perceptually aware of does not 'look' like at any temporal distance from us.

---

[31] Mellor (1998) seems to have something like this strategy in mind. However, he is ambiguous with respect to whether the 'projection' happens within perceptual awareness, or it is rather that we are aware of our own mental episodes as present and therefore we *judge* the events of which we are perceptually aware through them as present as well.

[32] Bayne seems to advocate a version of this view: 'On this conception of experiences, we are aware of our experiences as such in being aware of which phenomenal properties we instantiate' (2010: 33).

Matthew Soteriou upholds a different version of the Maquis strategy.[33] According to him, '[. . .] it seems to one as though the temporal location of one's experience depends on, and it is determined by, the temporal location of whatever it is that one's experience is an experience of' (Soteriou 2013: 89–90). What we are perceptually aware of is not the temporal relation (of simultaneity) between our mental events and what is presented to us through them, but rather of the relation of dependence (or determination) between the location of my experience and that of their content. This manoeuvre can be seen as an application of the *Inheritance Principle* (Section 2.4.2), which is the inverse of the Projection Principle. It states that the temporal properties of the content of experience are inherited by the experience itself. If an experience presents us with an event that has a certain duration, for instance, the experience itself has that very duration (at least in the 'normal' cases). Applied to temporal location that means that if what we perceive happens in the present, so does our perceiving it.

Now, crucially for this version of the Maquis strategy to work, it does not suffice that the Inheritance Principle holds, but we must also be *perceptually aware of that*, namely we have to somehow 'see' the dependence relation. In other words, we need an explanation of how we are aware of the temporal properties of our own experiences in virtue of being aware of the temporal properties of what we perceive. Soteriou has an explanation, based on his relationist account of perception, but he does not focus on presentness, and our indirect reports on how we experience it. Rather, he is interested in accounting how we are aware of the fact that the temporally extended events that we perceive occupy the same temporal width of the mental episodes through which we are aware of them.

But there is a difference between duration and topological properties (see Section 2.2) on the one hand, and presentness on the other. The former are content properties; experience does present us with events as having certain durations.[34] If we are aware of the duration of the events that we perceive in virtue of a *relation* we bear with them (rather than in virtue of some intentional

---

[33] To the letter he may seem to defend a Jungle strategy. Hoerl (2018) takes him as Jungle on the surface, but argues that it should be construed to be a proponent of Desert in order to avoid contradiction (as for Phillips 2014a and 2014b). Lee (2019) and Richardson (2019) construe him as a defender of the Maquis strategy, in line with my interpretation.

[34] There is a lot of disagreement on the correct theory of the phenomenological structure of this datum, but not on the datum itself. At any rate, if an extreme Reid-style view were to be correct—so that our direct and indirect reports on the phenomenology are mistaken, we are never presented with extended events, but only judge events to be extended, on the ground of memory and not on phenomenal awareness—this means that the strategy fails not only for presentness, but also for other temporal properties.

property our mental states instantiate), then it makes sense to claim that we are thereby also aware that their duration determines the duration of our experience (Soteriou's story is, of course, more complex than this, but in the same spirit). The latter, presentness, if my arguments in the previous section are on the right track, is not a content property (or a vehicle property, for that matter), hence it cannot be inherited by the experience itself in the same way—or, more precisely, *if* it is inherited in some way, we cannot *be aware of this fact* in the same sense in which we are aware of the sameness of temporal location of the extended content and the extended experience (since we are not aware of the presentness of what we experience by entertaining a certain perceptual relation with it).

This version of the Maquis strategy contains a good explanation of the lack of phenomenal discriminability between our position in time and the position of the events we experience perceptually, but it is not an explanation that we can exploit to account for the ground of the narrative present. One may still insist that even if nothing looks present, we could be indirectly aware of the presentness of our own perceptions through our awareness of the position in the phenomenal present of the events we are perceptually presented with.[35] As in the spatial case we are aware of being *here* at the centre of the spatial perspective where the things we perceive are located, in the temporal case we are aware that our perceptions happen *now*, at the centre of the temporal perspective where the events we perceive occur. The problems with this move are analogous to those we encounter by considering the hypothesis that the relation of simultaneity could be presented to us in a perspectival manner. Consider the spatial case, in which—I argued—we are only indirectly aware of our position in the sensory field through our awareness of the ways in which the other positions look from the position that we occupy. The indirect way in which the subject is aware of her spatial location is *entirely determined* by the way things (locations) around look. But in the temporal field things do *not* look like a different temporal location from us. Even if the temporal field contains a represented present, *our* temporal location—the time at which our perception happens, *as it appears to us*—is that of the temporal field itself and not of the represented present within it. This is what I meant when I said, in Section 3.4.2, that our awareness of our temporal position does not have presentational phenomenology.

---

[35] This idea is in line with modal retentional approaches, such as Almäng's (2014).

Those considerations, if correct, make the third strategy the more promising. Desert entails that perceived events do not look like at any temporal distance, not even at a zero temporal distance, from us. Therefore, we cannot have an indirect awareness of our own temporal position from an awareness of their position in the temporal field. Hoerl (2018) explicitly defends such a 'lack of temporal viewpointedness' in perception. The temporal field—that is, the phenomenal present—has a less rich structure than the sensory field in their spatial aspect; in particular, it does not display perspectival features. How Desert can be used to explain the lack of phenomenal discriminability is straightforward. There is simply no perspectival information encoded in the phenomenal present, neither indirect information concerning the temporal location of the experience itself (as there is with respect to its spatial location), nor direct information concerning the temporal location of what we perceive (as there is, presented in a perspectival way, with respect to spatial location). Therefore, there are no resources in perceptual phenomenology to distinguish between them. It is not the case that we are aware of the same location as presented in two ways, it is not the case that we are aware of two entities being in the same temporal location, and it is not the case that we are aware of the location of one as the location of the other in virtue of being aware of the location of the latter. Rather, we cannot distinguish between the two because we are not perceptually aware of there being two aspects in the phenomenal present whose temporal location can be considered.

But the lack of phenomenal discriminability is not what interests us the most here. How can Desert be exploited to explain the origin of the narrative present? Is it not in an even worse spot than the Maquis strategy? After all, if Desert is correct, there is no perceptual information about temporal location of experiences and their content, and thus no grounds for our talking and thinking about them as present. In what follows, I will argue that, by appealing to the embodied uses of narrative thoughts, we can provide an explanation of why perception has a privileged relation with the present. It is not what makes the present special, since the phenomenal prominence of the present is not perceptual in nature, but it does relate to the narrative present in a way that distinguishes it from mental episodes of non-perceptual nature.

Before getting to the details of the theory that I defend, which is a form of the error theory strategy (Section 1.3) and is based on Desert, let me clarify the distinction between mine and Hoerl's use of Desert. I share with

Hoerl the idea that lack of temporal view-pointedness in perception explains the lack of phenomenal discriminability between the temporal position of the content and that of the experience itself. But I part company with him in two further respects. Firstly, as will be clear in Section 4.4.1, while discussing what I call locational awareness, I think that we are aware of other (non-perspectival) structural features that pertain to the temporal aspect of perception, and indeed phenomenal experience in general. Hence, I maintain that at best positive—rather than full—temporal transparency holds for the temporal case. Secondly, and perhaps more importantly, Hoerl is looking for an explanation of a purported commonsensical belief in an objective present. His diagnosis is that the belief arises abductively from the fact that we lack a phenomenal basis to explain how it would depend on us (on the fact that we happen to be in a certain location in time) that we experience what we find in the phenomenal present 'to the exclusion of [other events] that happen earlier or later' (Hoerl 2018: 146). As I have pointed out above, the existence of a commonsensical belief in an objective present may be an academic prejudice.[36] But even if we (or some of us, at any rate) do have this belief on the ground of commonsensical elements, I maintain that there is a more basic feature of temporal cognition which is grounded on the phenomenal prominence of the present. That is, the fact that we talk and think of the present moment as the one in which we are and act. My aim, thus, is to put to work Desert in an explanation of this datum, rather than of an alleged commonsensical belief in an objective present.

4.4 From locational awareness to the narrative present

The fact that there are no structural elements in the temporal aspect of perception that carry the marks of perspectival presentations does not mean that there are no temporal structural elements in perception at all. Two such elements are relevant here: temporal *finitude* and *locatedness*. I put awareness of those two structural features of the temporal field under the label 'locational awareness'. As we will see, locational awareness does not pertain solely to perception, but it is a structural aspect of the phenomenology of experience more generally.

---

[36] Hoerl himself is now exploring an analogous claim; cf. Shardlow et al. (2020). See also Lee (2019) for some criticism of the idea that a belief in this metaphysical thesis could be grounded in experience in the way that Hoerl maintains.

4.4.1 Locational awareness

The first element of locational awareness is *finitude*. The phenomenal present comes with a limited width. In the case of perception, the finitude in question is that of the temporal field. If snapshot theorists are right, the width of the phenomenal present in perception is virtually zero; if specious present theorists are right, we apprehend events all at once in a wider berth. But even if the phenomenology of the width of the phenomenal present in perception is in some sense ambiguous with respect to where the boundaries of the temporal field are, it determinately carries information about there being such boundaries.[37] This can be explained by the fact that we are aware of the boundaries only vicariously (being structural features) through being aware of what we perceive within them, and thus we cannot put them in the focus of attention. The situation is analogous for the spatial case. The spatial boundaries of the sensory fields are structural features of the field itself of which we are aware, and not a further object presented to us, and that we can further inspect. Spatial finitude and temporal finitude seem to be phenomenally linked, and thus not merely accidentally analogous. Only by appealing to the finitude of *both* the temporal field *and* the spatial aspect of the sensory fields can we explain why perception comes with what I have called the *phenomenology of synchronic fullness*. We are aware that what is phenomenally present happens in the utmost borders both with respect to the past and the future, and with respect to any spatial direction. Like a cat in a cardboard box, the phenomenal present takes up all the available room that there is. Finitude is felinitude.

The second non-perspectival structural feature of the temporal field that pertains to locational awareness is its *locatedness*, and in a sense it is in tension with the phenomenology of synchronic fullness that is connected with finitude. Although, if Desert is correct, we do not have any information about the temporal location of what we perceive (and of our perceptions themselves), we are aware of it being located. It is not just that we are aware of the temporal field having its own boundaries, we are also aware that those boundaries cut a portion in a larger 'arena', where other things happen. This aspect of temporal

---

[37] Not everybody agrees. Rashbrook-Cooper (2011, 2016), for instance, endorses a position in which we lack awareness of the boundaries of the phenomenal present. Cf. 'On my view, the explanation of the difficulty in discerning the extent of Time-Windows [i.e., the phenomenal present] is that their boundaries are simply not manifest in the phenomenology at all, rather than merely being manifest in a way that renders their locations difficult to discern' (Rashbrook-Cooper 2011: 630). However, in one reading of what he is saying, he claims that we lack awareness of a determinate location of the boundary (something still different from being 'manifest in a way that renders their locations difficult to discern'). This reading is compatible with my claim that there is a determinate awareness of there being a boundary.

phenomenology is strictly connected with the awareness of succession, but it is nonetheless distinct from it. It is not an overarching phenomenal character, but it is likewise connected to an expectation of there being more to the temporal field than what we are currently experiencing. Also, here there is an analogy with space. Consider a visual experience: we are not surprised, when we turn our head, that space does not finish, but we encounter more space.[38] Analogously, in the temporal case, we are not surprised, when we find ourselves in a new phenomenal present, that time did not come to an end.

The tension between those two elements of locational awareness may in part explain why the fact that perceptual experience is openly limited has been taken to support the thesis that we take ourselves to be passive with respect to the temporal aspect of it (Hoerl 2018), as much that we are not entirely transparent with respect to the temporal features of experience itself (Soteriou 2013; Richardson 2014; Prosser 2016). From a third-person point of view, what results in a tension in the phenomenology is the unproblematic (and almost trivial) fact that we are aware of being presented with *all* what happens within the boundaries of *one* temporal location. However, in order to understand how the narrative present originates from locational awareness, we need to move on beyond these merely perceptual considerations.

To be more precise, we need to go beyond perception in two senses. Firstly, we must keep in mind that finitude and locatedness are features of non-perceptual mental events as much as of perceptual ones. It is not just the temporal field of perception that is finite and occupies only one 'slot' at a time in the temporal dimension, it is the phenomenal present more generally that does not extend indefinitely into the past and future, and that comes with an awareness of being one among many. Secondly, although finitude and locatedness are strictly connected, while one can probably be aware of the finitude of the phenomenal present merely on the basis of perceptual experience, in order to be aware that the phenomenal present has a temporal location we need more than perceptual information (especially if Desert is true), since we need *somehow* to be aware that there are things outside the phenomenal present, in a way that it is plausible to think that requires abstract thoughts of some sort. One may even argue that locational awareness is a form of (possibly fast and

---

[38] Michael Martin draws our attention to this phenomenological fact to support the idea that the boundaries of the visual field are a structural feature of the field itself, and not (a feature of) an object we are visually presented to. Notice that according to him, also bodily awareness, which is presupposed by touch (a sense for which, he argues, the idea of a sensory field only partially applies), comes with something like an experience of locatedness: 'We are aware of ourselves as bounded and limited within a world that extends beyond us' (Martin 1992: 201).

very natural) inferential belief. I do not want to take a stance here. Suffice to say that if locational awareness is a belief, it is one that is strictly based on (non-perceptual) phenomenological features, and if it is a non-doxastic state (a phenomenal awareness of some sort), it is one that requires non-perceptual mental capacities. In particular, my hypothesis is that *it requires the capacity to entertain narrative thoughts* (Section 3.5.2).

If my hypothesis is on the right track, in which sense are abstract mental capacities *required* for locational presentness? The issue is surely partly empirical, and I do not wish to speculate here. However, there are several considerations that are not empirical and relevant. Consider again the problem of accounting for our experience of not being aware of a distinction between our location in time and the location of the events we are perceptually aware of. The explanation of how we are aware that the location of *two* factors involved in perception are indistinguishable requires more than perceptual information. It is only through non-perceptual mental episodes that we can formulate various ways of *addressing* the sole temporal location of which we are aware. Hence only in thought can we become aware that this location is both: (i) the location of my perceptions and actions; and (ii) the location of what we perceive and of what is affected by our own actions. According to my hypothesis, we have awareness of those various conceptualizations of *the* temporal location we are presented with in perception thanks to our capacity to entertain narrative thoughts.

Remember that what is perceptually presented to us has phenomenal prominence merely in the sense that it is the only phenomenally accessible temporal location, but it is not presented to us as a *privileged* moment in the temporal series: presentness is neither a content nor a vehicle property. And even if one can maintain that it is a perceptual mode property, that does not mean that in perception the present moment is presented as distinguished from the past and the future. The fact that we perceive-as-present as opposed to remember-as-past (as the Brentanian would have it) means that we are aware that the temporal location of what we perceive in this moment does not contain the temporal location of events that we remember, as the breakfast that we had this morning or anticipate, as the night at the opera to come.

The perceptual contribution to presentness falls short of providing comparative information between the phenomenal present and other temporal locations. In order for the phenomenal present to be presented as privileged, we need to consider information from *other* mental states too. It is tempting to say that those other mental states are past and future perceptions. But the contents of past and future perceptions are not accessible to us, neither in the phenomenal present, *nor in memory or imagination*. Whatever is precisely the link between a perceptual content p had at a time t, and the content of a connected episodic memory experience m had at a time $t'>t$, the kind of access (if we are allowed to talk of access at all) we have to p when we are presented with m is surely different from the one we have when we are presented with p (cf. Debus 2007). The mental states that allow us to grasp a comparison between a moment that is phenomenally present and others that come before and after it are narrative thoughts. We cannot be perceptually aware of the phenomenal present as privileged in the temporal series, but we can think of the phenomenal present as the only moment accessible to perception when we think of it in narrative thoughts. The phenomenal present is the only *locus* of perception; past and future moments have an experiential dimension only outside perception, in thought.[39]

It is important to point out that locational awareness, and in particular the locatedness part, is not just another way to rephrase positive temporal transparency (or the Maquis strategy in general). The awareness of having experiences of limited width in the background of a wider field of possibilities is a feature that does not pertain only to the temporal field in perception, but more generally to any experience, also non-perceptual ones. Hence, insofar as our thoughts and our 'inner life' are phenomenally presented to us, we are aware of the content of non-perceptual mental episodes, too, as occurring in the same temporal location. Consider whatever you, reader, are experiencing now, this temporal location is not only (i) the location of your perceptions, (ii) the location of what you perceive, but also (iii) the location of your thoughts and non-perceptual mental life—vivid memories and burning desires included.

If so, the spatial and the temporal features of perceptual experience play a somewhat inverse role in phenomenal objectivity. Spatial perspectival features in perception are sources of phenomenal objectivity because through them we are aware of entities that dwell in locations that are *distinct from our own location* in the space that is presented to us. Yet, we are aware of the *subjectivity* of how something looks like from where we are, as soon as we move around. Contrariwise, the *way* in which we are perceptually presented with events happening in time is not perspectival, hence it does not change 'as we move in time', and in this sense is *not* subjective. Yet time cannot look objective in the same sense space does, since *what* is presented to us in perception is temporally located where we also find what is presented to us in memory, imagination, affective life, and thought in general. Hence, if we bracket the fact

---

[39] Cf. 'Whether we can observe events, and what we can observe of them, does indeed depend on their A-times' (Mellor 1998: 15).

that *spatially* the content of perception seems 'out there', it is not presented to us in a different way than the way in which what *clearly* depends on us is presented: our thoughts, moods, emotions, and desires. Indeed, if it were perspectival features that give *temporal* transparency phenomenal objectivity, as in the case of space, then the temporal position of the events we witness would not seem objective at all.

I think that at a perceptual level, it is plausible to think that the phenomenal objectivity of presentness as a temporal location is indeed ambiguous. Even if there are elements in perception that suggest the existence of an objective present, such as the lack of perspectival features in the temporal field, the most basic belief in a privileged present cannot be put in terms of a *metaphysical* privileged, as Hoerl seems to maintain.[40] The privileged is locational and not very tightly connected with an awareness of objectivity: the present moment is singled out from the past and the future, because it is the only moment where we find all what we are phenomenally aware of, our perceptions and actions in the first place, but also thoughts and the rest of our inner life. Maybe an explanation of the non-perspectival way in which perceptual contents are presented to us in the temporal field in terms of an objective present that warrants its unique availability, rather than an explanation in terms of causal constraints on accessibility and locational awareness, is very natural, and hence many people believe 'naturally' (scare quotes to allow for some philosophical reflection) this theory; yet, if my comments are on the right track, phenomenal objectivity is a kind of awareness that is primarily grounded in the spatial, rather than temporal, aspect of perception.

Indeed, I think that it is not implausible to think (although I am not going to defend this thesis in detail here) that phenomenal objectivity *entirely* originates from the perspectival way we are aware of the spatial elements of the sensory fields. After all, spatial phenomenology is primarily perceptual: sensorial awareness of a space presented to us through a very abstract thought (e.g. imagining the distances between different quantities) is always metaphorical, whereas we are aware of the temporal location of the occurrence of a very abstract thought in quite literally the same way (in so far as there is a what it is like to have it) in which we are aware of the temporal location of a perception. Hence, on the ground merely of temporal phenomenology it would be difficult to see how the idea of an external space, which we ourselves inhabit, could a rise.

---

[40] There is, of course, the further fact that we are also aware of *not being free* to move around in time, and in this respect our temporal experience does not seem subjective at all. This is an interesting aspect of our temporal phenomenology, which I am not investigating in this book. Note also that this awareness plays no explicit role in Hoerl's (2018) explanation of why we come to believe in an objective present, only the lack of temporal viewpoint does.

4.4.2 Embodied and detached presentness

In Section 3.5.1, I argued that a narrative is an abstract entity that represents a series of events, which can be used to model the content of narrative thoughts—mental states that are about series of events and their temporal and possibly causal relations. Having narrative thoughts with a certain minimal structure, encompassing a narrative present, is the grounds for our way of speaking, through experience-based claims, of things as happening in the present, or actions initiating in the present. Whatever happens in the present is privileged in the sense that it shares the temporal location with us. The connection between the narrative present and perceptual experience is not itself perceptual, at least not in the sense in which the connection between thinking of the roses on the table as red and being visually presented with red roses on the table is perceptual. It is, rather, *inferential*.[41] However, it is not inferential in the same sense in which by looking at the red roses on the table and remembering that my husband had told me that he would have got flowers for the house, I infer that he chose red roses, got them, and put them in the vase on the living room table.

It is not just that the kind of inference I am talking about is implicit or 'fast'. The point is that the inference involved is *not* based on information that is specifically perceptual; it is based on locational awareness, which, as I have pointed out, is a kind of awareness that involves non-perceptual mental states (and possibly is itself a kind of belief-like state). But then there seems to be an explanatory gap problem here. If locational awareness pertains to the limitedness of our experiences themselves, which we encounter in perception and in other phenomenal states, how exactly can we infer that, when we have a narrative thought, there is a moment in it that is privileged in virtue of being the moment in which experience happens, and things are accessible to us via perception and action?

The problem of the bridge between the phenomenal present and the narrative present can be understood also in terms of how we should understand the connection between the series of events that we perceive and the series of events we think of. Now, intuitively there is only one temporal dimension, and thus it is the same series of events that is both perceived and conceptualized. However, strictly speaking this cannot be true, not even in the sense

---

[41] This seems to be suggested also by a proponent of a version of the Maquis strategy: 'The temporal location from which one apparently perceives things is most naturally *thought of* as the temporal location of the experience one has. *What else could it be?*' (Richardson 2014: 497; italics mine). Cf. also Frischhut (2013).

that in thought we entertain a representation of the events we have—through successive perceptions—experienced. It is not just that our narrative thoughts are based on memory, which is often unreliable. But, more seriously, narrative thoughts are based on processes of simplification and 'editing', and when they are about the future, they essentially involve explicit exercises of imagination. However, undoubtedly by having narrative thoughts we aim—when we are not contemplating utterly alternative realities—to *target* the same series of events we had experience of, and we expect to have experience of in the rest of our life.

It is tempting to try and capture the idea that we use narrative thoughts to aim to represent the series of events that we have perceptual experience of in terms of two kinds of narratives: the narrative about *one's own life*, and the narrative about *the world* that each of us experiences in their life. Maybe by elucidating the connection by those two kinds of narratives we can provide a firmer grasp of how thoughts and perception can be both about the same temporal series, as it is natural to think. This way of proceeding leads to the consideration that depending on the broad outline in which the relation between the two kinds of narrative is understood, we end up with two opposite *weltanschauungen*, which indeed seem to characterize part of the history of thought, or, at least, part of the history of modern Western thought. According to the idealist worldview, the narrative about the inner mental life is more fundamental than, and contains the narrative about, the world. According to the realist worldview, the narrative about the world is more fundamental than and contains the narrative about one's own life.

I think the temptation should be resisted, though. Narratives are mere *heuristic tools* to model mental states that are about more than one moment. And in answering the question about the bridge between the phenomenal present and the narrative present, there is no particular role for the idea of a grand narrative about one's life in connection with a grand narrative about one's world.[42] Indeed, it may be that there is no psychological or philosophical significance attached to the idea of a narrative about one's life, or about the world experienced in one's life. Even if the sceptics about the appeal to narrative to elucidate the concept of personality or personal responsibility

[42] Of course, this does not mean that the relation between the experienced time and the time of the world (as we have reason to think it is, after our best scientific theories) is trivial or irrelevant. Even if the account of temporal experience given in this book is correct to the last detail, the picture of time that science (general relativity and quantum gravity in particular) delivers to us is so radically different from the one suggested by our experience that one can (and should) still wonder how the two are related. In Chapter 6, I will say something about this issue.

are right (as I tend to think, incidentally), the implementation of the error-theoretic strategy about experience-based claims concerning presentness that I am exploring here remains untouched.

The relevant distinction in the explanation I propose is that between the *embodied uses* of narrative thoughts, and the *detached uses* of narrative thoughts, which I have already touched upon (Section 4.4.2). An embodied use of a narrative thought is one in which the narrative is focused on an occurring phenomenal present. To capture how the narrative, an abstract object that we use to model the content of the thought, is focused on it, we can specify the abstract object in terms of having, as a part, the concrete mental event in question. That way of specifying the narrative does not make the narrative less abstract. Think of the construction of a set, in which all the members are sets (hence abstract entities) but for one, which is a concrete entity. To be more specific in the example, a set made of the singletons of the capitals of the European states, but for Lisbon, being the only city showing up itself as a member of the set. Such a set is mixed (concrete/abstract) in its composition in the sense that it contains both members that are abstract and members that are concrete, but it is an abstract entity as much as a set of all the singletons of the European capitals.

Analogously, a narrative that is used to model a narrative thought when it is used in an embodied manner will contain a series of abstract representations of moments that come before and after the moment that is represented as present, that is the narrative present. In this embodied case, the narrative present is a specific concrete entity, a mental episode, and it is represented *by identity* in the narrative—that is, it represents itself.[43] Of course, this way of specifying the narrative is just a stratagem to capture how the thought is used. It does not reflect anything deep from an ontological point of view (remember, the whole narrative machinery is just a heuristic aid for the explanatory theory), but it reflects the fact that embodied uses of narrative thoughts essentially exploit indexical ways of referring to the phenomenal present.

This indexical element is what distinguishes the specific connection of the phenomenal present with perception from its phenomenal prominence, which is a feature that is explained in terms of locational awareness, and hence not in specifically perceptual terms. The phenomenal prominence is given by the locational awareness that pertains to any phenomenal mental state, but only

---

[43] Cf. the formalism in Bourne (2005) for capturing his 'ersatz presentism', in which all but the present times are abstract entities. There is clearly an analogy between embodied uses of narrative thoughts and singular thoughts in Evans's (1982) tradition and with Perry's (1986) thoughts without representation.

perceptual state allows it to be *anchored* to a content in an indexical way. A narrative thought can contain an indexical element, and thereby be centred on a specific, concrete, mental episode. The thought is centred in virtue of its perspectival way of representing the series of moments. Notice that 'perspectival' has a *phenomenal* reading (cf. Campbell 1994), as in the case of the structural features of the visual field with respect to space, but also a *conceptual* reading, as in the case of the tensed format of thoughts (and linguistic representations).[44] A narrative thought is (temporally) perspectival in the conceptual sense, but when it has an embodied use, it is centred on a moment through an indexical mechanism based on a perceptual state. Yet, if Hoerl and I are correct, we do not experience this moment perspectively in the phenomenal reading. Narrative thoughts in their embodied uses represent the temporal succession that are about from the point of view of the moment in which our perceptions and our actions happen. In this sense, we can have experiences of events that 'from the present recede more and more into the past' or that 'from the future keep on approaching the present', even if our perceptual content is not in a (temporally) perspectival format.

This means that, if you use narratives to model narrative thoughts in the way I have suggested so far, the concrete moment that shows up in the narrative is the centre of the temporal perspective, and all that comes before is a representation of the past, and all that comes after is a representation of the future. Therefore, even though locational awareness is not specific to perceptual states, there is a difference between temporal awareness in perception and temporal awareness in non-perceptual mental states (e.g. imagination and memory). If we take the primary focus of a narrative to be the one indexically determined by its embodied use, then the time at which the content of memory and imagination is presented as occurring is not the narrative present (where the experiences themselves are), but somewhere 'out of' the primary focus in the narrative. Narrative present has thus a *distinguishing potential*, unlike any of the phenomenological features that we have investigated. The potential is given by the narrative structure (it being a temporal sequence) and its role in it.

Those considerations are crucial, because on their basis we can understand how the embodied uses can lead to detached uses. When we make an embodied use of a narrative thought, on the one hand an indexical, perception-driven mechanism determines its focus (this is captured in the heuristic by 'appointing' the concrete mental event through which this happens as a representation

---

[44] Hoerl (2018: 142) also notices this duplicity of perspectives. See Hartle (2005) for an account on how the construction of a conceptual type of perspectives could be implemented in a physical system.

of itself), and on the other hand the focus is that of a non-perceptual representation of a sequence of events in a tensed format. Given that the representation
is perspectival in a conceptual sense, and it is not a perceptual presentation of
a sensory field, it makes implicit reference to the whole temporal dimension.[45]
Therefore, also in the embodied use of narrative thoughts, the information that
the narrative present is the dividing point between the past and the future is
conceptual and not intrinsically attached to any perceptual content. We can
thus distinguish three roles of the narrative present in the embodied uses of
narrative thoughts; it is: (i) what perception latches onto, as the uses of indexical mechanism to refer to it shows; (ii) what has phenomenal prominence,
as locational awareness shows us to contain any phenomenal aspect we have
access to; and (iii) what has an *intrinsically temporal* kind of privilege, by being
the centre of a temporal perspective.

Only the third element is essential to the detached use of narrative thoughts,
and this fact explains how in detached uses of narrative thoughts the notion
of a narrative present can be applied *recursively*, as one would expect from an
abstract form of representation. Past and future are absolute determinations
in embodied uses of narrative thoughts. The present moment is the focus in
virtue of the role that it plays as index for perception and action. It cannot be
arbitrarily shifted along the temporal sequence of events that we are considering, and it cannot be represented from the point of view of another moment.[46]
As used in an embodied case, the tensed format cannot be recursively applied
to a tensed representation of the temporal series. But in a detached use of a
narrative thought a past moment (in this absolute, embodied sense) of the
narrative can represent a temporal focus—the narrative present of the narrative thought in its detached use. *Relative* to this narrative present, events can
be described as past and future (in a non-absolute, detached sense).[47] And in
detached uses of narrative thoughts we are free to shift our focus along any
direction of the temporal series of events that we are considering and to apply
recursively the tensed format, thereby ending up with a new narrative present.

---

[45] That is why it is in some sense wrong to characterize presentism as a form of tense realism. Tallant
(2014) provides a deeper explanation of this remark. See also Iaquinto and Torrengo (2022a) on the
distinction between factual and ontological presentism.

[46] Why it is so is an interesting question. Roughly, this 'rigidity' should not come as a surprise, given
that there are various causal constraints on the relation between our experiences and our surroundings.

[47] See Perry (2013: 499) on de-indexing: 'We have an expression, like "tomorrow", that has two features: (a) it is associated with a relation between days; and (b) it is indexed to the day of utterance. When
we "de-index" the expression, we preserve (a) but give up (b).' Also, for Ismael, temporal perspectival
(non-perceptual) representations have recursive applications: 'it is not just the events, but also the
perspectives themselves that we represent. Later perspectives have earlier perspectives as constituents.
Earlier ones have later ones as constituents' (Ismael 2017: 28).

In order to capture this crucial element of narrative thoughts in their detached use, we need to model them as abstract representations of sequences of moments. No part of the abstract object is concrete, as in the embodied case. The centre of the representation is determined merely in a relational way: it is the one that represents all the others as past or future in the detached sense. And yet presentness is an intrinsic feature of the representation of the series *as a whole*. Whether in the narrative present we find the moment of perception and action initiation, as in the embodied case, or the phenomenal present in which a certain memory is lived by a protagonist, or merely an event thought of from a third-person point of view, depends on the content of the narrative, and not on any of its structural features; in particular it will not depend on having a transcendental narrator and hence a focus that encodes a temporal privilege.

4.5 Conclusions

When Bill Murray, while playing the elderly Don Juan protagonist of *Broken Flowers* (2005: dir. Jim Jarmusch), gives advice to a teenager whom he thinks might be his son, he ends up with words that sound like a carpe diem: 'The past is gone. I know that. The future. . . isn't here yet, whatever it's going to be. So, all there is, is—is this. The present. That's it.' The clumsy attempt at the fatherly figure fails, but the end-of-the-movie message passes through. The present is not preferable over the past and the future per se, but we had better come to terms with the fact that the present is the only place where we can be— as the grotesque experiences of meeting his former lovers and their new lives after many years have shown. In this chapter I have argued that presentness is a property that does not carry phenomenal weight (while in Section 6.2, I will argue it does not carry metaphysical weight either). When we talk of the present and think of moments as present, we are merely describing from the standpoint in time that we happen to occupy what is close enough for us to perceive and act upon. Even if this is a shallow property for moments to have, the experiences that happen in the present are the only ones that we can enjoy, the only ones for which, literally, life is worth living. For our own existence the present is thus of paramount importance, and indeed is all we have.

5

The passage of time

> But at my back I always hear
> Time's winged chariot hurrying near
>
> Andrew Marvell, *To His Coy*
> *Mistress* (first publ. 1681)

In this chapter I focus on what I take to be the core element of temporal phenomenology: the experience of time passing. From Section 5.1. *Purported experience as of passage* to Section 5.5. *The belief that time passes*, I explore various accounts of the purported phenomenology of time passing (a more detailed roadmap is given at the end of Section 5.1). I will criticize several of them and defend what I call the phenomenal modifier view (Section 5.4.2), according to which there is a sensational element in our experience that suggests that our experiences are in flux, without presenting us with a world in which time passes. In Section 5.6. *Awareness of succession and passage phenomenology* and Section 5.7. *Passage and duration*, I complete my atomistic model of temporal experience, by explaining how our awareness of succession is modified by the feeling of time passing.

5.1 Purported experience as of passage

If you have read the chapters of this book as they are ordered, you may wonder what else is left to say about the experience of time passing besides what I have already covered in talking about experiences of change, succession, and presentness. This worry is understandable. However, it should also be clear why I need to say something more about our awareness that time passes. If our experience-based claims about the passage of time are cogent, namely if there is some element in our phenomenology that suggests that time passes, it seems obvious to think that being aware of the passage of time is in some sense being aware of the present *moving* from one temporal position to the next. But this cannot be correct, if what I have argued so far is on the right track and our experience of presentness is entirely cognitive. I do not see that something is

Temporal Experience. Giuliano Torrengo, Oxford University Press. © Giuliano Torrengo (2024).
DOI: 10.1093/9780191937804.003.0005

present as I see that the apple in front of me is red; rather, I see that something is present as I see that the apple in front of me is of the same colour as my bike. Somehow, I need to think of my own experiences as forming a succession to 'put presentness' in what I see, hear, feel, smell, and taste. Presentness comes with no cogent phenomenology of its own. Therefore, I think that understanding our experience of time passing in terms of an experience of change in what is present is a mistake.

And also, it would be a mistake to think that the experience of time passing, although not a perception of the shift of the present, is still an experience of a change in what we take or understand to be present. According to the atomistic model, we do *not* experience the connection between temporal locations as we experience the spatial relations between the locations in our visual field. The temporal location of our occurring experience is presented to us usually as containing an external world. Although it is presented to us with an overarching phenomenology, as a location within a (mono-dimensional) space of ordered locations, we do not 'see', or 'hear', or 'feel', or otherwise experience their connection, let alone their becoming present one after the other. And yet we almost literally constantly *find ourselves* in a new temporal location, where the external world and its spatial structure is presented to us together with our inner thoughts and sensations.

Brian O'Shaughnessy, while arguing against the conception of experience as constituted by states and in favour of the idea of experience as a process unfolding in time, concludes that '[n]ecessarily experience itself is in flux, being essentially occurrent in nature. Then being as such occurrent we can say, not merely that it *continues* in existence from instant to instant, but that it is at each instant occurrently *renewed*. Indeed, the very form of the experiential inner world, of the "stream of consciousness", is such as to necessitate the occurrence of processes and events at all times' (O'Shaughnessy 2000: 43). Although rarely noticed, there is a tension between the metaphor of the flow and the idea that experience always renews itself. It is somewhat paradoxical to think that at each time there is a new experience, but also that experience continues over time. In my atomistic model, there are feelings of persistence that pertain to what in the external world phenomenally appears to us, but the temporal locations of which we are aware, those of our own experience, are disconnected from one another. Therefore, experience does not continue, although it often presents us with things that do. That experience renews itself means that each experience is literally a new experience, although, through the overarching phenomenology, we are aware that it is not 'alone'. What my account still misses is an explanation of how we get from the overarching phenomenology to the experience that time *has passed* between the old and the new experiential reality in which we find ourselves.

We have to be careful here and be clear on the space of possible explanatory projects. As I have argued elsewhere, we should distinguish between the *ordinary belief* that time passes (see Section 5.5) from the purported *feeling* as of time passing. The former is part of experience only in the broad sense of the term, which includes not only presently occurring perceptions, but also memories, thoughts about the future, and our cognitive life in general. The latter is supposed to be a feature of experience in a stricter sense—one that includes only presently occurring sensory mental episodes. As the cautionary expressions 'purported' and 'supposed to be' indicate, we should not take for granted that talking about such a feeling is a cogent description of our phenomenology. And as I have already sketched in Section 1.5, we should not take the Priorian Belief that time passes in some metaphysically robust sense as so widespread as certain philosophers like to think. However, I find it hard to understand what one's experience as a whole would be if one did not have the Metaphysical Lightweight belief that experience undergoes constant renewal. We can thus give a neutral, commitment-free, characterization of the purported phenomenal character of temporal passage — let us call it E_T— as in (NC) below.

> **(NC)** E_T is that aspect of our experience in virtue of which we have the ordinary belief that time passes.

Even though NC is neutral with respect to the nature, and indeed the existence, of E_T, it rules out certain options, for instance, one in which we have to learn an abstract theory to come to believe in the passage of time. Those exclusions, and with them NC, are plausible as long as it is hard to think of a scenario in which our experience is like we are used to and we would not form the belief in the passage of time. Certain characters in artistic works, such as the Tralfamadorians in *Slaughterhouse N.5*, or the Heptapods in *Story of Your Life* (or the movie based on it, *Arrival*), are presented as not experiencing the passage of time at all, but rather as experiencing all times 'at once'. Others are presented as experiencing the passage of time not as humans do, but in a non-phenomenologically charged way, such as Data in *Star Trek: The Next Generation*, or Isaac in *The Orville*. In both cases what seems difficult to imagine is not the relation between those characters and the events in the external world, but rather *being* one such being. What would it be like, if anything, to be a Tralfamadorian, or Data? If we do not know how to answer that question, then it is plausible to think that E_T is a part of experience either in a strict or in a broad sense.[1]

If E_T is part of experience in a strict sense, there are at least two general options to consider. The first is based on the idea that the phenomenology that triggers our belief in the passage of time is *perceptual*. Our perceptual experience of time is dynamic in a sense in which our perceptual experience of space is not. In seeing the spatial arrangement of the shelves in the library in front of us, we have no impression that there is something to space over and above this spatial arrangement. Our perception of space is exhausted by our perception of the spatial relations among those objects. In observing a frog hopping on the grass towards a pond, however, the temporal aspects of our perceptual experience are not exhausted by the fact that the hops happen one after another. Our perceptual experience of the leaps in succession is also an experience of time passing. Obvious theoretical developments of this idea are *representationalism* in its various forms (Section 5.2) and *naive reductionism* (see Section 5.3.1). Representationalism is the thesis that either our experience tracks the passage of time, if the passage of time is something out there, or, if time does not really pass, our experience is a systematic perceptual illusion that represents to us the world as containing the passage of time. Naive reductionism is the thesis that the experience of passage of time is reducible to the distinctive phenomenology of change and movement. Another option is that E_T is a distinctive phenomenological character which is not perceptual in nature. There is a sense of passage specific to temporal experience, but it is a feature of conscious experience as such, due to factors that are not merely perceptual. The theoretical options to articulate this intuition are various forms of *sophisticated reductionism* (Sections 5.3.2–5.3.3) and of *structuralism* (Section 5.4). I will argue in favour of a primitivist version of structuralism: the phenomenal modifier view (Section 5.4.2). If E_T is part of experience in a broad sense, then the belief that time passes is in some sense prior to the purported phenomenology of passage. This option opens the possibility of *deflationist* approaches to the experience of temporal passage, according to which it is fundamentally

---

[1] In Torrengo (2018: 1047), I wrote '[. . .] NC is not neutral in two respects at least. Firstly, it presupposes that the ordinary belief is about the passage of time as some "purely" dynamic phenomenon, which should not be identified with temporal but "qualitative" phenomena, such as change or movement. Secondly, NC is not neutral in taking the experiential base of the belief as a feature of experience in a strict sense, namely as a feature of our occurrent mental episodes, rather than of experience in some broad sense, namely as a feature of our common sense narrative about reality.' I am here dropping those restrictions.

mistaken to describe our phenomenology as suggesting the passage of time (Section 5.5). Let us then begin by discussing representationalism.

5.2 Representationalism

Many people seem to agree that it would be very implausible to give up the idea that the phenomenology of passage is cogent. It seems obvious to them that the feeling of time passing imposes on us the description that the passage of time itself is presented to us, as experiencing visually the redness of apples or auditorily the la_5 pitch played by a flute imposes on us the corresponding descriptions. Here is a frequently quoted passage by Robin Le Poidevin:

> We are not only aware of the passage of time when we reflect on our memories of what has happened. We just see time passing in front of us, in the movement of a second hand around a clock, or the falling of sand through an hourglass, or indeed any motion or change at all. (Le Poidevin 2007: 76)

Although Le Poidevin ends up defending a different account of such an experience, an obvious continuation of this starting point is to endorse what I have called a content strategy to accommodate experience-based claims about the passage of time (Section 1.3). According to it, experience-based claims about the passage of time, such as 'the afternoon has flown away', are indirect characterizations of what the phenomenology of the experiences that prompt them to present to us as happening in the world. Although in principle a weak relationism version of the strategy could be elaborated, I will discuss only representationalist versions of this idea; partly because they are prominent in the literature, and partly because they are illuminating of the general idea.

5.2.1 Naive representationalism

There is a prima facie convincing argument to the effect that the belief in the passage of time is grounded in perceptual experience. It goes like that. The belief that time passes is strictly connected to the belief that we perceive the present.[2] But the belief that what we perceive is present is clearly perceptual, and so must be the belief that time passes. I have argued that the belief that

---

[2] Cf. Paul (2010). Torrengo and Cassaghi (2022) stress that it is not obvious to spell out what exactly the connection is.

what we perceive is present is *not* perceptual, and thus I reject the argument. However, those who are not convinced by my criticism of presentness as a phenomenal property will probably take seriously the idea that we *see, hear,* and maybe even *taste* the passage of time—as we note the raspberry hint disappearing and the citrus aftertaste surfacing. When we say things like 'two weeks have passed', we are making experience-based claims which are at least in part based on the fact that perception connects us to a world in which time passes.

This is the position that I call *naive representationalism*. One has to be careful not to conflate the view with others in the vicinity, which are forms of deflationism and reductionism respectively. Consider the claim 'two hours have passed since we arrived'. One way to read it is as a claim about a temporal distance. If so, there may be nothing specific to the passage of time in the phenomenal character that is cogently and indirectly described by such an expression. This view is a form of what I call deflationism, and I will discuss it in Section 5.5.[3] Consider the claim 'the clock is ticking', pronounced while looking at the second hand moving in quick jerks. Specious present theorists will explain the experience-based claims by resorting to some form of content strategy. However, it would be the phenomenal character of *movement,* or *change,* here that brings in dynamism into the picture. The position that we get by adding the further assumption that the feeling of time passing is identical to, or reducible to, the phenomenology of change or movement is what I call reductionism (to be discussed later), and again it has to be distinguished from naive representationalism.

Distinguishing naive representationalism from deflationism and reductionism allows us to understand that we should not characterize naive representationalism as a view according to which we are perceptually presented with temporal distances, or changes, but rather as the thesis that we are perceptually presented with the passage of time, *independently* from, although often along with, movement, change, or persistence. If we bear in mind this important difference, naive representationalism can be understood in the context of a functionalist analysis of the notions of temporal locations and distances. Talking about our spatial and temporal concepts, Chalmers (2015: 326–36, 2021) casts some doubts on the idea that we should understand them as primitive, namely as referring to some 'edenic' spatial and temporal properties which are exactly as presented in experience. Rather, as in the case of colours, we should understand spatial and temporal concepts in functional terms, as picking up

---

[3] Besides, most temporal distances of which we are aware require memory, and not just perception, and it seems that we can be aware of temporal distances even independently of perception, as when we imagine an event taking up some time.

whatever entities that play a certain role. Such a role can be either merely theoretical, namely a role played in physical theories, such as quantum gravity, or it can be given both in theoretical and phenomenal terms. In the second case, spatial and temporal properties are whatever entities that play the role of the typical stimuli of spatial and temporal experiences.

This idea has a certain plausibility if applied, as Chalmers does, to concepts, but whether it can be exploited to characterize experiential contents depends (among other things) on whether we are presented phenomenally (and not just able to represent in thought) with temporal distances between external events and their positions in time. If I am right that we are presented with dynamical state properties rather than with temporally extended events (Section 2.6.2), and that the only temporal position we are perceptually aware of is that of our own experience, we have no reason to think that we are. Indeed, we have no reason to think that experience presents us with primitive, edenic temporal distances. We may be presented with edenic movement and change, as it is encoded in dynamical state features, but there are no temporal distances of which we are immediately aware, as there are spatial distances and positions.

However, this is not really a problem for naive representationalism, since—as I have just stressed above—the position is not committed to us being perceptually aware of temporal distances (although it is not incompatible with the claim either). What is crucial for naive representationalism is that the passage of time be captured by the content of our current experiences. The naive representationalist maintains that when we say 'a few seconds have passed' or 'an hour has passed', the phenomenology that is cogently described is that of a perceptual experience that presents us with the passage of time, besides change, movement, and (if it does) temporal distances. And indeed, Chalmers seems to be inclined to think that something like naive representationalism may be true, when he claims: '[. . .] the intuition that Edenic properties are presented in experience is especially attractive in the temporal case, where many have noted that experience presents time as passing: it is natural to hold that there was passage of Edenic time in the garden of Eden, even if there is not in our world' (Chalmers 2015: 335). That there was edenic time 'in the garden of Eden' is just a way to say that E_T is a phenomenal feature of representational content of our ordinary perceptions, namely that we are presented with a world in which time passes.

If we take NC in the context of this view, the conclusion is that we believe that time passes because we perceptually experience the passage of time, either through (a combination of) the sensory modalities, or through a dedicated perceptual system, and regardless of whether there is passage of time, namely whether our perceptions are veridical or illusory. The origin of the belief in the passage of time is explained in the same way we explain why someone believes that there is a red apple on the table in front of them, given that they are awake and attentive, have ordinary conceptual capacities, and are looking at a red apple on the table in front of them. Because they *see* a red apple on the table over there.

The main problem with naive representationalism is that—as many have noticed—it is difficult to make sense of the idea that our experiences *track* something like the passage of time, as they (if they do) track properties like colours. (I discuss an analogous problem for presentness in Section 4.2.1.) Having a certain reflectance gradient is a property of surfaces of middle-sized solid objects which, although not very interesting as such or for the purpose of a physical theory, is causally relevant for our perceptual and cognitive systems. It is causally relevant because when we are in the presence of a surface that has the yellow reflectance gradient, say, our visual system reacts in a certain way, which is different from how it reacts when we are in the presence of a surface with the red reflectance gradient. And the causal relevance at issue has phenomenal import, since being a system that reacts in that way to a surface that has a yellow gradient means undergoing an experience with a phenomenal character that is discriminately distinct from that of an experience of seeing a red surface. But what would it be for our experience to be such that it tracks the passage of time?

Suppose that there is real passage in the world, whatever it is exactly. If so, and we are perceptually presented with it, then we are plausibly presented with it in *every* perceptual experience we have. Maybe the existence of passage is not something that holds of metaphysical necessity (although some believe that it does), but anyway it is not something that, like the yellow reflectance gradient, we are sometimes in perceptual contact with (when there is a ripe lemon in full sight in front of us, say) and sometimes not (when there is no yellow object in plain sight in front of us).[4] Even if time passes, but not out of metaphysical necessity, it would still plausibly be a strong and stable contingency, something our sensory systems would constantly be reacting to. Therefore, it is difficult to see how our experiences could represent it in the same way in which (assuming representationalism for colours) it represents the colours of the objects around us.

---

[4] Prosser (2016: Chap. 2) developed an analogous argument at full length, but his argument relies on the assumption that metaphysical realism with respect to passage, if it holds, holds with metaphysical necessity. See also Braddon-Mitchell (2013). More on this in Section 6.2.

Moreover, there is also an evolutionary worry here—even though, to my knowledge, it is rarely noticed. Why would a cognitive system that tracks something so pervasive as the passage of time be *selected* at all? Would it not be a pointless use of cognitive capacities, a feature that brings in cognitive costs but no clear advantage, to constantly *compute* that there is passage out there, given that we can take for granted that there is? It is not surprising that the capacity to track colours has been selected, since it is clearly useful in a variety of ways and contexts. But an analogous awareness of the passage of time would not be equally useful. Awareness of the passage of time, *as the result of a perceptual capacity*, would be pointlessly costly. This is not to say that coming to believe that time passes simply on the grounds of how our experience happens is not useful for *cognition*. Indeed, I will argue that E_T is an element of the phenomenology of our experience in a strict sense that it is hardwired to trigger the belief that time passes (Section 5.4.2). But we have no analogous reason to believe that, as an experience of perceptual tracking, E_T would be evolutionary advantageous. It is fair to say that the perception of the passage of time may be a *by-product* of adaptive capacities. There are, after all, certain bodily sensations of which we are probably constantly aware at some level, such as our blood flowing or our breathing, even though there is no clear advantage in having them. But plausibly if we had not them, we would also lack other perceptual capacities important for survival. This is true, but in the case of the passage of time, it is unclear what important perceptual capacity could have been 'reused' to track the passage of time.

Suppose instead that metaphysical antirealism with respect to the passage of time is true, for instance because something like the block universe view is correct. We live in a relativistic spacetime, and our life is a world-line (Section 3.5.1), namely a time-like trajectory in it. Our proper time is nothing over and above the temporal distances between the various events that make up our life, and time in general is nothing over and above the temporal aspect (relative to trajectories or to system of coordinates) of spatiotemporal relations between space-time points or events. It is coherent to maintain that in such a scenario our perceptions represent the world as containing real passage. This is indeed what Chalmers suggests above: our experience presents us with a world in which there is passage of edenic time, 'even if there is not in our world'. And as in the case of colours, nothing in the world corresponds to the primitive edenic concept. However, it is still possible that there is something that the *functional* concept of passage picks up. Plausibly, spatio-temporal distances, or something kosher for the metaphysical anti-realist with respect to passage (Chalmers 2021: 168).

But this does not really make naive representationalism better off. Unlike the case of colours, in the case of passage, the functional concept applies to things such as durations and changes that are, for independent reasons, plausible objects of awareness. I have argued that we are not phenomenally aware of temporal distances, but if we were, it is not clear in which sense they would appear to us as the passage of time. Maybe they appear to us in a certain *way* that leads to the belief in the passage of time (they appear as 'flowy', say), but then the account is no longer a form of representationalism, because it is no longer what is presented to us that plays the role of E_T (as we will see, it is a form of structuralism, close to what I defend). And if what the functional concept picked is movement and change, stimuli that are typically connected with dynamic phenomenology, then the proposal begins to look almost indistinguishable from a form of reductionism, which is the family of positions I explore and criticize in Section 5.3.

5.2.2 Rich content, complex content, and sophisticated representationalism

Maybe naive representationalism is too limited in the sense that it does not allow for a content that is rich enough to explain the experience of passage, but nothing prevents us from understanding representationalism in terms of a *rich content*, one that contains more articulated conceptual features than those involved in tracking colours or movement. Think of the analogous case of causality. It is widely agreed that the psychologist Albert Michotte (1946) showed convincingly that there is a specific phenomenology connected to our causal beliefs motivated by perceptual experiences. If we construe those results in terms of a content strategy, we can say that we are presented with causal relations. This does not mean that we can veridically perceive causal links. Maybe there are *no* causal links, or maybe there are but we cannot be responsive to the occurrence of those links, and thus they are not what our experience tracks. And yet there is a phenomenal contrast between the experiences that present to us causation and those that do not, such that it justifies the claim that our experiences represent causation. This rich content version of representationalism is not very convincing for the experience of the passage of time. Even if the experience in question does not track the passage of time, it should still track certain conditions in the stimuli, as the experience of causation tracks certain temporal and spatial thresholds between events. In the case of causation those conditions are, roughly, event c appears to cause event e when c

is before *e* and they are at the right spatial and temporal distance from one another. But what would those conditions be in the case of temporal passage? I do not see any plausible response forthcoming. Any situation is one in which time passes, so it is difficult to see what could *trigger* the phenomenology of passage.

However, another option is open to the representationalist, and does not seem to fall prey to the objections just raised. Although to my knowledge this position is not defended in the literature, one could take inspiration from Susanna Siegel's idea of *complex content* and understand the experience of passage of time as part of the representational content, although *not* a form of experiential tracking (Siegel 2010). Roughly, a complex content is one in which we represent not only something being in a certain way, but also the connection between what we represent and ourselves. Although this idea can be elaborated as a form of structuralism, a position I will turn to later (Section 5.4), there is room for a purely representational reading of it. The idea is that representing phenomenally the connection between the object of perception *o* and ourselves is the consequence of entertaining certain expectations. In the visual case, and considering spatial features only, it is the expectation that by changing perspective on *o*, it will not move, but it will rather change its appearance in certain ways. The position is a form of representationalism because there is a phenomenal difference between an experience that present to us such a connection, as the typical cases of object-seeing, and the cases in which we are not so presented, as in the typical cases of visual sensations (seeing 'the stars' as an effect of standing up too quickly or having an after-image), and such a phenomenal difference is captured by difference in adequacy conditions. If a visual experience presents to me an apple on a table two metres from me, but what I am looking at is a mirror reflecting an apple one metre from me, there is a clear sense in which my experience's adequacy conditions fail, namely it is illusory. But it is difficult to account for its illusoriness without considering as parts of its adequacy conditions the perspectival relation in which I stand to the apple.[5]

Whatever the merits of this position with respect to the spatial case, it is not obvious how to apply it to the temporal case, and whether such merits would still stand. In the spatial case, the content is complex because it has a part concerning how the object appears: the apple is represented as being red and round; and it has a part concerning the relation between how we

---

[5] For instance, imagine that behind the mirror there *is* an apple on a table. If I do not qualify the representational content also in terms of the perspectival relation with the apple, my experience would turn out to be veridical, and not illusory (Siegel 2006: 366).

represent it and us: it will not move if I move around it, and it will change its appearance accordingly. Assuming that in the temporal case the first part of the content is the same, namely the object appearing as having some visual quality or others, what would be the relation between the object and me that is represented? One idea is to consider a limiting case of a temporal perspectival relation. We represent the objects we perceive as being at a zero temporal distance from our own experiences, namely as being present. Setting aside my previous criticism of this idea (Section 4.3.2), if what we are after is an account of the experience of time passing, it is not enough to perceptually represent something as being present, or where our experiences occur, to account for the dynamic element in our phenomenology. But maybe the relation is represented as *unfolding* through time (as in certain relationist accounts the perceptual relation *is* unfolding through time, even if it is not so represented). We are aware of the transition from one experience to another, and indeed we perceptually represent this transition, although as part of complex perceptual content in which it is not the relation between the experiences themselves that is presented to us, but rather the transition from us being in a relation to a certain content to us being in a relation to a different content. This position is somehow specular to that version of sophisticated reductionism according to which the experience of passage is reduced to our awareness of the 'movement' of presentness across the specious present (i.e. distributionism, see Section 5.3.3). According to complex content representationalism, the experience of passage is the experience of *us* moving from one experience to another.

This view is compatible with the eliminativist view about presentness that I have defended before (Sections 4.2.4 and 4.4), and I think that there are aspects of the view that are worth pursuing. However, I think that eventually what is good in the view can be better captured in structuralist terms. The main limitation of the view is that it is built entirely around the perceptual case, and it is not clear how to expand or complement it with an account of the feeling of passage of time with respect to our inward-directed experiences.

Related to the complex content view is what I call *sophisticated representationalism*. Rather than understanding the content as encompassing a relational element between what is perceived and the perceiving subject, one may assume that we are aware of successions, or temporally events, in a *perspectival* mode of presentation. Consider the spatial case in the visual modality. Assuming what we are presented with is spatially extended, we are aware of spatial extension always and only from the point of view that *we* occupy in that very space. It is difficult to understand what it would even mean to be visually aware of a spatial distance or a spatial relation in itself, and not as a distance from where we are, or from something that is 'over there' with respect to where we are. If I am right in believing that we are presented with the temporal location of our own virtually instantaneous experience, then this view does not get off the ground. First, if we are presented with virtually instantaneous events, then there is no room for any perspectival mode of presentation that does not collapse on a tenseless form of awareness. A content of perception that is presented in a tensed way must have temporal parts, so that one can be presented as present and the other as past or future. Of course, what is presented in perception can be represented in thought as present in relation to what we remember, and we expect, but this is immaterial to sophisticated representationalism whose aim is to capture the feeling of time passing in terms of the tensed way our perceptual contents are presented to us.

Second, and more deeply, even if the contents of perception are temporally extended, the view cannot be articulated. To see why, consider that if the temporal location of what we are presented with is the temporal location of our experience (Section 4.4.1) and we are presented with temporally extended contents, then our experience is temporally extended, namely molecularism (Section 2.4.2) is true. Moreover, we cannot represent within the temporal location of our own experience the temporal viewpoint that *we* occupy. If our experience is temporally extended as what we are presented with, and we are presented with *its* temporal location, we cannot occupy a viewpoint *within* the specious present; rather, we are spread out across it.

Only if it is not true that we are presented with the temporal location of our experience (be it punctuate or temporally extended) can we make sense of a tensed mode of presentation for perceptual contents. According to sophisticated representationalism, we are not presented with our own temporal location only. Our temporal location is *contained* in the perceptual content, as the temporal standpoint from which we are presented with (brief) temporally extended events. This view entails a form of atomistic specious present. Although the view is coherent as a view to explain how we experience change and succession, I have argued elsewhere that as an account of the experience of the passage of time it is untenable. Roughly, there is nothing in tense as a perspectival ingredient of the phenomenology for them to play an explanatory role with respect to the origin of the belief in the passage of time. If the perspectival elements were what explains the dynamicity of our temporal representation, then given that we experience shifts in spatial perspectives (e.g. while walking towards a streetlamp) we should also naturally form the belief that space equally flows, which we do not.[6]

5.3 Reductionisms

Someone who accepts that E_T is part of experience in the strict sense may still think that, although there is an ingredient of our phenomenology that gives rise to the belief in the passage of time, such an ingredient is reducible, *in some sense*, to some other aspect of our temporal experience—such as change, succession, duration, persistence, or some combination thereof. One way to make precise the idea of reduction is to understand it in terms of identity. Matt Farr (2020), for instance, identifies E_T with E_M—the distinctive dynamic phenomenology that characterizes seeing something moving, or hearing a tone changing, as opposed to inferring that it has moved or changed. As in the case of the identification between phenomenal presentness and temporal presentness, we can distinguish an *elimination* version and a *conflation* version of the view (Section 4.1.2.1). According to the elimination version, perceiving change is nothing over and above perceiving temporal relations or successions of events. This version of reductionism is indistinguishable from deflationism, the thesis that there is no phenomenal character of occurring experience that is responsible for the belief that time passes. According to the conflation version, perceiving change is interpreted as involving a dynamic element over and above the temporal relations. This is the core of what I call *naive reductionism*, a view that can be articulated also if reduction is not carried out through an identity relation, but some other relation such as realization, being responsible for, or grounding. More generally, according to naive reductionism, E_T is reduced to E_M in the sense that having E_T is explained in terms of having E_M. Non-naive forms of reductionism follow this pattern, but involve temporal elements of our phenomenology other than E_M.

5.3.1 Naive reductionism

Few doubt that we perceive 'impure' or qualitative temporal properties, such as change, movement, succession, and duration (Section 2.2), and that those

---

[6] Cf. Torrengo (2018). In that paper, I also consider a similar view, which I label *attitudinalism*; cf. Kriegel (2015).

experiences are ways of being in connection with temporal reality. Naive reductionism is the idea that those are, at bottom, the *only* ways in which time is revealed in our phenomenal awareness. As I argued before (Section 3.2), if we admit that there is an overarching phenomenology through which we are aware of the connection between the experiences that succeed one another, and that our experience is not as cogently continuous as we tend to think, we can have a partial reduction of (b) to (a). But what about (c)?

(a) Being aware of a continuous motion/change
(b) Being aware of having a continuous experience
(c) Being aware of the passage of time.

The idea behind naive reductionism is that (c) can be reduced to (b), assuming (b) can be reduced to (a). Intuitively, it seems that no matter how what we experience is discontinuous, and our own experience gappy, we are still aware of the flow of time. But perhaps this intuition does not reflect the deep nature of our phenomenology. Laurie Paul (2010) appeals to the phenomenon of apparent motion to explain how our brain can elaborate an experience with a dynamic element, from a series of static presentations. She does not plainly claim that our experience of the passage of time just is our experience of real or apparent motion. Rather, we can explain our phenomenology of passage E_T with the same means with which we can explain the phenomenal character E_M connected to motion and smooth qualitative change, because the feeling of the passage of time is a by-product of change detection. If the correct metaphysic of time is the block universe view, or other form of B-theory (as Paul thinks it is), we have an explanation of the pervasive *perceptual illusion* we all live in. And if the A-theory is true, no better explanation of our experience is available (on the A-theory and B-theory see Section 6.1). According to Paul, if our experience of passage were a consequence of our brain tracking the ever becoming present of events (or some other 'reaction' to a real and robust passage of time), then both when we are presented with an optimal stimulus of apparent motion, and when we are presented with a discrete succession of static scenes, we should have the same dynamic phenomenology. But this is not true; as soon as we go below the threshold above which the discrete succession of flashes is presented to us as a smooth movement of a dot, the dynamic phenomenology is disrupted. This is a sign that our brain, out of a succession of discrete and static inputs, in optimal condition, constructs the representation of a persisting object that moves (and continuously changes) along with an animated character, the *quale* of the passage of time.

I think naive reductionism is wrong, but it is very instructive to see where its problems are. First, there is what Hoerl (2014) calls the *intelligibility problem*. If experiencing the passage of time is a *perceptual* illusion, then we must have an idea of what is an illusion of, namely of what it is like to have the corresponding veridical experience. But how can we have an idea of what it is to perceive the passage of time if time does not pass? The contrast between the illusory and the veridical case involves merely the experience of change and movement, but not that of passage. There are experiences that possess E_M (for example, the direct perception of the movement of the second hand of a clock), and there are experiences that lack E_M (for example, watching the hour hand of a clock). There are experiences with E_M that are correct or veritable (such as watching the second hand moving), and there are illusory ones (such as watching a phi-motion setting). But the illusory cases of E_M are not experiences as of a reality in which there is no passage of time; there are merely misrepresentations of an object moving and changing, when in fact there were only two flashes over there.

One may think that the intelligibility problem has bite for naive representationalism only on the assumption that time does not really pass. But that would be a mistake. The intelligibility problem brings to the fore a deeper problem of naive reductionism, which is one of circularity. Although the aim of the position is to explain the phenomenology of passage in terms of the phenomenology of change and movement, its explanation works only if we *assume* that the phenomenology of passage is present only when the phenomenology of change and movement is. Consider again Paul's criticism of the view that our experience as of the passage of time is a consequence of our capacity to track an objective passage of time. Her point is that if that were the case, then both an optimal motion stimulus (be it apparent or real) and a discontinuous stimulus would give rise to the same dynamic phenomenology. But since that is not the case, the hypothesis is incorrect. But in which sense *is that not the case*? If the aim is to reduce (c) to (b), we should not assume that an experience of a slow sequence of static, disconnected, experience is not one in which we have that kind of phenomenology that explains our belief that time passes. But this is exactly what we need to assume to conclude that the experience of the passage of time *cannot* be due to the tracking of real passage. Remember, the reasoning is that since we do not have such a phenomenology in the 'staccato' case, the experience of the passage of time cannot be due to a tracking of real passage—something that is supposed to take place also in the 'staccato' case.

I think that we have good reasons to discard the hypothesis that we need to appeal to the A-theory to explain our temporal phenomenology in general.

Even bracketing independent evidence against the A-theory, as I pointed out in Section 5.2, it is hard to make sense of our sensorial system to track something like the passage of time or the 'movement' of the present. But the fact that when a sequence of motion or change stimuli is not optimal it does not seem to us that something moves or changes is not one such good reason. And precisely because in such an occasion, introspection seems to suggest that we would still have an experience whose phenomenological character could be cogently described by an experience-based claim such as 'time is passing'. If there is a specific E_T that gives rise to the belief that time passes, then it is difficult to make sense of the idea that E_T is *missing* when we are presented with a reality that does not contain smooth change or movement. Picture yourself in front of a discrete sequence of flashes of light, alternated by brief klaxon outbursts and from time to time the feeling of someone briefly touching your shoulder. Would that be an experience in which 'time stands still', or in which we would think that nothing in what we experience suggests that time is passing? I do not see why one should answer that in the affirmative. Of course, it is always possible to point out either that there is always an inner change in our train of thoughts, or that there is always some underlying continuous bodily sensations, such as the feeling of our blood circulating, of us breathing and standing, and so on. But in the first case, we are appealing to an explanation of the passage phenomenology which is fundamentally different from that suggested by the reductionist approach in general, especially if I am right in thinking that 'inner change' is not us being presented with a change in an inner theatre but rather us being aware of our own inward-directed experiences changing (see Section 3.4.2). And in the second case, if I am right that what is not in the focus of our attention contributes only amorphously to the content of our experiences, we are simply appealing to the overarching phenomenology of our awareness of succession. And I agree that the overarching phenomenology is part of the explanation of our experience of passage, but—as I will argue (Section 5.6)—it cannot be the whole story.

5.3.2 Sophisticated reductionism: succession and duration

An alternative take on reductionism is to look for something different from the *quale* of motion and smooth change E_M to be the reduction basis of E_T. Natalja Deng (2013, 2019), for instance, argues that our experience of the passage of time is nothing over and above our perceptual experience of *succession* and *duration* that we have when we sensorially experience something changing or persisting. In other words, experiencing temporal relations—i.e. that something comes before or after something else, or that it has a certain duration—*is* experiencing the passage of time. This form of reductionism entails that the temporal aspect of our experience is exhausted by our experiences of temporal relations, and thus it collapses on deflationism (see Section 5.5). However, one can think of approaches in the same spirit which do not make the further identification and thus resist collapse.

One (relatively) early example in this direction is (or can be articulated starting from) the so-called *ecological approach* to perception championed by the psychologist James J. Gibson over fifty years ago. According to the ecological approach, in order to explain vision (the only case Gibson is taking into account in detail), we need to look not at the retinal image of a subject whose head and body movements are impeded (as was customary in psychological practice of the time), but rather at the *ambient optic array*, the rich incoming stimulus that we obtain from moving around and exploring the environment in which we live. Crucially, the difference between the two is that the former contributes static and impoverished information to the visual system, while the latter contributes a 'flow of change', a continuous stimulation from which the visual system extracts invariants (colours, shapes, and so on), which is what we are presented with in our phenomenology, and what we are interested in for our survival. Gibson is not interested in the experience of passage per se, but seems to suggest a conflation approach, in which the experience of flow is reduced to the constant variation in the 'stimulus flux'. For instance, in the introduction to his 1966 masterpiece, he states:

> In this book, emphasis will be placed on events, cycles, and changes at the terrestrial level of the physical world. The changes we shall study are those that occur in the environment. I shall talk about changes, events, and sequences of events *but not about time as such*. The flow of abstract empty time, however useful this concept may be to the physicist, has no reality for an animal. We perceive *not time but processes, changes, sequences*, or so I shall assume. The human awareness of clock-time, socialized time, is another matter. (Gibson 1966: 12; emphasis mine)

The claim that we do not perceive time as such, but rather events and processes happening in time, is compatible with many views on temporal experience apart from naive representationalism. But the reference to 'awareness of clock-time' right after suggests that there is no further phenomenal awareness of the passage of time than the awareness of the change in the content of our experience as we move around and things in our sight move around us. Although in the ecological approach this idea becomes somewhat central, since the approach individuates the purpose of vision itself in extracting information about the invariant in the environment from this ever-changing flux, the origin of it can be traced back at least to the classical empiricists; Hume, for instance, writes: 'Five notes play'd on a flute give us the impression and idea of time; tho' time be not a sixth impression, which presents itself to the hearing or any other of the senses' (1739: Book I. Part II. Section III).

What makes the position based on Gibson's stance 'sophisticated' in my terminology is that it is not based on the idea that the experience of passage can be explained in terms of our tracking movement and change, and indeed not even pure succession of events. Rather, it is explained in terms of the phenomenology that comes with having a stimulus in flux, out of which we extract information about a world that is comparably 'stable', even when it contains things that move and change. I have not seen this idea elaborated much in the literature, and thus I will not discuss it further. However, it is worth noticing that there may be a sort of ambiguity lurking beneath the concept of a *stimulus* in flux. The problem is that this view requires a third option between tracking change and being aware of the succession of experiences themselves. To see why, consider that if the change in content to which the experience of time passing is reduced to is the tracking of change and movement, then the view collapses on naive reductionism; and if it is change in experience, then the view is a form of structuralism after all. But without a more articulated theory, it is not obvious that such a third option exists at all. Fascinating as it may be, I think this proposal is better understood in terms of a structural explanation of the experience of passage, as I will clarify in Section 5.4.1.

5.3.3 Sophisticated reductionism: distributionism

In this section I discuss *distributionism*, which is a form of reductionism to sui generis, non-qualitative change. Since in my jargon, reductionism is sophisticated when it is not simply a reduction to the experience of detecting *ordinary*, qualitative change and movement, distributionism counts as a form of sophisticated reductionism. Distributionism's starting point is the distinction (see Section 4.1.2.1) between the phenomenal present (present$_P$, that is, what is phenomenally presented to us) and the represented present (present$_R$, that is, what is felt as temporally privileged), and two theses about *perceptual* experience: Privilege and Distribution.

> **(Privilege)** My perceptual experience presents$_P$ me with one moment that is felt as privileged (the present$_R$)
>
> **(Distribution)** My perceptual experience presents$_P$ me with a change in what is felt as privileged (the present$_R$).

If we are presented with a moment as privileged (the present$_R$) within a temporally extended succession of moments (the present$_P$), then we can also be presented with a *change* in what is present$_R$ in a given present$_P$. Such a change is substantially different from ordinary, qualitative change, such as the change in colour of an LED light or the change in position of an orange rolling on a table; it is a change in tensed status of the temporal positions that are presented to us (in succession) within the present$_P$. If it is true that we are aware of such a 'pure' change above ordinary qualitative change, then it is not implausible to think that the experience of the passage of time is (explained in terms of) the experience of being presented$_P$ with the present$_R$ as changing. I have criticized in detail various forms of distributionism elsewhere (Torrengo and Cassaghi 2022); here I will point to the main limitation of the approach in general. Assume a specious present approach to motion detection (namely, one in which the present$_P$ is temporally extended) and consider a perceptual experience e_2 in which we are presented with a ball b having been at location l_1, being now at location l_2, and being about to reach location l_3:

$$e_2 \, [\text{WAS}\,(b \text{ is at } l_1) \;\&\; \text{NOW}\,(b \text{ is at } l_2) \;\&\; \text{WILL}\,(b \text{ is at } l_3)]$$

As we have seen by discussing and criticizing sophisticated representationalism (Section 5.2.2), the mere fact that different temporal parts of the specious present are presented in a perspectival, tensed format does not suffice to bring about a 'time is passing' element to the presentation of the movement of the ball b. It is not thus the change in the position of the ball as presented from the point of view of a 'now' that is to be identified with E_T, but rather the change in where the 'now' is in the specious present. However, the 'now' in e_2 does not change or move in any sense. And this is so because no temporal part of the specious present (no moment in the succession of moments with which we are presented) is presented *more than once over*, as persisting objects, such as the ball, are. The change of tense status (e.g. from future to present, or from present to past, or from past to more past) can be 'presented' only in a *succession* of specious presents. But then the experience of passage is not reduced to being phenomenally aware of a sui generis change in what is present$_R$ in the present$_P$, because nothing like that can be presented in the width of the specious present. And the problem is not one of extension of the phenomenal present. Even if the phenomenal present were extended, several seconds would still be an experience in which a succession of events is presented *from the perspective of a present focus*. We may be aware of persisting entities as located at more than one temporal location within the specious present, and having different spatial location or qualities at each of them, as thus as moving or changing, but if a *temporal location* is presented as present, or just past, say, it is only by *changing the content of experience*, namely 'moving' to another experience, that we can be aware of the change of its tense status. Everything seems to point towards an explanation in which we have to take into account our overarching awareness of succession in order to account for experiencing time passing. I will now move to a family of positions in which this is, in various ways, explicitly thematized.

5.4 Structuralisms

In discussing sophisticated representationalism and distributionism, I have already touched upon the idea that certain perspectival features of our awareness are responsible for the experience as of time passing. As long as perspectival features count as structural features of our temporal phenomenology, those accounts are, partially at least, forms of what I call structuralism. However, if I am right, there are no temporal perspectival elements at the level of the phenomenology of experience in the strict sense. In this section I explore approaches that appeal to structural features other than perspectival ones.

5.4.1 Structural reductionism: pure update and perspectival shift views

One idea that qualifies as structuralism is to appeal to our awareness of succession and to identify the sense of flow with the awareness that *our own experiences constantly change*. It is not only a matter of being aware that our experiences are not 'alone' in the temporal dimension, but also that they are not stable, as it were, that one experience is always on the verge of giving way to, or being substituted by, the next. However, notice that the experience of our own experiences changing, in and of itself, is not trivially identical to a purported phenomenology of passage. We could be aware of the change in our experience upon reflection, for instance because we take it to be a consequence of experiencing change, without having a phenomenology of passage. For theories of this sort to be reductive theories of the phenomenology of passage (and not forms of deflationism), it is necessary to have an explanatory machinery bridging our awareness of a change in our experience with a reductive base for the experience of passage. One version of this is what I call the *pure update view*.

Consider our perceptual experiences. As we have seen criticizing distributionism, we cannot be phenomenally presented with the change of tensed status of a moment within the specious present. It is in the passage from one specious present to the next that such change can take place. Now, change can be said to happen in at least two ways. There is change when something that exists at various successive times has different properties at different times, and there is change when a certain role that is played by something at different times is played by different things at different times. Change in the first sense happens when an apple changes from green to red. Change in the second sense happens when the president of an enterprise changes: it was Mrs Wong, it is now Mrs Ho. The difference between distributionism and pure update view can be understood as a difference in which a kind of sui generis change constitutes the reductive basis. According to distributionism, the reductive basis is change in tensed status and thus change in the second sense. According to the pure update view, it is change in the first sense: there is something that persists through different experiences and of whose change we are aware in being aware of the succession of experiences. Thomas Sattig has elaborated a view of this kind (Sattig 2019a, 2019b). His aim is to reduce the experience of passage of time to the phenomenology of renovation of the content of our own experience. He focuses on the perceptual case and individuates the 'thing' that changes in the content of the experience of passage with what he calls the simultaneity field of perception, the *simfield* for short. In a succession of experiences, the *simfield* is presented as containing different things. For instance, first a leaf on the branch of a tree, then floating right beneath it, and then closer and closer to the ground. Here I consider the pure update view in the context of a B-theoretical metaphysics of time.[7]

According to the pure update view, the change in the *simfield* (or in whatever has the role of the object of change in the experience of the passage of time) is not part of a perceptual content. We are not presented with the passage of

---

[7] I have discussed and criticized the pure update view in the context of an A-theory of time in Torrengo and Cassaghi (2021).

time as we are presented with the movement of Petunia the guinea pig towards the fresh bell pepper; rather, we are aware of the update of what is in the *sim-field* by having an overarching phenomenology. The question here is how to understand the 'by' in the previous sentence. In which sense can an overarching phenomenology make us aware of a change in the *simfield*? As I understand it, the pure update view here reaches its fundamental explanatory brute fact. Roughly, according to the pure update view there is nothing more to the experience of the passage of time than the fact that the phenomenal present is updated as time goes by.

The problem with the pure update view as a reductionist account is apparent if we think again of the parallel with experiencing qualitative change. A succession of experiences can make available information about changes in the environment around us thanks to our ability to recollect in memory past instantaneous experiences and notice that what is now in a certain position (or has a certain quality) was not in such a position (or had not such a quality) then. However, in and of itself, the fact that our experiences succeed one another cannot ground any specific phenomenology of motion or change. The specific phenomenology of motion or change requires experiences of motion or change that are not the result of a comparison between temporally distinct experiences. It requires a specious present or a dynamic snapshot.

Similar remarks can be applied with respect to the experience of time passing. What the pure update view puts us in a position to explain is the inference to the flow-like character of experience based on the comparison between past and present experiences. A succession of experiences can make available information about the passage of time in the environment around us thanks to our ability to recollect in memory past experiences and notice that what is present now was not present then. Without postulating some further element of the phenomenology, such cognitive awareness is the *only* awareness the pure update view can explain, and yet the view aims to yield a reductive account of a phenomenal awareness. In other words, the pure update view is only compatible with either deflationism or a view in which the phenomenology of passage is otherwise accounted for, but it is a non-starter as a form of reductionism *of the experience of passage*.

Another reductionist form of structuralism is what I call the *perspectival shift* view. B-theorists, as antirealists with respect to an objective flow, can endorse a position according to which the experience of the flow is explained by the fact that in a succession of experiences we are presented at different times with different temporal perspectives. And, as a matter of a non-further-explainable fact, this suffices to give us a phenomenology of passage. It is not merely the pure update of our experience, but a richer phenomenology that comes from being aware of having had experiences and going to have new ones along the way. A forerunner of the perspectival shift view can be identified in Mellor's (1998) pivotal work on temporal experience in a B-theoretic world. In Mellor, we experience change by virtue of having, remembering, and expecting different states at different times. In his theory, E_T is an aspect of experience in the broad sense. However, Mellor is also clear that we come to believe that time passes on the basis of some non-inferential aspects of our psychology. The basis of the belief is thus not a phenomenological feature, but it is not some mere theorizing either. However, even if Mellor points at a structural aspect of experience to account for our experience of passage, he also does not clearly distinguish between experience and judgement. Therefore, it is difficult to evaluate his explanation in the present context.

Jennan Ismael is more sensitive with respect to the need for accounting for a specific phenomenology of passage, rather than merely for the belief or judgement that time passes. She identifies the experience of the passage of time with what she calls a 'Temporally Evolving Point of View (TEvPoV)—that is, not just the view from a particular moment in a life, but the progression of views over a life as a whole [. . .]', which we obtain 'by stringing together temporally embedded points of view in an order defined by their frame-defining temporal parameter' (Ismael 2017: 28). Ismael explicitly takes the issue of whether the content of our perception is punctual or extended as immaterial to 'the phenomenology of the flow' (2017: 29), thereby suggesting that the phenomenology in question depends on there being TEvPoV, and by perception having a perspectival nature, rather than by some feature of the content (such as representing the flow of time). However, it is unclear whether the experiential features her account relies on are overarching phenomenal features of experience in the strict sense (and if so, whether they are cogent or interpretational), or are higher-order feelings triggered by the pure update that our experience constantly undergoes.[8]

Although I am sympathetic towards the spirit of such accounts, I think the perspectival shift view faces an explanatory gap between the reductive basis, namely the shift in temporal perspectives, and the explanatory target, namely the phenomenology of passage. The problem is that the obvious ways to fill in the gap are precluded by the approach. The reductive basis cannot be a representation of the shift of perspectives which the experience of passage consists

---

[8] See Hoerl (forthcoming) for some criticism of Ismael's theory. Something similar holds also for Craig Callender's (2017) interesting and inspirational account of the experience of temporal passage. Hartle (2005) can also be seen as a project in this spirit; but see Hoerl (2023) for a criticism.

of. Such a theory would be a higher-order form of representationalism and suffer from the same problems of representationalism plus having the burden of justifying meta-representations as essential to an experience which is plausibly a quite basic one. Neither can the view be that the only thing we have to account for in the experience of passage is how the belief in the passage of time is generated. For the view to be a form of structuralism, the ground of the belief must be genuinely phenomenal, and accounted for in terms of a reductive basis that is not necessarily restricted to the phenomenal character of an occurring experience. But this consideration leads us to an even deeper problem for the perspectival shift view, which is answering the question what exactly the structural reductive base of the experience of the passage of time could be. There are several problems in trying to articulate a coherent answer to this question. First, if I am right that perceptual experience is not temporally view-pointed, talking about a perspectival shift is ambiguous. It could be a shift in the focus of a concurrent narrative thought (Section 3.5.2), but then the account is entirely cognitive and something more is required to fill in the details of how we get the phenomenology of time passing from a shift in the content of thoughts. Or it could be a structural element involving an overarching phenomenology. I am sympathetic towards this option, but as such this is merely the beginning of an account, and it is not clear to me how to continue it in the context of a reductionist view. In Section 5.4.2 and in Sections 5.6 and 5.7, I will develop a similar idea in the context of a non-reductionist version of structuralism.

Second, even if we grant that there is a temporal perspectival element in experience in the strict sense, the explanatory gap does not go away without a story about how we become aware of the shift of the perspectival element. Hohwy (2013) has given a Bayesian story to account for the shift. According to the account in Hohwy et al. (2016), our phenomenology of passage is an effect of the prediction that our perceptual system makes about the world, namely that it will not stay the same. This is an interesting hypothesis about the cognitive origin of our phenomenology of passage.[9] However, note that this account does not entail that the shift of perspective is presented to us (or if it is, then it is a higher-order representationalist account). The shift is given merely by the fact that our perceptual system generates alternative hypotheses (incompatible with the present state of the system) about the incoming input. And if the shift cannot be presented to us, it must be something of which we are

---

[9] An alternative account is to appeal to protention. Cf. 'protention plays an important role in the self-movement of the flow' (Gallagher and Zahavi 2008: 82).

aware through a non-presentational phenomenology. But then we are where we started. Either we bite the bullet, and we insist that the mere shift is enough for being aware of our temporal viewpoint shifting, and thus of the passage of time, or we appeal to some overarching phenomenology. In the first case, we are stuck with a version of the pure update view; in the second case we have merely begun to explain the experience of the passage of time.

5.4.2 Structural primitivism: phenomenal modifier

Although structural reductionism cannot deliver what it promises, the idea that the experience of time passing has to do with a structural element of experience is on the right track. My bet is that the problem with structural reductionism is not with the 'structural' side but rather with the 'reductionism' side. I will explore the idea according to which the phenomenology of the passage of time is structural *and* primitive, and thus not reducible. The fact that it is primitive does not mean that we cannot say anything about it, but only that we cannot provide a definition or a reductive account. A theory of the experience of the passage of time E_T in terms of a primitive structural element of our experience must settle several issues about E_T, and thereby give a characterization of E_T. I call the account that I am giving here, based on some of my previous work, the *phenomenal modifier* view. I will elaborate it here in some details, and then, after having discussed the main deflationist approaches (Section 5.5), I will put it to work, as it were, in the context of the account of change, succession of experience, and presentness that I have developed in the previous chapters (Sections 5.6 and 5.7).

The first thing to settle about E_T is whether it pertains to the outer flow or to the inner flow. Remember how I defined *worldly* any phenomenal character that corresponds to the 'what it is like' to be presented with an external world as being in a certain way, typically as containing objects and events located in space. According to the phenomenal modifier view, E_T is *not* worldly: it is neither a representation of a pure flow of time, nor of movement, change, or the like. If we take representationalism to entail that all our *perceptual* experience is worldly, then the phenomenal modifier view is in tension with it and can be seen as a form of sensationalism (Section 1.3).

Second, in which sense does this non-worldly feature of experience modify the content of our experience, including that of our perceptions? Suppose you are looking at a red sphere in an ordinary situation. You visually perceive the world as containing a red sphere in front of you—that is, you are having an experience with worldly phenomenal ingredients such as E_{RED} and E_{SPHERE}. If representationalism is true, all your experiences are characterized by phenomenal ingredients that are worldly. If sensationalism is true, there may be features of your perception that do not appear as part of what you are presented with. Consider the case of blurred vision, discussed by Paul Boghossian and J. David Velleman: '[B]y unfocusing your eyes, you can see objects blurrily without being able to see them as being blurry. [The] description [of such an experience] requires references to areas . . . that . . . become blurry without anything's being represented to you as blurry' (Boghossian and Velleman 1989: 94). Analogously, if the illumination under which we observe the sphere is particularly strong, we may experience the perception as vivid without mistaking the brightness of the colours around us as characteristic of the surfaces that we are observing. A non-worldly phenomenal character, such as being blurred or vivid, is an intrinsic property of the vehicle through which experiences represent the world to us as being in a certain manner. The claim that the sensationalist makes is that we can be aware of such non-worldly phenomenal characters, just as we are aware of what we see, smell, and hear. When we attend to such aspects of our perceptions, we are aware of aspects of what it is like to perceive something that does not represent the world as being in one way or another. There is a sense in which we can be aware of our vision being blurred even if we do not pay attention to the fact—as when our vision continues to be blurred for a long time—but we can also direct our attention towards the blurriness of our experience—as when near-sighted persons realize that they are not wearing glasses.

At least some non-representational features of experience are phenomenal modifiers in the sense that they make a difference to the way the concurrent mental episodes feel to us. Although phenomenal modifiers do not represent the world as being one way or another, they typically have an influence on our beliefs based on the content of the concurrent experiences. Having a blurred visual experience rather than a non-blurred one leads us to a certain kind of indeterminacy in the judgements based on the content of our representations. For the purpose of introducing my main thesis about E_T, I assume that the experiences of blurriness and vividness are a phenomenal modification of a content, in the sense that they modify the way the content is felt, and thereby ground beliefs that come along with the usual perceptual judgements.

How close the connection is between the modified phenomenology of the representational elements and what the mental episodes represent the world as being like is a matter of dispute. In the case of blurred vision, a representationalist may claim that the phenomenal character in question is connected to the fact that we represent the boundaries of objects as indeterminate,[10] whereas the sensationalist can insist that there is a difference between representing the boundaries of objects as indeterminate (as when we see a fuzzy object) and having a blurred perception that feels as if the object is indeterminate even though it does not represent it as indeterminate. Typically, a representationalist account of blurriness and analogous features will interpret the seemingly sensationalist elements to ways the content represents (Martin 2002; Tye 2003b), whereas the sensationalist will argue that such features must be primitive—that is, non-reducible to, or supervenient on, elements of the content. I do not mean to enter this debate here, but I merely make the following conditional claim: if blurriness is a primitive phenomenal modifier, and so is an ingredient of the 'what it is like' to have an experience e, then it makes a difference for the judgements that we make on the grounds of having e, even though it is not an experience of the world as possessing certain features or others.[11] Thus, by having a blurred perception that feels as if the object is indeterminate even though it does not represent it as indeterminate, we can judge the boundaries of the object as appearing indeterminate, or even as being indeterminate, if we do not realize that our vision is blurred. What I call the phenomenal modifier view is the claim that E_T is a primitive phenomenal modifier in this very sense.

Third, what is it that the phenomenal character E_T modifies and how does E_T modify it? Imagine again you are looking at a red sphere in front of you. You will have a perception with phenomenal ingredients E_{RED} and E_{SPHERE}. If the sphere is moving at a visible pace, an experience with E_M is triggered, and you represent the sphere as moving. If not, you do not experience motion—that is, your experience lacks E_M. But in both cases, you perceive the sphere while you also feel that time is passing. For all that it is difficult to imagine an experience in which it does not seem to us that time passes, the experience of the red sphere would be different if it were not modified by the sensation that this is not an isolated experience, but one that was succeeded by a previous one (in which the apple was there) and will be followed by another one (in which we will find the apple). It is a plausible working hypothesis that any experience is an experience of passage in this sense, even when in its content, features such

---

[10] For instance, in a paper that defends representationalism against the objection from the case of blurred vision, Michael Tye claims that '[i]n the cases of seeing blurrily, one's visual experience [. . .] makes no comment on where exactly the boundaries [of the object in front of us] lie' (Tye 2003b: 7–32).

[11] The claim that mechanisms underpinning perceptual judgements can be affected by non-representational concurring feelings is not unheard of. For instance, Sizer (2000) argues that we have empirical evidence for the fact that moods, while not representational, can influence representational contents.

as movement, changes, and the like are *not* represented, and even when the attitude is not that of perception, but rather that of a recollection, an act of imagination, or of conscious but non-perceptual thinking. Therefore, what E_T modifies is the overarching awareness of succession itself, namely the awareness that by being presented with the temporal location of our own experience we are not presented with an isolated temporal location. It modifies it because it brings in the awareness that, as I put it elsewhere, my own experience is about to get older and abandon me (Torrengo 2017: 187). Both in the case in which the mental episode in question is a perception, and in the case in which it is a non-perceptual experience, E_T makes us aware that what we are experiencing is about to be renewed, that we will very soon be experiencing a new temporal location. The modification, thus, involves primarily the presentation of our occurring temporal location and the awareness that it is part of a succession. It is not the world around us that we are aware of as 'flowy', but the succession of our own experiences.

Fourth, something must be said about the relation between E_T as a modifier and its role in triggering the belief that time passes. Even a perceptual experience of a sequence of discrete events (like there is a red dot on the left of the screen, and then there is a green dot on the right of the screen) can make us phenomenally aware that time passes, and even when we are lost in our recollections or abstract thinking, so much that we 'lose track' of time, we are still in some sense aware that time passes (more on this in Section 5.7). I have already noticed that a phenomenal modification can at least in certain circumstances modify our perceptual judgements: for instance, even if we are not presented with an ectoplasm, we may judge that a certain human silhouette is indeterminate, when having a blurry visual experience of a person in front of us. If E_T is not a worldly representational feature of our experience, then the illusion that, according to the B-theorist, besets us should *not* be understood as a perceptual illusion but rather as a cognitive error. It is not a perceptual illusion because the content whose phenomenal character E_T modifies may be (and often is) veridical. However, by influencing the way an experience *e* feels, a phenomenal modifier may also influence the beliefs based on the content of *e*. My hypothesis is that it is hardwired in the mechanism that realizes the modification that when we pay attention to the modification, we form the belief that our experiences are in flux. We are aware of the temporal position that we happen to occupy, of its not being isolated, and of its being transient. And since the temporal position of the things that appear to us in an external world is *our* temporal position, our awareness of an external flow is not fundamentally distinct from our awareness of an external flow. Each experience is modified by E_T, and this leads us to believe that both our experiences and the things we experience are in flux. The time 'in there' is one and the same with the time 'out there'.

5.4.2.1 Some objections and replies

In this section I discuss some objections to the thesis that the feeling of time passing can be accounted for in terms of a phenomenal modification of the awareness of succession. The first objection is that since the phenomenal modification generates the belief that time passes, it should be understood as part of the content, rather than as a non-worldly sensational element.[12] My first reaction to this objection is that it seems to be based on an uncollaborative interpretation of the phenomenal modification. Representationalists typically counter-argue to the example of blurred vision re-interpreting the case as if we were determinately presented with an indeterminate content (rather than being presented indeterminately with a determinate content). If so, blurred vision is not a counterexample to the thesis that every aspect of perceptual phenomenology is representational, because it is an experience that represents an object with indeterminate boundaries, and thus the blurred 'modification' is part of the content. One reason to believe in such an interpretation is that saying that the object in sight has indeterminate boundaries is a prima facie cogent description of the phenomenology.[13]

But regardless of whether this interpretation is correct for the case of blurred vision, it should be resisted for the case of experiencing the passage of time. The main reason is that the phenomenology in question is structurally connected to the metaphysically lightweight belief, and not the Priorian belief. The phenomenal modifier account entails that E_T invites a belief about our own experiences, namely that they update constantly, and not about the nature of reality around us. In order to account for the belief in an objective passage of time, we need to take into account also that the only temporal position that we are aware of is ours (see end of Section 5.4.2). So, if the main reason to think that the phenomenal modification is part of the content is that it elicits a belief about a way the world is presented to us, the reason is simply not there.

Moreover, this objection relies on a notion of content that is not the one that I have explicitly adopted, according to which a phenomenal character

---

[12] Graham Peebles (2017) has articulated a representationalist theory of perceptual content that substantially identifies it with perceptual belief, and used it to argue for experience in favour of the A-theory.

[13] Dretske (2003) gives a defence of representationalism from the blurriness objection that is more sophisticated than this consideration, but in the same spirit.

is part of the content when it has a tracking role with respect to an external feature of the world. Now, there are many legitimate ways of using the label 'content'. My claim is not about the use of the label, but rather about the distinction between mental events that track, in optimal cases, certain external conditions, and mental events that do not. I think that this distinction is crucial for temporal experience. If you want to use 'content' in a way such that the modification I am talking about is conceptualized as being a non-tracking part of content, rather than a non-representational element of the phenomenology, I will not put up a fight. However, the substance of my point stands: the 'flowy' ingredient of our ordinary experience does not track anything out there, and thus in my terminology is a sensation and is not part of the content.

The second, related objection is based on the idea that even according to my conception of content, the presence of a phenomenal contrast is a sufficient condition for being part of the content. To articulate such a phenomenal contrast in the case of the passage of time we just need a bit more abstraction than in trivial cases such as seeing red or seeing yellow. A content strategy is thus more coherent with my premises than a phenomenal modifier view. The contrast is between an experience that does not present us with a temporally extended event, and one that does. The idea is that we are phenomenally aware of the passage of time only when we are presented with something that unfolds through time. But if we consider an experience that does not present us with anything unfolding, then we have a contrast, because that would be an experience in which time does not seem to pass.

The problem with this objection is that it resorts to an unjustified abstraction. Maybe we can 'isolate in thought' an experience with a virtually instantaneous content and not considering certain aspects of its phenomenology. But in what sense can we have an experience of that sort without also having a phenomenology of succession that tells us that our experience is constantly refreshed? Even if nothing 'moves' in what is presented in a virtually instantaneous experience of that kind, no experience can be isolated in such a way that we are not conscious of its location in a flux of experiences, and still be an experience of the kind that we have ordinarily. I think that the initial plausibility of the objection comes from thinking of experience in terms of mental states rather than mental events. Maybe there is a mental state such that it is phenomenally isolated from its past and its future. But no instantaneous mental event, even if its content is both instantaneous and static, can lack overarching phenomenological aspects. If there is a phenomenal contrast here, it is not of the right kind.[14]

The third objection comes from the opposite direction. If the metaphysically lightweight belief is hardwired, why is it hardwired to a phenomenology? It would be more parsimonious to assume that we are hardwired to form the belief in the passage of time, regardless of our phenomenology. This objection has the flavour of deflationism, the approach I will discuss in Section 5.5. As such, it leaves it open what to think of the purported phenomenology as of passage. As long as we take attentive reports made in good conditions as prima facie evidence of there being a certain phenomenology (cf. Bayne 2010: 127), the conclusion of the objection has to be integrated with an explanation of at least our tendency to describe our ordinary phenomenology as involving a dynamic element. Maybe we tend to describe our experience as involving a phenomenology of passage because of the hardwired belief, or maybe the belief has an effect on our phenomenology; it somehow percolates into it so that our reports of feeling the passage of time are after all cogent. It doesn't really matter because this objection leaves a crucial aspect unanswered. If we are hardwired to form the belief, but not as a consequence of a certain phenomenological element, then we should expect that there are certain conditions that *trigger* the belief. But what could those conditions be? This objection is based on a hypothesis that is as problematic as the hypothesis that E_T tracks the passage of time, or it is somehow responsive to a certain feature of the external world.[15]

Finally, the fourth objection is based on the observation that spatial extensions, too, is a feature that we are always presented with, and yet there do not seem to be problems in saying that we track spatial extension, along with the objects that are located in space and their properties. The objection is aggravated by the fact that there seem to be many other features that share the destiny of spatial extension. For instance, 'colourness' (we are aware that our visual experience always comes with colour information), and temperature (we are aware that we always feel our body as having a certain temperature). I don't want to deny that spatial extension is something that enters our

---

[14] In Torrengo (2017: 186–7), I explore the possibility that we can imagine situations in which we would experience no passage of time (and thus understand what would be an experience that is not modified by the feeling of time passing), even if for us it is impossible to experience such situations or to imagine what it would be like to be in them.

[15] What if the hardwired mechanism of belief forming does not require any triggering conditions? That is a very different scenario. I will consider it in the context of an alternative interpretation of the amic model in Section 6.3.1.

phenomenology. However, for spatial extension, and all 'constant' features such as colourness and temperature, I see no reason to think that they must be understood as part of the content, and thus that we should say that our experience tracks them, as it tracks colours, rough but specific range of temperatures, shapes, and movements. Being aware of spatial extension is rather a structural feature of our phenomenology, it is the awareness of a perceptual field (or perhaps of a concomitance of perceptual fields), and not yet another entity that appears to us in sight or any of the other modalities. And the same holds for colourness, temperature, and any other candidate of a feature that is constantly presented to us in phenomenal awareness. I am not saying that they all have to be interpreted as phenomenal modification, but they are all structural features, and thus not obviously in the content as worldly features are. Before further elaborating my view in the broader context of temporal experience (Sections 5.6 and 5.7), I will discuss the deflationist approaches, which fail, but from whose failures I think we can learn some important lessons.

5.5 The belief that time passes

All accounts of the purported phenomenology of passage that we have seen so far take E_T to be an ingredient of experience in the strict sense. I will now consider deflationist approaches, according to which what triggers the belief that time passes is not an element of experience in the strict sense, but only the outcome of experience in the wider sense, something to which we arrive through reflection and reasoning of some sort. As I have already hinted at (Section 1.5), there is a potential ambiguity in the expression 'the belief in the passage of time'. It is important to distinguish at least two different beliefs that may go under that label, and which differ in their degree of 'metaphysical involvement', so to speak. The first is the *Priorian* belief that there is a constant and inexorable change in what is present *in reality*. Asking whether we have such a belief is asking whether human beings are naive A-theorists of some sort. I think the interest in this question is mainly empirical, and as far as I can see from the Ex-phi evidence available so far, the answer seems to be: y. . .es, but not as much as professional philosophers like to think.[16] In other words, the tendency to think of reality as being centred on a sweeping present is likely not to be constitutive of human beings, and although there may be convergence across cultures, there is variation at many

---

[16] Cf. Shardlow et al. (2020); Latham et al. (2021); Lee et al. (2022). Latham et al. (2020a) argue, on empirical grounds, that the folk conception of time is not *essentially* dynamic.

levels. The second is the *metaphysical lightweight* belief that our experience constantly and inexorably renews itself, even if nothing noticeable happens, or—to paraphrase O'Shaughnessy—the belief that there is a continuous alteration of the temporal location of experience.[17] I do not find it very interesting to ask whether we have such a belief, since it is hard for me to imagine what kind of understanding of one's own experience one must have to reply negatively. So, I take the thesis that we have such a belief as definitional of experience, and I am ready to negotiate other conceptual connections with someone who disagrees with my assessment, so that they can accept it. However, I do think that it is interesting to ask what the origin of such a belief is—either independently or jointly to the Priorian belief (assuming we have, or at least can easily form, the Priorian belief). I call the problem of providing an answer to such a question the *origin problem*, and I maintain that an account of the purported experience of passage should (among other things) have the means to face it.

In a sense, the accounts that we have seen so far do not have a difficult life in providing a solution to that problem. By definition, E_T's role is the pervasive aspect of our phenomenology that originates the ordinary belief in the passage of time. Therefore, although various details may be crucially different, for all non-deflationist accounts the answer to the origin question will be all but trivial. More precisely, what I call *non-deflationist* accounts easily explain the origin of the lightweight belief. Given the empirical status of the Priorian belief is in dispute, there is potential disagreement on whether the ordinary belief is the Priorian one, or the metaphysical lightweight one. Since the trivial explanation of the origin of the ordinary belief works for the latter only, the answer that the origin of the belief is E_T is partial, if the ordinary belief is the Priorian belief.

At any rate, what I call *deflationist* approaches to the purported phenomenology of the passage of time do not have an easy life even if we restrict the origin problem to the lightweight belief. It is important to be clear on what counts as a deflationist approach here. Since the experience of passage has become one of the main foci of attention of what can be called contemporary analytic temporal phenomenology, many scholars have argued that our perceptual experience does not present us with the passage of time.[18] This

---

[17] In comparing an experiencer with a non-experiencer, someone in a coma for instance, O'Shaughnessy comments 'And [the non-experiencer] cannot [direct a belief to the same instant as the belief itself] because he cannot do what an experiencer can do: pick out the present as "now"; and that because a non-experiencer is not conscious of "now", nor therefore of a continuity of "now"s, which is to say of "the passage of time" (which is nothing but the continuous non-phenomenal alteration of temporal location)' (O'Shaughnessy 2000: 51).

[18] Among the first ones: Prosser (2012); Braddon-Mitchell (2013); Frischhut (2013); and Hoerl (2014).

claim is true for all approaches that do not endorse a content strategy for experience-based claims about the passage of time, including the phenomenal modifier view that I defend. However, certain scholars construe the idea of presentation here in a stricter sense. It is not just that there is no cogent element of our phenomenology that presents us with a world in which time passes, but rather that our phenomenology does not suggest that time passes at all, although we might think otherwise. For all such accounts, it is *not* trivial to explain the origin of the belief in the passage of time, since none of them take seriously the thesis that E_T, along with its role of giving rise to the ordinary belief in the passage of time, is an aspect of the phenomenology of experience in the strict sense. And if it is merely in terms of experience in the broad sense that we come to believe that time passes, then replying to the origin problem is no longer a trivial deed.

5.5.1 Naive deflationism

If the purported phenomenology of time passing is indeed merely purported, then there is no aspect of our experience in the strict sense that can originate the belief that time passes. If so, and if there is an ordinary belief in the passage of time (be it the metaphysical lightweight one or the Priorian one), it is based on experience in a wide sense only, namely on our cognitive life broadly conceived and not on the 'what it is like' to have an occurring experience. One obvious idea to provide an answer to the origin problem, which surprisingly is not explored in the recent literature as far as I can tell,[19] is that we deduce that time passes from the fact that we are aware of change. By looking at a clock, we notice that the hour hand has moved forward; by remembering that in the morning we were in a bad mood we realize that now the bad mood has gone and life cheers at us. Experience in the wide sense can make us at any moment aware that either we or the world around us has changed. We thereby form an intuitive notion of change, and it is contained in the *intuitive notion of change itself* that if something has changed, then time has passed. In other words, the intuitive notion of change, the one that is suggested by very simple experiences, is a complex idea, such that upon reflection we can easily infer that change entails passage. Once we notice that the hour hand has moved forward, we can infer that some time has passed during which the hour hand has moved.

[19] I say 'recent' because early B-theorists, such as Smart (1949); Mellor (1998); and Oaklander (2004), sometimes speak as if they have something like this view in mind.

Once we remember how bad our mood was this morning compared with how we feel now, we can infer that some time has passed during which the change of mood happened. I call this view *extreme naive deflationism*. It bears some similarity to naive reductionism through identity (see Section 5.3.1), in the sense that, according to both views, there is no ingredient of our phenomenology that corresponds to the passage of time over and above the phenomenology of change and succession. However, according to naive reductionism with identity, the phenomenology of change is the phenomenology of passage, and thus reasonably we come to believe that time passes on the grounds of experience in the strict sense, and not as a consequence of an implicit or explicit reasoning, whereas according to extreme naive deflationism it is in the concept of change as we form it through experience that the idea of time passing is conceptually contained. There is no experience of passage (as in all forms of deflationism), there is only the belief in the passage of time, which is gained through a very simple inference.

I am presenting extreme naive deflationism only to have a foil for the other forms in the family of deflationisms. There is indeed a major problem of the view, which less naive forms seem to overcome. The problem lies with the purported explanation of the origin of the belief in the passage in terms of a simple inference from our observation that things move and change. It may well be true that we make similar inferences ordinarily, but this does not prove that the idea of the passage of time is contained in the idea of change, rather that we combine or connect the two ideas in reasoning about the world around us. In other words, the view merely assumes that the idea of passage of time is derived from that of change. It does not provide an answer to the origin problem thus; it merely states that the origin of the belief that time passes is the (commonsensical) belief that things change.

There are other forms of deflationism that are not so naive, in the sense that they do not simply postulate that the belief that time passes comes from the belief that things change, but that equally—it seems to me—do not possess the means to answer the origin problem. Consider Natalja Deng's remarks against the idea that the passage of time is an illusion, because time does not pass although it seems to us so: 'For there to be an illusion of passage, one would have to answer "Yes" and "No", respectively, to the following two questions: "(a) Does time seem to pass?", and "(b) Does it pass?". Assuming for present purposes that the answer to (b) is indeed "No", I'll suggest that the answer to (a) is also "No". The upshot will be that there is no illusion of passage: All we perceive is one thing after another' (Deng 2019: 4). According to this form of deflationism, our temporal phenomenology does not involve passage phenomenology, but 'just impressions of succession, order, and duration [. . .]' (Deng 2019: 7). Similarly, Christoph Hoerl has argued that we mistake our ordinary phenomenology of change and movement for a specific phenomenology of passage. The mistake is not a form of phenomenal illusion. Even assuming that the B-theory is true and thus time does not really pass, it is not our phenomenology that leads us astray and induces us to believe that the A-theory is correct. Rather, it is what we *take* our phenomenology to be that leads us astray. The mistake is thus a *cognitive error*; it does not have a phenomenal source. This is close to saying that we misdescribe our phenomenology as a phenomenology of passage while it is not. However, the problem remains, and the cognitive error we make, that of taking a phenomenology of change and movement for a phenomenology of passage, is not itself explained. Rather, it is used to explain why we believe that time passes, and why we believe that our experience tells us that time passes.[20]

5.5.2 Sophisticated deflationism

I call 'sophisticated' every form of deflationism that has the resources to address the origin problem. The most recent forms of sophisticated deflationism have been labelled 'misdescriptionism' and 'inferentialism' by Kristie Miller and collaborators in a series of papers. In the abstract of one of those, they correctly lament that 'Cognitive Error Theory [what I call deflationism] is a relatively new view and little has been said to explain why we make such an error, or where, in the cognitive architecture, such an error might creep in' (Miller et al. 2020). Both according to misdescriptionism and inferentialism, the source of our mistake is the way we speak. Miller et al. notice that all natural languages are *minimally passage-friendly*, namely they contain temporal indexicals and other deictic expressions that make sense only if we think of ourselves in a temporally embedded perspective. Moreover, many natural languages are also *substantially passage-friendly*, namely they contain moving-present and moving-ego metaphors. The general idea is that the direction of explanation expressed by (NC) is incorrect (see Section 5.1), at least if we read it in terms of experience in the strict sense. We do not come to believe that time passes because our phenomenology tells us so. According to misdescriptionism, the fact that we have a passage-friendly language

---

[20] Cf. Hoerl (2014). See also Huggett (2014). In Torrengo (2017), I have discussed in some detail Hoerl's and Huggett's version of deflationism and argued that their view does not have the means to solve the origin problem.

is a common cause both for describing the world as containing passage and for describing our phenomenology as of passage. And given that we describe our phenomenology in this way, even if it is not, we also believe that our phenomenology presents us with passage. According to inferentialism, our language suggests that time passes, and since we also believe that the reason why we believe that time passes is that our experience tells us so, we infer that the content of our phenomenology is that time passes.

One obvious question to raise with respect to this proposal is why we have a passage-friendly language (a question somewhat even more urgent if we assume that the B-theory is true). Miller et al's answer is evolutionary. Every language needs the means to express how things are from the point of view of the speaker, and thus requires temporal deixis and metaphors of time flowing through the ego, or the ego flowing through time. This reply is suspicious. First, they admit that not all languages are substantially passage-friendly and '[y]et, [as Deng rightly notices,] it's precisely these moving time and moving ego metaphors that drive the A versus B debate', namely that suggest that the world is dynamic (Deng 2019: 13).[21] Second, even if we pretend for the sake of argument that there are only substantially passage-friendly languages, the explanation from the evolutionary need to the passage metaphors is not very convincing. There is a confusion between the need to communicate effectively by exploiting information that is obvious given our temporal (and spatial) position (for which indexical language is sufficient), and the need to be aware that we cannot help but find ourselves always in a new present (capitalize resources for the future, rather than trying to change the past), which is what flow metaphors suggest. But the need for temporal indexicals per se cannot explain flow metaphors: we need spatial indexical too, but we do not have flow metaphors for space! Something is thus missing in the sophisticated deflationist reply to the origin problem. At the very least, to complete the explanation we need to postulate a further fact about the belief in having experiences constantly updated. But then either the belief has a phenomenal origin, and then the view is no longer deflationary, or it is a further brute fact that does not really require appeal to natural language in the first place.

Another possibility for the deflationist is to argue that the origin problem does not really arise at all. Certain deflationists have argued that it is empirically inaccurate to assume that there is a common sense belief in the passage of time (cf. Latham et al. 2021; Lee et al. 2022). Hence, we do not need to answer

---

[21] Moreover, 'using the moving time metaphors available in one's language is not the same as being committed to a particular metaphysical conception of time' (Deng 2019: 14).

the question where such a belief comes from. People who have the belief have acquired it because of cultural influence, as happens with many other beliefs concerning the environment around us. As I have already pointed out, it is possible that the Priorian belief in an ever-changing present is not as deeply rooted in common sense as certain professional philosophers seem to think. However, the lightweight belief that we are always updating our temporal location does not need to follow the same fate, and indeed I have suggested that we should take it as constitutive of experience itself. Although the two beliefs are easily confused with one another, the difference between them should not be underestimated. As Natalja Deng notices, 'It's true that once one is in the business of [. . .] doing metaphysics [. . .], A-theoretic ideas tend to have some intuitive appeal. But that's not to say that human beings in general walk around with tacit A-theoretical models in their heads' (Deng 2019: 14). In other words, having the metaphysically lightweight belief does not entail having the Priorian belief. Or, at least, whether the metaphysical lightweight belief in some sense suggests to us that the A-theory is true partly depends on what is the correct theory of the origin of the metaphysically lightweight belief. Moreover, it may be that the lightweight belief is often perceived as the same as the Priorian belief, perhaps in virtue of the tacit inference that if our experience changes, it is because what is present changes. Although not everybody makes such an inference or finds it compelling.

Another, even more radical, deflationist option is to argue that it is not the case that everybody believes that they themselves have an experience of the passage of time, contrary to what certain scholars assume.[22] David Braddon-Mitchell (2013: 213, 221) articulated this idea, which has been empirically supported in later studies (cf. Latham et al. 2020b; Shardlow et al. 2020). However, the empirical results are not so univocal as those authors seem to concede. For instance, in the conclusions of their empirical investigation, Shardlow et al. (2020: 16) state: 'Our results suggest that people tend to claim to have a phenomenology as of temporal passage and that this is most often construed as a process of movement through time or a changing present. Our results also provide evidence that people represent these construals as a function of subjective experiences rather than as a function of memory or of agency'. And even the authors of a more critical study admit 'Arguments that intend to show that there is defeasible reason to endorse a dynamical theory of the actual world because most people represent actual time as dynamical, are consistent

---

[22] 'To date, [. . .] there is no evidence that people report having a phenomenology as of time passing, beyond first-person reports by philosophers and physicists' (Latham et al. 2020b: 357).

with [previous empirical] results (though whether such arguments are good is another matter)' (Latham et al. 2020a: 29).[23]

But more importantly, it is not clear that those studies contain evidence against the idea that the metaphysically lightweight belief is constitutive of experience.[24] Shardlow et al. (2020) test how people take their own phenomenology to be like *and* what they believe it is for time to pass. The reason why they focus on those two parameters is that they want to individuate the *passage non-experiencers*, namely the people who disagree that they experience time passing, and at the same time 'endorse a description of what it means to say that time passes that is distinctively A-theoretic' (Shardlow et al. 2020: 5). About 5 per cent of the test subjects fall into that category.[25] But it may be that people who have only the metaphysical lightweight belief have it in virtue of what their experience is like, although they would not describe it as being as of time passing, since that is a description apt for a phenomenology that suggests the Priorian belief, which they do not have.

Moreover, that experience suggests or triggers the metaphysical lightweight belief is a claim that needs to be qualified in various ways. As I have argued throughout the book, our phenomenology may be cogent sometimes, when certain aspects of it are in the focus of our attention, but the very same stimulus situation can be related to a merely interpretational phenomenology, when we are not attentive to certain aspects of what we experience. Therefore, the claim that E_T is responsible for the belief in the passage of time does not entail that E_T is a constantly cogent aspect of our experiences, but only that *when* we are attentive to E_T we are in a position to form the belief that time passes (more on this in Section 5.6). Consider the interpretation that Latham et al. (2020b) give of the contrasting results that they find. Differently from Shardlow et al. (2020), they do not focus on spotting 'passage non-experiencers', but rather they are interested in testing how strongly people agree with direct descriptions of their phenomenology that involve either moving ego or moving present metaphors (e.g. 'It feels like the future is ahead of me and I am moving

---

[23] And they continue: 'By contrast, arguments that intend to show that dynamism is necessarily true because non-dynamism is conceptually impossible—because a non-dynamical world would not satisfy our representation of time—are not consistent with our results. These results suggest that the folk do not represent time as essentially dynamical.'

[24] Even when it comes to subjects with pathological profiles that are typically associated with temporal disorders (depression and schizophrenia), it is the Priorian belief and the belief in having the purported phenomenology associated with it that seems to be lacking.

[25] Cf. also 'we asked them about their understanding of what it means to say that time passes; this was because we could only confidently classify participants as passage-experiencers if they both (i) claimed to experience time as passing, and (ii) understood "time passing" in a distinctively A-theoretic way.' (Shardlow et al. 2020: 17).

towards it' [Latham et al. 2020b: 374]), and whether their confidence correlates with what they believe about temporal passage in the world. The result is that there is no *strong* convergence between firmly reporting a feeling of passage and the belief in the passage of time. They interpret the conclusion as supporting what they call the *ambiguity hypothesis*, namely 'the claim that there is ambiguity somewhere, either in the content or character of the phenomenology, or in what its character tells us about the world' (Latham et al. 2020b: 381).[26] Now, let's grant that the results do support the ambiguity hypothesis. There is still a lot of leeway in how to interpret the 'somewhere' in the previous sentence. It may be that phenomenology does not *always* unambiguously suggest that time passes, because when we are not particularly attentive to certain aspects of our ordinary experience, our experience is largely interpretational on whether it suggests that time passes or not. However, when we are attentive to it, it is unambiguously suggestive of the metaphysically lightweight belief in the passage of time.

Finally, let us go back to the first form of deflationism I have discussed, the position according to which we mistake experience of change for experience of passage. One can think that what we exchange for an experience as of passage is rather our awareness that *our experiences* change, or renew, over time. Close to this idea is Nick Young's theory of agentive phenomenology as inviting the belief that time passes. In acting, we are not merely aware of changes that happen in the world, as when we observe something moving, but we are also aware of ourselves as changing the world and when our experiences are inwardly directed as changing ourselves. This is 'the experiential ingredient which tells us the present moment is changing' (Young 2022: 2630). The core thesis of Young's theory is that the belief in the passage of time is the consequence of an indirect projection of this phenomenology: 'agentive experience does not present us with a reason as to why we are active, and so can be thought of as inviting the idea that there must instead be some fact independent of ourselves which accounts for this instead: if I am not causing it, and do not experience anything else as causing it, it must be something else' (Young 2022: 2634). That something else is, of course, the moving present. I think that this deflationist manoeuvre goes one step further towards a plausible picture. However, it crucially rests on the assumption that the Priorian belief is constitutive of temporal experience. As I have pointed out, there is empirical evidence against the thesis that the Priorian belief is the common sense belief in the passage of time, since

---

[26] Shardlow et al. (2020: 17–19) cast doubt on the fact that the result supports the ambiguity hypothesis. Cf. also Graziani et al. (2023), who argue that there is empirical evidence in favour of the fact that the commonsensical temporal ontology is presentism, which is an A-theoretic position.

around 30 per cent of people do not have it. If so, it is unlikely that it plays a structural role in temporal experience, as Young's theory seems to require.

The conclusion is that rather than deflating the experience of passage on awareness of succession, we should combine the overarching aspect of our experience with a primitive passage element. In the last two sections of this chapter, before the short conclusion, I articulate this idea.

5.6 Awareness of succession and passage phenomenology

The Persian medic, philosopher, and theologian Ibn Sina (980–1037; known also by his Latin name Avicenna) is credited with a thought experiment—the so-called floating man—that many have seen as a forerunner to Descartes's cogito. Here is the relevant passage from the *Kitab Al-Shifa*, the book *Concerning the soul*:

> We say anyone among us must make himself believe (*yatawahm*) that it is as if he is created all at once and as a whole (*kamila*), but his eyes are prevented from seeing anything external, and he is created floating in the air or a vacuum in such a way that the substance of the air does not collide with him so as to allow him to perceive; and his limbs are separate and do not meet or touch each other. He then reflects on whether he affirms the existence of his self. For he will not have a doubt in affirming the existence for his essence, yet he will not along with this to affirm [the existence of] the extremities of his limbs, nor his innards, his heart, or anything external to him. Instead, he will affirm [the existence] of his essence, without affirming that it has length, breadth or depth. Nor, if in that state he were able to imagine there to be a hand or other body part, would he imagine that it was a part of his essence or as a condition for his essence. (Cf. Alwishah 2013: 51–2)

The text focuses on the lack of access to spatial information through the senses of the floating man. The main point seems to be that although nothing in the floating man's experience presents him with things in space (or with spatial features of some sort), such an impoverished experience would still suffice for him to form the belief that he exists. Now, it is not trivial to generalize this conclusion if we shift the focus from the spatial to the temporal aspect of experience. If we had no access to time whatsoever, would we still be experiencing *at all*, and thus be aware of our own existence (assuming something like the cogito argument is sound)? From what I have said so far, it seems plausible to think that if we had no access to the unfolding of our own experience, we could not have experiences. At the very least, we would live a very different life. However, that intuition is prompted by the idea that an experience without awareness of the passage of time would be a very different form of awareness than ours. And whether the unfolding of experience itself is structural to experience in some deep sense is not settled by such considerations.

Although it is tempting to take as a brute fact that the unfolding of experience itself is an explanatory basic element of experience, I think this temptation should be resisted. Let us call the *molecularist model* of the experience of passage the theory according to which: (i) we need nothing more than our experience actually unfolding in time to be aware of our experiences succeeding one another; (ii) being aware of our experiences succeeding one another is being aware of the passage of time; and (iii) something without which our experience in general would not be possible. I oppose the molecularist model with my *atomist model*, according to which: (i) we are aware of the unfolding of our experience through an overarching phenomenology; (ii) which as such does not suffice to account for the experience of temporal passage; since (iii) we are aware of the passage of time in virtue of our experiences in succession being phenomenally modified; (iv) something without which our experience in general would not be possible.

The two models do not differ much with respect to the level of fundamentality in which they postulate their respective more basic explanatory facts. For the molecularist model, it is the succession of experiences themselves, for the atomist model is the awareness of succession together with the phenomenal modification, the dynamic feeling. However, dialectically I take the molecularist model to be more problematic. More precisely, the model seems to be in a sort of an explanatory impasse. Either the awareness of our experience unfolding is identical with the experience of passage, and then the account is a form of reductionism with identity after all, or they are different, and then we have an explanatory gap similar to what I have discussed for structural reductionism (Section 5.4.1). Second, the explanatory gap in the case of the molecularist model is deeper than in the case of structural reductionism. To see why, consider that the phenomenological fact that we are aware of the passage of time is supposed to be explained by the metaphysical fact that experience essentially unfolds through time. As you cannot derive an 'ought' from an 'is', you cannot derive a 'seems' from an 'is'. The mere fact that our experiences are in a succession does not support the thesis that we are aware of the succession of our own experiences *in a specifically phenomenological way*, as opposed to being aware of them in a cognitive way, through recollection and imagination. Moreover, as we have seen by talking about the experience of movement and change, taking extended experiences as the more fundamental bearer of phenomenological features (upon which the phenomenological character of the temporal parts depends) is not a very promising move. And any further addition of phenomenological elements to virtually instantaneous experiences to 'fill in' the gap would make the molecularist model suspiciously close to the atomist one. What else could those additions be, other than some form of overarching phenomenology?

It is important to stress, though, that the awareness of succession is not the whole story for the atomist model when it comes to account for the experience of passage. We need to postulate something that explains our awareness that what we are experiencing now is part of a larger succession in order to begin an explanation of the experience of the passage of time. But such an awareness is not enough to put us in a position to come to believe that time passes, since an overarching phenomenology is not as such a feeling of transition or renewal. If we cannot deflate the phenomenology of passage or reduce it to a worldly experience of some temporal feature such as change, we have to acknowledge that we are phenomenally aware not only of the succession of experiences, but also of the fact that each experience is bound to get updated. It is, after all, trivial to say that if you ask me at any time whether I believe that I just was in a different experience and that I soon will be in another, my answer will be positive. But is this something that I come to believe as I come to believe that the hour hand of a clock has moved, upon reflection on what I see and remember, or rather as I come to believe that the second hand of a clock is moving, since I see it moving?

The idea of a phenomenal modifier of the awareness of succession is that such an awareness is phenomenal rather than cognitive, but it is not worldly, namely it does not come from what our experience presents us as occurring in the environment around us. As in the case of the awareness of succession, such a phenomenology is ordinary even if not necessarily common. Indeed, it would be a mistake to think that we are constantly aware of the passing of time. Recall the discussion of the phenomenology of diachronic fullness as the tendency to describe our own experience as smooth and continuous, even if we are not constantly experiencing a cogent flux, and our experience contains many gaps of interpretational phenomenology (Section 3.3.2). The situation is analogous with respect to our awareness that time is passing. We are always in a position to become aware of the passage of time, although we are certainly not always paying attention to the passage of time. We may not pay much attention to the fact that the mental episode that we are having is dynamic, but we may also direct our attention towards this fact, as happens with other phenomenal modifiers. We can notice how vivid a certain visual perception is, but we can also experience its vividness outside the focus of attention, as it were. Analogously, we can notice that time passes, but we can also have a dynamic experience while our attention is directed towards what is going on around us—as is often the case.

In other words, the phenomenal modifier explanation of the origin of the metaphysically lightweight belief requires an appeal not only to the overarching phenomenology and the phenomenology of diachronic fullness, but also to the idea of an anarchic flow (Section 3.3.1). In the example that I gave of a disunified flow, I am watching very attentively a fly flying around, when I realize that Petunia the guinea pig has been whining for a while. In that moment I probed my stream of consciousness and came out with an interpretation of its phenomenology. Although there never was a unified phenomenal field in which Petunia's third squeak (say) was experienced together with the fly getting onto the fridge's door, I can interpret my experience by describing it in that way. And although I was not paying attention to how much time I was spending in watching the annoying fly flying at the moment that Petunia's loud whine caught my attention, I can make a rough estimate that it was some twenty seconds. But crucially, neither the interpretation of the disunified flows as unified, nor the awareness of the duration of the events (nor their conjunction) exhaust the experience of the passage of time. To see why, consider that when I probe the stream of consciousness, I normally also realize that I am in a new present, and that nothing from the past or the future is presented to me. This is not something that becoming aware of having heard Petunia whining for some time without realizing it, or that the flight of the fly lasted twenty seconds, can explain. Unlike spatial experience, which entails that we are presented with spatial locations and their connections (from the perspective of the spatial position we occupy), temporal experience presents temporal locations as fundamentally disjoined one from another. And the feeling of renewal, the phenomenal modification that connects to the overarching awareness of succession and is hardwired to the belief that time passes, is what characterizes it and distinguishes it from spatial awareness. The phenomenal modification is not always in the focus of our attention, but obtains prominence when we probe the stream (Section 3.3.3), and we can easily reconstruct our past experience as one in which we have been constantly aware of the passage of time. But according to the anarchic flow model, this aspect of the phenomenology is largely interpretational when it is off the focus of attention, and the phenomenology of the succession of experience that we just had is only completed post hoc, when, and if, we direct our attention to it.

This sort of diachronic a-modal completion is particularly interesting because of the distortions that it can bring about. Although the distortions pertain to awareness and judgement of durations, they can be connected and implicitly motivated by a variation in the phenomenology of passage, as in the case of life-threatening situations (e.g. car crash), in which the survivors often report a 'time slowing down' phenomenology. If those reports are to be taken as cogent, they are evidence for an alteration of the experience of the passage of time itself, rather than a postdictive interpretation (motivated, for instance, by emotions). However, those rare situations are not the only ones in which our durations and temporal passage judgements can be distorted, and we have to be very careful in evaluating how seriously we should take our ordinary way of speaking. I will do that in Section 5.7, while discussing the relation between the experience of passage and the experience of duration. Here let me add a few further considerations by directly addressing the theory of the phenomenal modifier.

As I have already stressed, the fact that E_T is primitive does not entail that we cannot say anything about it. In particular, it is possible to investigate whether there is a cognitive mechanism underpinning the phenomenology of the passage of time, and whether this mechanism is connected to other mental activities, such as an inner and an outer flow. If the hypothesis that the sensation of the passage of time is not given by what we represent in perception or imagination—because it is primitive—is correct, then the hypothesis of a cognitive mechanism independent of the perceptual system, but not isolated from it, seems plausible. After all, one could argue that one of the reasons for taking blurriness to be primitive is that it is due to a certain condition of our visual system that induces the vehicle through which our conscious experiences represent having intrinsic properties—properties that are independent of those constituting the representational content. Now, if E_T is a primitive phenomenal modifier, then the output of such a cognitive mechanism is both independent of the representational content of our mental episodes (it is primitive) and has an influence on it (it is a phenomenal modifier, we have experiences that feel as if reality is dynamic when our attention is outward-directed). More interestingly, the influence of the feeling of the passage of time on the representational content may not be invariant. For instance, if the felt 'pace' of the passage of time can be influenced or can vary through experiences, then there will also be a variation in the way the concurring mental episodes feel to us. A sensation of a slowed-down time will make the perceived durations of the event represented longer—roughly as a vivid visual perception makes the perceived colours brighter, and a blurred vision represents the boundaries of things indeterminately.

These hypotheses about a cognitive mechanism that underpins the feeling of the passage of time are empirical and can, at least in principle, be investigated within a larger framework that encompasses results for other cognitive and neural phenomena. Interestingly, there exists a large body of literature on the variational effects in duration perception and time estimation.[27] In those studies, both the reports and the theoretical elaboration of the data often resort to the vocabulary of 'time seems to slow down/speed up' to describe or gloss duration misperception and time misevaluation, which are connected to certain conditions of stress (such as the perception of danger, the repetitiveness of stimuli, or the effect of drugs such as dopamine agonists).

Consider Ian Phillips's criticism of the internal-clock model for explaining time estimation and duration perception and his proposal of a different model based on the perception of the duration of external events relative to the amount of mental activity experienced (Phillips 2013, 2014a). According to the internal-clock model, the effect of a spike in the dopamine level (as a consequence of a sudden perceived threat, for instance) is a speeding up of the internal pacemaker, which leads us to misperceive durations as being longer than they are. According to Phillips's model, the spike causes an acceleration in mental activity, and hence, the *relative* duration of external events is perceived as dilated. One reason that Phillips gives to prefer his view is that the internal-clock view supports an unsatisfactory explanation of the developmental advantage of the 'time expansion' effect. If durations are perceived always in relation to the amount of mental activity going on, then it follows that in correspondence to a time-expansion scenario, an unusually large amount of mental activity occurs—hence, our mental activity is actually (and not just phenomenally) faster than usual. This explains why pondering alternatives for action and reaction can be quicker (and more efficient, if not disrupted by other factors such as a mania). On the internal-clock model, on the other hand, the speeding up of the internal pacemaker can explain a misperception of the duration of the external events as longer, but it is left unclear whether this would lead to a quicker preparation for action (and if so, how). After all, the world around us is *not* slowing down.

It is not my aim here to establish which model is better placed to explain perception of duration, time estimation, and their distortions. What I wish

---

[27] See Carson (1999); Hancock and Weaver (2005); Tipples (2011); and Arstila (2012).

to highlight is that neither model is able to provide an explanation of why a speeding up either of our internal pacemaker, or of our internal stream of consciousness, leads to a variation in how we *feel* time to pass while we are having these experiences. If the phenomenal character connected to experiencing a mental episode as a perception that lasts one second (say) is different from E_T, then there is no reason to think that a misperception of the duration of an event as lasting longer than it does is also an experience of a reality in which 'time slowed down'. Of course, there is a logical connection between the two representations of reality that such phenomenological characters suggest. Once we reason about the speed of a certain movement that we have misperceived as lasting a certain amount of time that we know is more than it usually takes for the movement to occur, we conclude that the movement must have seemed to be slowed down (absolutely speaking, or relative to our internal flow of thoughts). But it does not follow from the fact that we can perform this reasoning (or from the fact that we do perform it, for that matter) that when we misperceive the duration as longer than it is, we also have a 'time is slowing down' sensation. If there is such a sensation, as it seems phenomenologically appropriate to claim once we accept that E_T is a specific aspect of our experience, then it cannot be given rise to by the misperception of a duration as such. It is, rather, the other way around: we have the impression to misperceive the duration of a certain event as longer (or shorter) than usual because we are experiencing an altered sensation of the passage of time while we perceive these durations.

One can think of the issue at stake here in the context of the alleged first-person infallibility. We tend to think that although we can be wrong as to the actual temperature of the room we are in (because, for instance, we did not realize we are ill and feel cold, while the room is twenty-four degrees Celsius), we cannot be wrong about feeling cold or not, namely its perceived temperature.[28] An analogous tendency is there with respect to the perceived temporal length of the events we experience. Although we may be wrong as to the actual length of an event, we cannot be wrong about its perceived length. Notice, however, that there is an ambiguity in the temporal case that is not there in the temperature case. What exactly is the infallibility claim? The claim that the perceived length of the event occurring in the environment is the length of our experiencing it, or the claim that the perceived length of the event occurring in the environment is the *perceived* length of our experiencing it? As we have seen so far, when it comes to short timescales, at the level of the phenomenal

---

[28] There are counter-examples to this prima facie obvious claim; cf. Williamson (2000: 95).

present, it is not obvious what is the best theory about the relationship between our awareness of temporal length of our experience and our awareness of the temporal length of what we experience. It may be that we are not aware of the temporal length of our own experiences independently from the perceived temporal length of what we experience (the length of the experience is inherited from the perceived length of the event). Or it may be the other way around (the length of the experience is projected on the event).

Cases of mismatch between the actual length of an experience and the felt temporal length either of the event or of the experience itself are puzzling also because of this ambiguity. If, when we fall off a cliff, the fall feels longer than it actually is, it is not because our experiencing the fall continues after we have landed on the ground (cf. Phillips 2014b). Or to give another example, when in a sequence of events all of the same length, we misreport the 'oddball' event as lasting longer, it is unlikely that this is so because we continue to experience the oddball stimulus through half or so of the following event.[29] And yet if our description of the phenomenology of the experience as of an experience lasting more than it actually did is cogent, there is something in what it is like to have it, *while we are having it*, that is responsible for this judgement. Phillips's theory entails that it is the felt relative duration; the phenomenal modifier view entails that it is an alteration on the feeling of the passing of time that leads to a misjudgement both of the temporal length of the perceived event (e.g. the fall) and of our own experiencing it.[30] I think a look at a third competitor may be useful to understand which view has more chances to approximate the truth.

The psychologists Stetson Chess, Matthew Fiesta, and David Eagleman designed and executed an experiment aiming to establish whether in a situation in which it is reported that time seems to have slowed down, we also perceive events with higher temporal resolution (Chess et al. 2007). The idea is to attach at the wrist of a subject an LED display showing alternate random numbers and their negative image. If the alternation rate is behind a certain threshold, the subject is unable to report the digits that are shown on the display, since the image of the digit and its negative are perceived as simultaneous (and thus the display appears as uniformly illuminated). The experimenter then secured the subjects with a harness on top of a 46 metre

---

[29] Notice that the problem arises also with the simple case of habituation (which is an experimental condition preliminary to the oddball experiment, incidentally). Once we are habituated to a sequence of stimuli, we tend to underestimate the length of the sequence, but this does not mean that we experience the end of the sequence before the sequence actually ends! More on those cases in the next section.

[30] See also Arstila (2012).

tower. 'Participants were released from the top of the tower and experienced free fall for 2.49 seconds before landing safely in a net. During the fall, they attempted to read the digits for subsequent report. If higher temporal resolution were experienced during the freefall, the alternation rate should appear slowed, thus allowing for the accurate reporting of numbers that would otherwise be unreadable' (Chess et al. 2007: 2). The results indicate that the subjects do not experience a higher temporal resolution, since they were not more able to discern the digit when the alternation rate was slightly above their threshold. Participants were also asked to imagine retrospectively their own fall and evaluate its length. On average, they overestimate it by 36 per cent, 'consistent with their verbal report that their fall had "seemed to take a very long time"' (Chess et al. 2007: 3).

There is a series of considerations that the experimenters draw from those results. One is that 'while duration estimates increase during a high-fear situation [. . .] duration estimates are not directly linked to temporal resolution' (Chess et al. 2007: 3). Note that Phillips's explanation is in tension with this result. If the 'time slows down' phenomenology is explained in terms of an increase of the amount of internal processing, then some influence on our discriminatory capacities should be expected. Phillips himself seems to suggest it when, by appealing to the evolutionary advantage of the reaction, he states that '[. . .] the effect of the fear-based dopamine spike is to speed mental activity. That, in and of itself, is an adaptive response' (Phillips 2013: 246). However, the experiment does not obviously bring grist to the mill of the phenomenal modifier explanation either. Chess and colleagues' interpretation of the result is, in fact, a different one. From the abstract of the paper, it is clear that they assume that a link between an increased time resolution and an overestimation of the length of the fall can be justified only if 'time as a single unified entity can slow down—the way it does in movies [. . .]' (Chess et al. 2007: 1). Therefore, they take the fact that people who report to have experienced duration expansion did not gain increased time discrimination capacities as evidence against there being a unified subjective time, which can accelerate or slow down by certain factors.

Notice that there are two assumptions at work here in their consideration. The first is that if there is an (alterable) feeling of time passing, it has to be unitary. The idea is that a unitary feeling of passage entails that our experience is structured as a synchronically and diachronically continuous phenomenal field. But it is not obvious that a disunified experience, both at a synchronic and diachronic level, with 'gaps' of non-cogent phenomenology (see Section 3.3), is incompatible with a feeling of passage of time. It may be that when we probe our experience, we reconstruct our experience as one in which we experienced the passage of time unitarily, although such a feeling is seldom a cogent part of our experience. This is what I have suggested above. The second is that we can disregard the reports about our phenomenology also in the case in which we are attentive. Chess et al. assume this because their interpretation of the data is in terms of interpretation of the memory of the event. They say: '[. . .] we speculate that the involvement of the amygdala in emotional memory may lead to dilated duration judgments retrospectively, due to a richer, and perhaps secondary encoding of the memories [. . .]. Upon later readout, such highly salient events may be erroneously interpreted to have spanned a greater period of time' (Chess et al. 2007: 3).

If we abandon the first assumption, the data can be interpreted differently, in a way that does require us to take neither the direct descriptions of the experience of the passage of time (e.g. 'it felt like time slowed down'), nor the indirect ones (e.g. 'the fall had seemed to take a very long time') in terms of an error theory. It is true that such judgements or descriptions are not sacrosanct, but they are prima facie evidence of a cogent phenomenology (cf. Bayne 2010: 98). More to the point, the reasons Chess and colleagues give to reject such evidence are not sound. It is not true that the only alternative to their interpretational take on the phenomenology of the fall is a situation in which a phenomenology of a slowed time temporal passage is due to, or is paired with, an enhanced time resolution. The phenomenal modifier view, in the contest of the atomist model, allows for an alternative interpretation of the results. The dopamine peak affects the phenomenal modifier in a way that means we cogently report a distinctive change in the phenomenology of the passage of time. This variation leads to a misjudgement of the duration of the experience of the fall. I will now turn explicitly to the relation between the feeling of time passing and our awareness of how long an event lasted.

5.7 Passage and duration

Situations in which experienced time is sped up or slowed down 'online'— namely apparently and while we have the experience—are unusual. Much more common are situations in which we misjudge durations or temporal intervals *without* having the impression that our sensation of time passing is altered. If the hike to the top felt like it never finished, it is not because while I was walking everything appeared slowed down to me. And yet it *felt* everlasting; it is not just something I arrived at after speculating.

What I have discussed in the previous section is (a), an alteration of a specific phenomenology of the passage of time, which happens in unusual situations, like those created by a dopamine peak. The phenomenology involved in (a) should be distinguished not only from that of (c) and (d), namely estimation of durations, but also from what in the psychological literature has somewhat only recently[31] been individuated as the phenomenon of passage of time judgements, namely (b).

(a) Sensation of the slowing down and speeding up of time
(b) Passage of time estimation
(c) Estimation of duration based on (recent) perceptual evidence
(d) Estimation of duration based on long-term memory.

Although there is awareness in the psychological literature of those distinctions, the main focus of interest is usually how duration judgements based on *prospective* tasks differ from duration judgements based on *retrospective* tasks. The prospective/retrospective divide is an operationalization of James's contraposition between experienced or felt time and remembered time, carried out on the basis of the kind of experiment performed. If the participants are told in advance the task (usually an estimation of duration), it is a prospective judgement. If they are asked to evaluate the length of the experience only after it, it is a retrospective judgement. The idea is that in the prospective case we are less prone to distortion effects due to memory, and thus the estimation of the duration is more likely to be based solely on the perceptual experience just had. This may well be true, as far as I can tell. However, the distinction does not capture James's characterization, because both prospective case and retrospective case are postdiction phenomena. After all, the judgement in both cases is made *after* the relevant experience (since it is an estimation of the overall duration of something, when else?). More importantly, neither does such operational distinction map onto (c) and (d) above. Even if it is more likely that a retrospective task is influenced by memory elements, there is still a difference between evaluating the duration of a relatively short event right after it (even if we were not prompted in advance to do it), and the judgements about the length of significantly longer events, for which it is likely that what

[31] As Jones (2019) notes. Cf. Zakay (1992) and Wearden (2016).

it was like while we were experiencing them does not play a significant role. Indeed, uneventful weeks may feel like they do not pass while we live them, but, given the little variety of information to remember, be judged afterwards to have passed very quickly (a familiar example is the months during Covid confinement).[32] What characterizes (c) is thus the fact that when we talk of how it *felt* that a certain event lasted, what we say is largely cogent of the phenomenology at issue. A duration judgement based on a retrospective task can thus be an example of (c).

More interestingly, both cases are not obviously connected with (a), which, as we noted, is something that shows up in unusual situations only. Take a phenomenon like the 'return trip' effect. Once we arrive back at the starting point, we are surprised to be already there, and we can comment that the way back felt shorter, but we do not tend to talk of a situation in which time speeded up, certainly not in the sense that while we were returning to the starting point, we had the impression that time was going faster. A very boring afternoon may be such also because during it we think that time does not seem to pass. However, this generally means that we have looked at the time on several occasions and were surprised that so little time had passed since the last time we checked. It does not mean that during the weekend we had a slowed-down experience of the passage. Indeed, our retrospective judgement may be that now (in the evening) it seems that we had lunch just one hour ago.

The relation between (b) and (c) is less clear. Passage of time judgements are sensitive to two factors: stake of the situation and insecurity elements (cf. Wearden 2016). If we are waiting for an event that is important to us, and the timing of the event is uncertain, we will tend to judge that it felt like time was passing slowly. If we are just biding our time and engaged in some recreational activity, time is likely to fly. Both high stakes and high insecurity lead to overestimation of the amount of time passed. Does that mean that in those situations experienced time slows down? It is probably wrong to think of a deformation of the sensation of the passage of time, like in the case of the car accident. However, it may be that in those situations the duration of the events in question is indeed experienced as longer than it is, as is shown by the fact that we may be surprised by how little time it lasted when looking at the clock. The feeling that it lasted more (or less) *does not go away* (neither is it, somehow, postdictively rectified) once we come to know how long it actually lasted. The situation is

---

[32] James notes the opposite case when he comments '[. . .] a time interval filled with varied and interesting experiences seems short in passing, but long as we look back' (1890: Chapter XV).

made more complex by the fact that retrospective tasks are usually underestimated as compared to prospective ones, and this is tentatively explained by the fact that fewer attentional resources are devoted to the estimation of the passage of time during the experience. An explanation that can be expanded to account for the fact that prospective tasks in which attention is devoted to a non-timing task, while the experience occurs, are also underestimated.

This last phenomenon is known as *dual task interference effect*, and it has received attention both from psychologists and philosophers. The general idea is that a subject who has to evaluate the duration of an event while they are also involved in another task, such as sorting a deck of cards by colour, will, in general, underestimate the length of the event compared to a subject who is attending uniquely to the duration of the event. While the details of the received explanation, involving an attention gate and a counter, do not concern us here, it is important to stress that philosophers have criticized it on the grounds that the effect is there also when the 'distracting' task involves attending to temporal features, such as listening to music. This is puzzling because if by attending music we are focusing on durations, then we should overestimate the overall duration of the event, or at least not underestimate it. The issue is of course largely empirical. One issue, for instance, is whether by attending to something that shows temporal features, such as the rhythm and succession of notes in music or actions in a movie, durations go into the focus of attention, rather than some other aspects, such as the pleasure that follows in experiencing it (Droit-Volet et al. 2010). But the problem is also how to understand the distinction between attending to the duration of a perceived event, and to *the duration of our experience of perceiving it*. Even if it turned out that we can only be aware of the duration of our experience by inferring it from the duration of the events that we are experiencing, the two tasks are different, and as long as the judgements are based on concurring phenomenology, they may be based on different phenomenal elements.

If we focus on the thesis that listening to music or watching a movie 'makes time go faster', it is difficult not to wonder whether the experiential basis of such an experience-based claim is something inbetween a mere judgement of duration (as in 'the weekend felt like a month') and an actual phenomenological distortion (as in the car crash cases). As I stressed, the case (c) is distinct both from (d) and (a), in that it involves how the experience *felt* like it lasted. One way to make sense of the cogency of the experience-based claim is in terms of a *past-oriented overarching phenomenology*, a present awareness of how long a recent past event lasted (cf. Pelczar 2010). Another option is that durations are dynamic state features (Section 2.6.2) of events with which we are presented, mainly in perception. This has some plausibility for short durations, but if there is phenomenal awareness of longer durations, then it is gained through a quasi-metric past-directed feeling of persistence. But should we think of it in terms of awareness of succession (Section 3.1), which involves features of our own experience, or in terms of feelings of persistence (Section 2.6.3), which involve temporal features of the event and object we experience?

There is probably room for both interpretations, as the case may be. Let us assume that it is correct that I am aware of the temporal location of my experience (Section 4.4.1). Even when I am focused on what happens around me, it is not the temporal location of the events that I perceive that appears to me, but rather my own temporal location as occupied by events in space out there. Considerations about (c) suggest that I am also aware of the durations of the events that I perceive, through a past-directed feeling of persistence. But from the fact that I am aware of the temporal location of my experience, and that I am aware of the duration of the external events that I experience, it does not follow that I am aware of the duration of my experience; or, at least, that I have the same phenomenal awareness of their temporal length as I have of the event that I have just experienced (Frischhut 2014: 46).

First, if it makes sense to think of one's experience as virtually instantaneous, then it is not really the duration of our experience that we are aware of when we are aware of having experienced something for an extended period. Second, even if experiences are not virtually instantaneous, the purported overarching phenomenology of how long something just past lasted does not concern merely durations in the order of magnitude of the specious present or less. That the train ride felt like twenty minutes while I was watching a one-hour episode of *Star Trek: Picard* does not mean that each of its one-second-or-so parts felt shorter. Third, and more importantly, even if experiences are not virtually instantaneous, and even if we grant that we can be somehow aware of the durations of events that over-span the specious present, it is difficult to make sense of the idea of being aware of the duration of my own experiences independently from what I am presented with while having them. And unless perhaps there is cognitive phenomenology, I am aware of any duration at all only insofar as I have experiences with either outward-directed or inward-directed presentational phenomenology.

However, those considerations do not yet explain the dual task interference effect and the puzzling fact that attending to temporal features of perceived events does not disrupt the underestimation effect. Carla Merino-Rajme (2022) has lately elaborated a model in which felt time is 'fragmented'

in the sense that the formation of an internal timeline and an external timeline can part company. In a train ride in which you are engrossed in watching
an episode of *Picard*, the train ride will receive much less attention than
the episode, and as a result the ride will feel much shorter, twenty minutes
say, than what you know it actually lasted when you look at the clock on
arrival. Merino-Rajme correctly insists on the phenomenological source of
this judgement. When you learn that an hour has actually passed, you are baffled, because that is not how it *felt*: 'the twenty-minute felt duration persists
despite the formation of an explicit belief that the ride took about an hour'
(Merino-Rajme 2022: 6). Adapting her example to mine, this is roughly how
her explanation of this phenomenon goes. 'As the train departs, you start
[watching an episode of *Picard*]. At this point, you are not yet absorbed by the
[episode] and so [...] you experience the [first scenes] as partaking in external
time. [...] You experience time as passing for [*Picard*] and for the train ride,
increasing the duration of both timelines by the same amount. A bit later, you
become absorbed in the [episode] and remain so for most of the trip. While
absorbed in the [episode], it feels to you as though time passes only for [the
episode], and only its timeline increases' (Merino-Rajme 2022: 12).

Although her talk of fragmented timelines resonates with my idea of a disunified anarchic flow,[33] I have a different explanation of the phenomenon.
Merino-Rajme is of course right in insisting that we do not have a 'compressed'
experience of the episode of *Picard*, simply because the train trip felt only
twenty minutes long, rather than an hour. However, her account entails that
the internal time, that in which we were engrossed in the vision of *Picard*, felt
one hour long, as opposed to how the duration of the trip felt. Therefore, 'by
the end of the trip, the timeline for [*Picard*] is much longer than that of the
train ride'; and this is why 'this proposal can hold that it felt to you as though
the train ride lasted twenty minutes without holding that it also felt to you
as though [*Picard*] lasted only this much' (Merino-Rajme 2022: 15). I find this
consequence of the model a bit puzzling. I am certainly aware that I was riding
the train while I was watching *Picard*, and if I am baffled by discovering that a
whole hour has passed since we left, I may also be baffled that a whole hour has
passed since I began watching *Picard*. It is true that most of the scenes of the
episode were not experienced as part of the trip, since I was engrossed in its
vision, but that does not mean that I did not *experience* both the vision of the

---

[33] From what I can tell, one crucial difference with my view is that she does not take there to be
interpretational diachronic gaps in the flows. In her view, phenomenology is always cogent, even when
off the focus of attention.

episode and the trip as having the same duration.[34] After all, when things like that happen, we are *not* surprised that the train trip and the episode had the same duration, we are surprised that so much time has passed. This situation leads also to a tension that is internal to her account. Merino-Rajme (correctly, I think) denies that we have an experience with contradictory content in such cases. But it is difficult to understand how we would not have it, since according to her account, we feel that something lasted one hour and we feel that something lasted twenty minutes 'at the same time'.[35]

My starting hypothesis is that passage of time judgements are judgements about the temporal length of our own experiences. Or at least the two things are strictly connected. In a sense, the overarching phenomenology of succession fuses with the phenomenal modifier of the passage element and with the past-directed feeling of persistence. As stressed above, we are not presented with the duration of our own experiences as such, although we can become aware of the duration of our experiences by being aware of the duration of what we experience. And yet the temporal location we are phenomenally aware of is that of our experience and not of what we experience. Perhaps we think of time as a dimension, but that is surely not how we live it. Although I agree that ununified flows may feel different with respect to their durations, I am not sure that the explanation is in the fact that we can track separately different temporal lengths. Rather, the parts of the inner flow that do not have presentational phenomenology do not contain *any* duration, and thus the more we are focused on them, the less we feel that time has passed.

I do not think that there is a sharp distinction between the inner flow and the outer flow of experiences that constitute our conscious life (or, at any rate, that it is easy for us to sharply distinguish them). However, there are both presentational aspects of our phenomenology, those that clearly are part of the outer flow if they have phenomenal objectivity, and there are non-worldly, non-presentational aspects of our phenomenology, which pertain to the inner flow. E_T is a modification of the awareness that involves our own experiences

---

[34] In response to a similar worry, she states: 'while you may well believe that you [watch] the whole of [*Picard*] while riding the train, this is not how you *experience it*' (Merino-Rajme 2022: 17; emphasis hers).

[35] To be fair, since Merino-Rajme thinks that I only believe that the experiences lasted the same, but I do not experience them as having the same length, there is no contradictory content. Another puzzling consequence of her model (which I think follows from her implicit assumption that the phenomenology of the various flows is always cogent) is that '[. . .] despite being objectively disjointed, we experience the separated segments of the train ride as continuous' (Merino-Rajme 2022: 13). Surely, we do not experience it as if the ride restarted every time we got distracted from watching *Picard* by something happening in the train, but it seems wrong also to say that we experience a *smooth passage* between them.

and thus part of the inner flow. It is non-worldly because not only it does not possess phenomenal objectivity, but it is not presentational either. That does not mean that we cannot 'find' the passage of time in the world around us. As I have stressed, the modification of our awareness of succession as dynamic can easily lead to the belief that we live in a world in which time passes, since the temporal location of the things that appear to be external to us is not distinguishable from the temporal location of our own experiences.

The reason why the way we experience time is very different from experiencing an extended space is that we are not presented, neither in the inner flow nor in the outer flow, with a connection between temporal locations. Nothing in the case of space corresponds to a phenomenology of diachronic fullness, an awareness of succession, a feeling of persistence, and a feeling of passage. We are aware of the temporal location of our own experience as containing external events, and we have an awareness of succession. But awareness of succession is not awareness of the relations between temporal positions either of the external events *or of our own experiences*. That the inner flow does not contain any duration does not mean that everything is still or timeless there. Consider the phenomenon of 'losing track of time' that hits us in daydreaming or mind wandering. Losing track of time is failing to become aware of the temporal distances between the events in the environment around us, it is not to 'exit' the flow of time altogether. When we mind wander, or meditate, most of the outer flow goes off the focus of attention. Later, we can interpret the outer flow as having been populated by changes and persisting things, but if the phenomenology was very faint, it is likely that little will remain in the feeling of how long we had been mind wandering. We only have the belief that so much time has passed as the clock says.

There may be inward-directed presentational elements that remain cogent while mind wandering: maybe mental imagery in the focus of attention, or bodily sensations or emotions that at times emerge as prominent. In general, we can be aware of various durations while not attending to 'normal' perceptions of things around us.[36] Indeed, not all losing track of time in mind wandering or daydreaming leads to underestimation of how long we have been absent minded. Sometimes the wandering feels as long as it is, as we discover by looking at a clock when something catches our attention. Since we can be aware of the duration of mental imagery and bodily sensations with which we are presented while mind wandering, we can also be aware of durations which

---

[36] Possibly, deep meditation is a state in which virtually every presentational phenomenology is absent. Sometimes deep meditation is characterized as a 'timeless state'. If I am right, it is a duration-less, but still temporal, state. On meditation, see Metzinger (2020) and Frischhut (*ms*).

are roughly the same as those of the events outside us. But barring those 'Get-tier' scenarios, we normally underestimate the time that has passed when we focus on the inner flow, because not all our inner phenomenology presents us with durations. Indeed, usually when we are focused on the inner flow, neither the duration of the external events nor of bodily sensations are very prominent, and thereby we can rarely be aware of the duration of our own experience through being aware of the duration of what we experience.

In the case of being engrossed in an episode of *Picard* during a one-hour train trip, both the train trip and the vision of *Picard* may feel shorter than they are, because, with respect to both flows, non-presentational aspects may be prevalent. This happens especially when one is 'swept away' by the narrative, rather than fixated on the visual detail. When the non-presentational aspects of our experience become the centre of our attention, when we are deep in our thoughts as it were, durations are no longer accessible to us, although if I am right, we are aware of the succession of our experiences and of the passage of time. Besides, since many aspects of the phenomenology can be interpre-tational but still quite prominent, for instance when the noise of the train is not in the focus of our attention, and yet it is somewhere in the background, or when we fixate on a chromatic detail of a scene of the episode, rather than on the plot, it is not implausible that we end up with an interpretation of our past experience in which both the trip and the episode felt more or less of the same (shortened) length. And even when we have been fully concentrated in watching *Picard*'s episode, paying little attention to most of the goings-on around us in the train, it is unlikely that either phenomenology imposes on us very strongly, such that we are surprised how different the trip's duration and the episode felt. If that really happened, then at least certain aspects of our experience *would* feel contradictory.

Notice also that there is a significant ambiguity in saying 'being concentrated on' attending something. It can mean that we pay attention to the individual passages of a symphony, or the images and sounds in a movie, or it can mean that we are engrossed in the plot or in the melody—swept away by some form of articulated thought, if not a fully fledged narrative. Moreover, we can also be concentrated on *doing* something, and also in this case there is an ambiguity between being concentrated on the detail of the action or being lost in act-ing. In both the perceptive and active cases, being concentrated in the sense of being lost means a prominence of attention to the inner flow, and thus poten-tially an underestimation of the duration on the ground of how it felt. The prominence of the inner flow can become a proper absence of mind, and in that case, we cannot just lose track of time, namely of the duration of the events around us, but also of the very activity in which we are engrossed. For instance, while reading a book one's thoughts can 'take over' and the activity of reading may switch to a background, up to the level that we have to come back several pages because the story does not make sense any longer (who is this guy? Why does everybody in the book act as if I was supposed to know? Wait, and Hildebrand is dead?). Indeed, someone who is doing something in a completely 'automated' fashion may look from an external point of view as if they are 'fully concentrated' on doing it.

This framework explains also why certain activities may have the effect of actually slowing down time rather than speeding it up, for instance when they are extremely boring and require a lot of attention that cannot be relegated to some 'autopilot' system that allows us to wander with our thoughts. In such activities, very little attention is given to the inner flow, and a lot to the external details. It is not a matter of attending to temporal features rather than non-temporal ones. Indeed, it is not even clear exactly what attending to temporal features means as opposed to attending to non-temporal ones. If we attend to a rhythm, is our attention split towards a merely temporal aspect, in which it is the temporal pattern that counts, and a qualitative one, in which we appreciate the difference in pitch or timbre of each 'beat'? Or is attending to the rhythm something that requires attending to both features as somehow fused together? Moreover, when we are focused on the duration of our own experience, is it only temporal elements that enter in the focus of our attention? It is not clear to me that clues that allow us to become aware of the duration of a certain just past event must themselves always be temporal in nature. Maybe we got used to associating the colour of a certain stimulus with a certain temporal length, and attention to the colour became an important clue for our immediate awareness of the duration of a past event.[37]

Finally, if I am right that evaluations of how much time has passed are evaluations of the length of one's experience, which in turn is something that we can phenomenally gain through presentation of durations, the two factors of high stake and insecurity must correlate with outward-directed attention, or with presentational phenomena more generally. It has indeed been noticed that those factors lead to attention towards the timekeepers, such as watches, but also other external clues (Jones 2019). A further (compatible with the former) hypothesis is that fixation on the (possibly uncertain) future may enhance the presentational aspects of our inner life, especially in emotionally charged mental episodes. This may also explain the cases in which time does not seem to

---

[37] Cf. also the considerations in Droit-Volet (2019).

pass because of anxious thoughts. Imagine that during the train ride, rather than enjoying an episode of *Picard*, a maniac on your side pulls out a gun and points it at your face for the whole trip, and threatens to kill you several times, in a long, delirious rant. My bet is that that one-hour trip would feel like an eternity (assuming you survive), and yet what you almost exclusively might have done during that period was thinking. But thinking with anxiety for the future brings in more presentational phenomenology and thus makes the passage of time feel slower.

5.8 Conclusions

We live in a world where time passes even underneath the sofas, as song-writer Paolo Conte notices (in the song 'Fuga all'inglese', *Appunti di Viaggio*, 1982), namely in which time passes also when and where we do not notice it to pass. This is something we are aware of in an intimate and yet obscure way. In this chapter I have argued that there is no shortcut to account for this experience. Our ordinary and possibly constitutive awareness that time passes cannot be reduced to a perceptual phenomenon or deflated to entertaining a certain belief about the world. It is a structural and primitive element of our experience, which combines with our awareness that our experiences succeed one another, and our (largely faulty) impression that the flow of our lives is smooth and continuous.

6

The tenseless sunshine of the conscious mind

Si nni jeru, si nni jeru li mè anni
Si nni jeru, si nni jeru, un sacciu unni
'Vitti na crozza', Sicilian folk song
(unknown author and date)

Although talking about experience is like building a sandcastle on top of another sandcastle, what we talk about when we talk about experience is not just a wishful figment of our imagination. Experience is part of reality. And reality has *its* rules, not ours. Maybe experience does not tell us that things are in any way (cf. Travis 2004), but the fact that in the world in which we happen to live experiences are in a certain way is not 'up to us' in any interesting sense. Specifically, it is not up to us whether we live in a dynamic, A-theoretic universe and experience reveals this fact or rather we live in a static, B-theoretic block universe, although our experience suggests otherwise. In this chapter, my aim is to show how the overall picture of temporal experience I sketched in the previous chapters does not require a dynamic universe and indeed sits better with a static, block universe view (and perhaps also with the timeless universe of certain versions of quantum gravity). Somewhat contrary to the typical attitude of B-theorists, according to whom there is nothing eerie in the general picture that comes out by combining the block universe view and our experience of the passage of time, I will argue that the final result *is* surprising.

In Section 6.1. *The sunshine model and the wave model*, I introduce the two rival models, based on the B-theoretic and A-theoretic metaphysics respectively, of temporal experience. In Section 6.2. *The explanatory vacuousness of the wave model*, I discuss two objections to the sunshine model that arise from the wave model, and I discard them, providing indirect evidence against the explanatory power of the latter. In Section 6.3. *The sunshine model*, I articulate the sunshine model into some of its more significant, and all but shocking consequences.

Temporal Experience. Giuliano Torrengo, Oxford University Press. © Giuliano Torrengo (2024).
DOI: 10.1093/9780191937804.003.0006

6.1 The sunshine model and the wave model

There is an argument that begins with the trivial existence of experiences in our universe to the conclusion that either experiences are temporally extended or there is an overarching phenomenology. It goes like this: we experience the world; experience requires some level of consciousness; consciousness requires some awareness of the passage of time; and awareness of the passage of time requires awareness of succession in the form of an inner flow. But to be aware of our own experiences succeeding one another, either experience itself is temporally extended, or we have temporally unextended experiences with an overarching phenomenology. If my reasoning in the previous chapters is correct, then there are indeed many overarching aspects of our phenomenology, even if our experiences are virtually instantaneous.

In this chapter it will not be important whether our experience is temporally extended or rather some form of the dynamic snapshot view is correct. The focus will be rather on the implicit assumption in the previous argument that *we* persist, namely we are, somehow, spread across time. In order to have a succession of experience, a person, a mind, an organism, something has to go through all of them and thus persist (or at least survive). Although the issue of how we persist (and how things in general do), and the issue of whether there is real passage, are orthogonal, I will work with the traditional partition of the logical space, according to which if time really passes then we are spread across time by being multi-located across the temporal dimension (i.e. by enduring), whilst if time does not really pass we are spread across time by being temporally extended, and having a temporal shape and temporal parts (i.e. by perduring).[1] Now, conscious entities like us have experiences by being persisting entities that are involved in processes of the right kind, that is, temporally extended mental events. The question is how the mental events that lead to our experience of the passage of time relate to the metaphysics of the passage of time. I will distinguish two models, depending on the stance towards realism about passage: the *wave model* and the *sunshine model*.

The wave model is based on the assumption that the passage of time is a genuine feature of reality, namely it assumes as background metaphysics the so-called A-theory. For ease of exposition, I will adopt a moving spotlight

---

[1] Later, I will also consider a variant of this view, the so-called stage view (or ex-durantism), according to which we have different counterparts at different temporal locations (Hawley 2001; Sider 2001). I will not consider the extended simple view (Parsons 2004), or the combination of temporal parts and real passage (cf. the presentist perdurantism of Brogaard 2000), or of endurance and passage antirealism (cf. Gilmore et al. 2016).

framework, namely a metaphysics according to which the passage of time is given by the 'movement' of the present on the temporal dimension. The word 'movement' here requires scare quotes because the present does not move from being in the living room to being in the bedroom as I do when I go to sleep. Rather, the present shifts temporal position, it is first in the evening, and then in the night. Movement thus is just a metaphor and the truth behind it is that the whole of reality changes constantly in virtue of the purported fact that the content of the present constantly changes. For this metaphysical picture to play an explanatory role for temporal experience, we need the further assumption that there is a connection between being present and being phenomenally aware of anything, namely conscious. Mental events become conscious (and thus we are aware of this and that) as they become present, and stop being conscious by slipping into the past. What tells us that time passes in our phenomenology is the effect of our consciousness being 'carried by the wave' of the moving present. To many, this model seems very natural and indeed close to the common sense narrative of how we relate to the world. We think of our own experience of the passage of time in terms of a constantly changing present of which we are phenomenally aware. And if the wave model is correct, it appears to us that our present experience constantly changes because this is what really happens. Experience may ultimately be a big illusion under almost all respects, but not with respect to the passage of time.

The sunshine model is committed to exactly the contrary. Our experience may be substantially veridical with respect to anything but the passage of time. Time is at bottom an arrangement of temporal or spatiotemporal locations in a manifold, and it does not pass or flow. The passage of time is not even a metaphor; it is at best a description of a certain aspect of our phenomenology that does not capture anything that goes on in reality. The sunshine model is thus incompatible with the truth of the Priorian Belief that there is an objective flow of the present, but it is compatible with the truth of the Metaphysically Lightweight belief that our experiences are constantly updated (cf. Section 1.5). The application of my atomist dynamic model to the so-called block universe view, or B-theoretic eternalism, is an exemplification of the sunshine model. According to my atomist model, we make a cognitive mistake in thinking that time really passes, but we are partially excused by the fact that an intrinsic aspect of our phenomenology, namely the fact that the awareness of succession is modified by the feeling that our experiences are constantly renewed, can be easily interpreted as suggesting that an objective passage of time is responsible for that.

Although the theory of temporal experience that I have articulated and defended in the previous chapter is incompatible with the wave model, it does not rule out the metaphysics underlying it (viz. the A-theory). The dialectic of this chapter can be put as follows: my theory does not need an ever-moving present to explain the experience of passage, or any other type of temporal experience. However, if the wave model were to be able to provide a good explanation of temporal experience by resorting essentially to the assumption that time really passes, then my theory would turn out to be comparatively more complicated. Therefore, there would be abductive reasons that support the A-theory. To contrast this, I need both to show that the wave model cannot deliver what it promises, and that the sunshine model delivers it by taking passage antirealism seriously. To this effect, first I argue against the wave model (Section 6.2), and then I provide a picture of the atomistic sunshine model in which it will become clear how it works within a B-theoretic framework (Section 6.3).

6.2 The explanatory vacuousness of the wave model

6.2.1 The objective present

In Chapter 4, I introduced several notions of presentness, but none of them carries serious metaphysical implications. I now introduce the metaphysically heavyweight notion of an *objective present*. The thought that there is an objective matter of fact with respect to which events are present is allegedly very natural.[2] What would it mean to take it at face value? An idea is to build upon the different implicit assumptions that the indexical mechanism for temporal reference and that for spatial reference encode. Firstly, the objective present is a time that is *privileged* or *special* among the other times that constitute the temporal series. Secondly, there are non-time-relative and non-subject-relative matters of fact with respect to which time is the objective present. The notion we are after is non-time-relative because whatever the 'specialness' at issue here, it is a feature that singles out *one* time among all others; if every time is special merely relative to itself, or privileged in the same way, then there is no objective present after all—no unique objective present at any rate. And it is

---

[2] In the words of someone who is sceptic that it *is* natural: 'The phenomenology associated with perceiving the world is taken as representing the present as special in some way' (Braddon-Mitchell 2013: 211).

not subject-relative because it is a form of *metaphysical* privilege we are seeking here. It is not special because I like it more than others, or because it smells good, say. However, typically someone who believes in an objective present believes also that we have privileged epistemic access to it. But this privilege is derivative of its metaphysical specialness. If we leave the nature of the relation between the objective present and the experiential present (Section 4.1.2) unspecified, we can say that the temporal index (Section 4.1.1) of the experiences of the participants to a given communicative exchange is shared *in virtue of* those experiences all happening at the (one) objective present.[3] And this differentiates the present time from the spatial location that each of us occupy. Your spatial location is epistemically privileged (to you) merely in virtue of the fact that it is your location, and not in virtue of some alleged metaphysical difference between it and my location (or anybody's else, for that matter).

With those preliminaries in mind, I will pinpoint three versions of objective presentness we encounter, often implicitly, in the literature: the *intrinsic* conception, the *extrinsic* conception, and the *tense-based* conception. They all can be seen as ways of formulating versions of the A-theory of time, which is a family of theories that aim at capturing the idea of an objective passage of time, and are opposed to the B-theory, which is a form of passage antirealism. According to the intrinsic conception, presentness is a property that a time or an event has *independently* from anything else. This conception is at work in so-called spotlight theories of time (cf. Cameron 2015; Deasy 2015; Skow 2015). The present time is special because it 'luminesces', it has a sui generis status that distinguishes it from all other times. Notice, however, that *nothing* in the notion of an intrinsic objective present can guarantee the *unicity* of the present, and hence its special status. If being intrinsic is being possessed independently of anything else, then the mere fact that a time is objectively present cannot exclude that other times are objectively present too. Thus, in order to be put to use to mark *the* present time as special, the intrinsic notion of an objective present has to be coupled with a *substantive* metaphysical principle of uniqueness, which states *no more than one time* can be objectively present.[4]

---

[3] *Nota bene.* I am merely giving an example of a rationale that could motivate the idea of an objective present; I am not claiming that facts about the communication and coordination between agents support the hypothesis that there is an objective present. Quite the contrary, I agree with Butterfield (1984) and Callender (2008, 2017) in thinking that we may tend to think (erroneously) that there is an objective present *because* we are coordinated. But the explanation of why we are mutually coordinated is free of an 'objective present' assumption.

[4] And possibly other principles governing the 'movement' of the present and avoid its being stuck or jumping in an erratic manner; see Cameron (2015). For further detail on this point and its experiential relevance, see Spolaore and Torrengo (2019). It is also worth noting that the metaphor of the spotlight, insofar as it suggests that the present moment 'receives' its special status from something else, is a bad

An extrinsic conception of objective presentness can avoid this extra metaphysical cost. In the so-called growing block theories of time, being objectively present is strictly connected with the topological property of *having nothing (temporally) ahead*. The present time is the 'last arrived' in an ever-growing reality. Notice that the mere *topological* fact of being at the utmost border of reality seems irrelevant to explain the kind of experience we have of the present. Hence the extrinsic conception of presentness too may need further substantive theses to 'fully' do its job.[5] An alternative notion that goes under the extrinsic conception as well is to identify the specialness of the present with *existence*. In many views that go under that heading 'presentism', the fact that there is a unique existing time is a consequence of its being the only objectively present. Existence, thus, essentially characterizes presentness (cf. Zimmerman 1996; Merricks 2007; Tallant 2014). What distinguishes and makes a certain instant special is either not a property at all (if we adopt the Kant–Quine notion of existence) or at any rate not a qualitative intrinsic property (if we adopt the Leibniz–Meinong notion of existence). By adopting this view of objective presentness we are denying that time is a dimension. There is no 'temporal arena' where various events are differently located and stand at possibly different temporal distances to each other. The present time is the *whole* of time (or the whole real, existing part of time, at any rate), and the flow of time is the global change in the content of reality.

The tense-based conception of objective presentness appeals to the idea of *real* or *metaphysical tense* (cf. Dyke 2013). Tenses, in the linguistic or mental sense of the expression, are representational features through which one can describe the temporal dimension in a perspectival manner, from the point of view of a given time that is the centre of the perspective. If tenses are real, then there are matters of fact about what time is (*simpliciter*, that is, not relative to a time), the centre of the metaphysically privileged perspective (cf. Zimmerman 2005). The theory of time that comes out of this picture is one in which there is only *one* real temporal perspective whose centre is ever changing; all other perspectives are only imagined or hypothetical temporal perspectives. Rather than being a property of times or events, presentness in this conception is a feature of facts (or of properties, or some other fact-constituent, if any). The crucial factor is that reality is partitioned along the temporal dimension in past,

---

metaphor of the intrinsic conception of presentness. See also Skow (2015: 209), who struggles with the metaphor when he writes 'the spotlight of *intrinsic* privilege *shines on* the red experiences but not the white ones' (italics mine).

[5] Forrest (2004), for instance, maintains that presentness comes with a metaphysical 'frisson' that ignites consciousness.

present, and future. This conception is compatible with different ontologies, that is different ideas on what parts of the temporal dimension exist: the one on the past-side of the objective present? The one on the future-side? Both? Neither? (Cf. Eker 2023.)

In any of these versions, the notion of an objective present is more contentious than the other notion of presentness introduced in Chapter 4. One well-known worry is the tension with views that are usually seen as more in line with, if not outright supported by, corroborated empirical theories. For instance, with minimal assumptions, an objective present entails absolute simultaneity. Although the Special Theory of Relativity does not rule out facts about absolute simultaneity, it predicts that they would be empirically undetectable. More generally, an objective present is incompatible with any plausible form of antirealism of the passage of time, which is a metaphysical view generally regarded more in line with most of our best science.[6]

6.2.2 The metaphysics of the wave model

Why is an objective present important if we aim at explaining our *experience* of the passage of time; which role can it have in the explanation? Roughly, it plays two roles. First, we need an objective present to 'anchor' the (alleged) phenomenal prominence of the present (Section 4.2) to an objective feature of reality. Second, the reality behind the metaphor of the 'movement' of the present is the constant change in the temporal position of the present. Therefore, by being reactive to the objectivity of the present, we are also reactive to its change of temporal position, namely to the passage of time. Or so the wave model tells us. In contrast with my eliminativist take on experiential presentness (Section 4.4), being in the present for the wave model is meaningful both for metaphysics and for experience.

There are at least three ways in which it could be maintained that the experiential presentness is metaphysically significant. Firstly, someone who takes seriously the idea of a phenomenal property of presentness, either as a content

---

[6] The problem of the incompatibility between an objective present and Einstein's relativity is thoroughly investigated in Costa de Beauregard (1981) and Savitt (2011). Although I think the problem is very serious, the philosophical debate is still very lively on both sides. See Markosian (2004) for a careful explanation of how the incompatibility charges can be resisted and Baron (2017) for reasons to believe that future scientific developments may overturn this aspect of relativity. It is also fair to point out that some have argued that although relativity is in tension with an objective present, other parts of our best empirical theories, such as cosmology (Lucas 1973) and quantum mechanics (Popper 1982), are rather favourable to it. See Bourne (2005: Ch. 6) and Hilgevoord and Atkinson (2011) for rejoinders. For consideration concerning general relativity, see Dorato (2002). The debate on what to make of an objective present and the flow of time in quantum gravity and other 'great unification' theories is ongoing; see Callender (2017: Chap. 4) and Baron, Miller, and Tallant (2022).

property (Section 4.2.1) or as a vehicle property (Section 4.2.2) and is a *phe-nomenal idealist*, would consider presentness in experience as direct evidence for *reality* including a robust notion of presentness, since in that methodolog-ical framework how reality *is* is one and the same with *how we experience and conceptualize it*.[7] This stance is a minority in the analytic tradition, but it is common in the continental one. I will just set aside it in what follows as too methodologically distant for my general approach to the philosophy of time.

Secondly, a *phenomenal realist* can take the represented present in our per-ceptual experience to be evidence for time itself being constituted by such a phenomenal property. If there are phenomenal facts that are irreducible to non-phenomenal ones, and if presentness (and possibly dynamicity with it) is an essential feature of such facts, then presentness is real after all. Its being 'merely experiential' is just another way to say that it does not constitute any non-phenomenal fact, but given that phenomenal facts *are* denizens of reality as much as non-phenomenal ones, presentness is real after all. Sympathizers of dualism and panpsychism, who are an ever-growing minority these days, may look at this option favourably.[8]

Regardless of whether phenomenal realism (and dualism, and panpsy-chism) is true, however, the rationale from the phenomenal reality of present-ness to the existence of an objective present is flawed. A *metaphysical antirealist* can point out that even if there are phenomenal facts about presentness, those cannot 'force' *objective* presentness onto the rest of the universe. One can admit that there are modes of presentation, or representational features that are correctly described by resorting to the notion of being felt as temporally privileged. But it would be incorrect to infer that given that our phenome-nal states are constituted by presentness *in this sense*, then they are *objectively* present. As the hypothesis that phenomenal facts are fully fledged denizens of the world does not entail that redness is an 'edenic' property of the stim-uli that impinge on our sense organs, it does not entail either that presentness extends from the realm of the phenomenal to that of the non-phenomenal.[9] Therefore, we should put this route to the metaphysical significance of the experiential present on a side. Besides, this route requires presentness to be either a content or a vehicle property, and I have given arguments against both characterizations (Section 4.2).

---

[7] Cf. '[For the idealist . . . t]he phrase, "time as it really is" is more suitably applied to the original phenomenologically manifest time than to the derivative time of the sciences' Smith (1988: 150). See Dolev (2007) for a book-length development of this methodological stance.

[8] Smith (1988) introduces the idea and applies it to his own view (1986). Here I enlarge it to other stances, such as dualism, panpsychism, and more generally anti-reductionism of the phenomenal sphere, e.g. Nagel (2012); Goff (2017).

[9] On 'edenic' properties, see Chalmers (2006).

Thirdly, someone may accept the rationale of the metaphysical antirealist with respect to the phenomenal realist but argue that metaphysical import of experience is indirect. More precisely, there is *abductive evidence* from the facts about the phenomenal prominence of the present to the existence of an objective present. That is, the best explanation of the prominence of the present in experience is that perception and awareness happen only at the metaphysically privileged time. If so, presentness is not *merely* an experienced feature, but also an objective feature of experience.[10] The change in what is objective present is also a change in what we are aware of. Our experience 'feels' dynamic because we are carried by the wave of time. Insofar as the wave model does not require construing presentness as a content or vehicle property, I take its viability to be a serious challenge to the metaphysical antirealist, and indirectly to my atomistic sunshine model. Notice that the atomist dynamic model is compatible with both the A-theory and the B-theory. But the wave model is incompatible with the B-theory, and the sunshine model is incompatible with the A-theory. In other words, it is not the A-theory per se that clashes with the explanation of the experience of the passage of time provided by the atomist dynamic model, but the explanation of the experience of passage in terms of the wave model. Dialectically, it is that explanation and not the A-theory that is my foil here.

6.2.2.1 Replying to the realist challenge: token-reflexivity

In line with the third strategy in favour of a metaphysical significance of the experiential present, a traditional tenet of the metaphysical realists about presentness is that the phenomenal prominence of presentness is *evidence* for the existence of an objective present. For the sake of the dialectics, let us bracket the negative results we reached with respect to the possibility of having a represented present in perception (Section 4.2), and see how a realist can argue. As far as I can tell, there is at least a version of the traditional argument that assumes the existence of a represented present in perception and can be reconstructed in two steps.

(1) The thesis that there is an objective present explains the existence of a represented present in perception.

(2) The thesis that there is a represented present in perception explains the existence of a narrative present.

---

[10] Notice that an analogous rationale can be adapted also to someone who denies that there is a represented present in perception but thinks that we need an objective present to explain the role that the represented present plays in our thoughts.

Since there undoubtedly is a narrative present, namely we have the conceptual resources to think of a moment as present in a temporal series (see Section 4.1.2.2), insofar as the explanations in (1) and (2) are good, there is abductive evidence for the existence of a represented present in perception and an objective present.

The traditional reply of the metaphysical antirealist is to question the explanations in both steps. Adolf Grünbaum well exemplifies this stance. His line of thought is as follows. No physical theory postulates a property of presentness. Therefore, we have no good reason to believe that there is an objective present, *but* for what common sense tells us. However, common sense is wrong about the mind-independence of presentness. For a time or event to be present is nothing over and above for it to be in the phenomenal present of some sentient being who is aware of the simultaneity relation between the perceived event and her own perception of it. In his words:

> What qualifies a physical event at a time *t* as belonging to the present or as now is not some physical attribute of the event or some relation it sustains to other purely physical events; instead what so qualifies the event is that at least one human or other mind-possessing organism *M* experiences the event at the time *t* such that at *t*, *M* is conceptually aware of the following complex fact: that his having the experience of the event coincides temporally with an awareness of the fact that he has it at all. (Grünbaum 1967: 16–17)

Grünbaum's point against (1) is that experiencing certain events as present is experiencing them as simultaneous with our awareness that we are perceiving them. No objective present hypothesis is required to explain this fact; the presentness of an event is merely its being in the right causal connection with a given mental episode. His point against (2) is that there is no need for a 'phenomenal oomph' in the mental content that originates the thought that what we are perceiving is present. Perception does not present us with things as present, we *think* of the things we are perceptually presented with as present. Crucially, *conceptual awareness* is not a form of perceptual awareness.

If this is the correct reading of Grünbaum, then he is defending a form of what I have called *presentness eliminativism* (Section 4.4), along with his metaphysical antirealism. Discussing Grünbaum's position about presentness, Ronald Hoy draws an analogy with colour antirealism:

> Just as common sense is wrong about the independent inherence of colours upon the surfaces of physical objects, so too it is wrong about the ontological independence of nowness. An object's having colour involves its ability

to stand in complicated relations with light and the perceptual equipment of sentient organisms. Similarly, for an event to become (for it to appear now) is for it to stand in whatever causal relation is necessary for it to be the object or content of a sentient organism's state of conceptual experience. (Hoy 1978: 271)

The analogy with colour antirealism is on the right track but does not go far enough. According to both a colour antirealist and a presentness eliminativist, the property that is attributed to external entities on the ground of our experience—being present and having a colour respectively—is mind-dependent in the relevant sense. Yet antirealists about colour do not usually maintain that there is no *what it is like* to see red or green, which is what Grünbaum denies by appealing to conceptual awareness rather than to *perceptual* awareness.[11]

By acknowledging that we have a commonsensical belief in the existence of a present moment, and yet maintaining that there is nothing in our perceptual phenomenology that suggests it, Grünbaum is giving us an example of an error theory strategy for our experience-based claims about presentness that is based on the hypothesis that the condition for attributing presentness to experiences and the entities we have experience of are *token-reflexive*.

Suppose at a certain time we have an experience *e* of hearing the loud squeak of Beep Beep, a hungry and demanding guinea pig. Under what condition can we correctly say that the squeak and our hearing it are present? Once we rule out that it depends on whether the time at which they happen is objectively present, the answer will necessarily involve the token experience *e* itself. Whether we can attribute presentness to something depends on what experience we are having. Each experience is present with respect to itself, and every event is present relative to a given experience just in case it is roughly simultaneous with the experience, as (usually) in the case of the moment experienced in the experience in question.

This token-reflexive theory of presentness attribution goes hand in hand with the combination of metaphysical antirealism and presentness eliminativism. It is important to stress that, as Callender and others rightly pointed

---

[11] Notice that I am not here making an assumption against cognitive phenomenology. The hypothesis that there is a what it is like to *think* of a moment as temporally privileged is compatible with presentness eliminativism. The point here is that there is no *perceptual phenomenology* of presentness such that it can ground the belief in a present moment. Cf. also the distinction that Chalmers makes between edenic concepts, towards which antirealism and eliminativism are justified, and functional concepts, for which some form of imperfect realism is usually acceptable (Chalmers 2021).

out, token-reflexivity is *not* meant to be an aspect of our phenomenology.[12] Who complains that 'we most decidedly do not experience events merely as tenselessly occurring simultaneously with some linguistic or psychological token nor on some given date at a given clocktime' (Craig 2000: 139) is barking up the wrong tree. What is token-reflexive is *not* the perceptual content, but the correctness conditions to *attribute* tensed descriptions through language or thought. The point is two-fold. From a metaphysical point of view, a correct attribution of presentness to an event requires a relation of simultaneity between the attribution and the experience or the event; no objective present is needed. From a phenomenal point of view, a correct attribution of presentness requires that what is deemed present is in the phenomenal present; no represented present in perception is needed (cf. Connor and Smith 2019). This second point is the key feature of presentness eliminativism.

If presentness eliminativism and the token-reflexive account of presentness attribution are on the right track, the phenomenal present is not felt as temporally privileged, and the experience-based claims that we make, thereby talking of events and experiences as happening in the present or now, are therefore indirect mischaracterizations of the phenomenal character of our own experiences.[13] One reason to take eliminativism as correct is that we cannot put ourselves *outside* the phenomenal present and contrast it with other moments—that is, the moments we experienced in the past and the one we will experience in the future. Even if there is, within the phenomenal present, a contrast between a present focus and the past tail of retention (and the future front of protension), there is no contrast between the present focus within the phenomenal present and something *outside* the phenomenal present (cf. also Section 4.1.2.1).

6.2.3 The temporal location problem

Another challenge that the wave model raises to the sunshine model is how to account for the fact that our experience seems to be always of a time at the exclusion of all others (Balashov 2005). The wave model has an obvious answer, or so it seems: it is because the presently occurring experiences are

---

[12] Cf. 'The token-reflexive account explains a correlation between a type of judgment, belief, or other propositional attitude about presentness and an experience, (it does not) account for or describe a psychological experience itself. But that was never (its) job!' (Callender 2017: 188).

[13] Remember that experience-based claims (Section 1.3) indirectly characterize the experience on which they are based, but they are not about those experiences. Hence, a 'now' claim can be true even if it mischaracterizes our experience.

the *only ones* we are having. It is not obvious how the sunshine model can account for that fact, since according to the model every experience enjoys the sunshine of consciousness, and thus the presently occurring experiences are not any different from the past and the future ones. In what follows I will defend a solution to this puzzle that I call the temporal location problem, and thus provide indirect support for the sunshine model.

6.2.3.1 Accessibility and availability

One feature of the phenomenal present that seems relevant for its alleged specialness is that the latter is the *only moment accessible* to our awareness. Even if the moment in the phenomenal present is not *felt* as privileged, it is still phenomenally prominent in its uniqueness, if compared to the moments in the past and in the future.[14] Imagine being all alone in a mansion that has a hundred rooms, all perfectly indistinguishable with respect to their interiors, and with closed windows. You walk along the corridor of one of the floors and decide to enter room 42. By assumption, there is nothing in room 42 that distinguishes it from the others, and yet it does phenomenally impose on you, since it is the *only* room that contains you and that you can explore. And it would be so even if the content of the rooms were different—different interiors and windows opened, say. What makes room 42 phenomenally prominent is not the peculiarity of its decor, but the fact that *you find yourself in it.*

If this analogy is on the right track, then eliminativism is compatible with the present being phenomenally prominent. Consider again the example of you hearing, out of the blue, a loud guinea pig squeak that captures all your attention. Perception does not present to us the squeak as present, but the phenomenal present that contains it is the *only* thing that is presented to us. And the same goes for non-perceptual cases; when we remember a certain past event, we are non-perceptually presented with it to the exclusion of what other past and future experiences (perceptions, memories, imaginations, etc.) did and will present to us. There are local accessibility constraints that make the occurrent phenomenal present phenomenally prominent. The fact that we can only access the moment(s) in the phenomenal present, and not those before and after, makes it that case that it imposes on us as the present. This seems to be what certain metaphysical antirealists with respect to presentness have in mind when they grant that 'presentness is an inextricable part of all sensory appearance' (Falk 2003: 221).

---

[14] Cf. '[. . .T]he present is experientially privileged in that we are only ever capable of experiencing that which occurs in the present' (Mozersky 2006: 442).

The idea that *local accessibility constraints* on experience bring about the phenomenal prominence (see Section 4.4.1) of the present requires some refinement, and again we need to take into account the metaphysical debate on the objective present. Let us begin with the case of perception, not because of its specificity, but for ease of exposition. Accessibility is definitely *not* a phenomenal property; we do not 'see' that what is presented in perception is accessible to us. Even less so we see that it is the *only thing* that is accessible to us. And yet phenomenal awareness comes with a *that's all* clause, as it were (cf. Sattig 2019a), which is what I have called synchronic fullness in Section 3.2.2. What can explain the accessibility constraints on perception? If we are focusing on the constraints on the accessibility of *what* gets presented to us in perception, an obvious candidate is causality.[15] Being available for perception means being in the *right* causal connection with a cognitive system capable of perception, something that only certain events in the temporal series are. When the system is 'active' (a conscious and attentive person, for instance), then certain mental content rather than others will be accessible to them. In other words, that there are local accessibility constraints on a cognitive system means that the *entire content* of a phenomenal present depends on the conscious mental episode we are considering and the events in its proximity.[16]

This causal construal of perceptual accessibility is particularly congenial to the metaphysical antirealist. It allows us to explain the phenomenal prominence of the present without assuming any metaphysical privilege of the present moment. The existence of local spatiotemporal constraint on the causal relations underpinning our conscious mental episodes is entirely kosher for the metaphysical antirealist. I think the core idea of the explanation is correct, but in this crude formulation there is a tenable objection that the metaphysical realist can rise. Causal considerations can explain why the content of a certain experience is thus and thus, rather than so and so, but it cannot explain why *this experience rather than a different one* (in the past or in the future) is the only one that is accessible to us, which is what is required to have the phenomenal prominence in question. The antirealist can rejoin that causality constraints do explain why through *this* perception I can only access the events located at a certain spatiotemporal distance from me. And that's all that we need to make sense of the phenomenal prominence of the

---

[15] Cf. Lepoidevin (2007: 86 ff.) and Grush (2005).
[16] Of course, in certain cases—as in looking at a distant star whose light has travelled in the vacuum of space for billions of years—what happens in the proximity of a cognitive system *informationally* depends on very distant events.

present. I doubt that the realist would be happy with this reply, though, since they still can insist that the fact that we can see and hear and smell and taste and feel only entities that are at the 'right' spatiotemporal distance is a fact that does not pertain to present mental events *more than* to past and future ones.

The realist counterproposal is that accessibility be construed as *availability*. This is a metaphysical heavyweight notion: objective presentness is what makes experiences available to perception.[17] Maybe this is the case because objective presentness is existence, and thus present experiences are perforce the only available to us, or maybe because the mental events that are objectively present are the only ones that can be conscious (cf. Correia and Rosenkranz 2018: 59–60). At any rate, the realist rationale is that we need this notion of availability to explain the phenomenal prominence of the present. Mere causal availability is of no use. Or so the realist claims.

6.2.3.2 The problem and its solution

A recent formulation of the temporal location problem[18] can be found in Balashov:

> [. . .] why am I finding myself at this particular time, with this particular set of experiences, to the exclusion of others, *rather than* at any of the numerous other times, with different experiences, to the exclusion of others [. . .]? (Balashov 2015: 64)

The metaphysical realist has a straightforward answer to this question. There are non-time-relative matters of facts concerning the present, and thus concerning what experiences are present among all the experiences that at one time or another I have. Therefore, I find myself having this particular experience *e* and not another *e'* (that I had or I will have), because *e* is the experience that I am having *simpliciter*, namely the only one available to me.

---

[17] 'Perception is the mode of awareness that relates to present events, whereas it is only possible to remember past events and to anticipate future events' (Smith 1985: 117).

[18] There are (at least) three related problems often discussed in the literature, and which I will not address here. The 'thank goodness that's over' problem (cf. Prior 1959): although I know that pain will be over after the visit to the dentist, I do not have an attitude of relief towards this fact while I am at the doctor's attention. The temporal knowledge problem (cf. Perry 2001): I know that the movie begins at 10:15, and that knowledge seems to exhaust all that one can know about the temporal location of the beginning of the movie. Yet when I look at my mobile and see that it's 10:00, I come to know a new fact about the beginning of the movie, namely that it is about to be present. And the 'how do we know that we are in the real present?' problem (cf. Braddon-Mitchell 2004): any theory that posits both more than one time and an objective present has problems in explaining how *we*, unlike Julius Caesar (say), know that we are in the objective present.

Antirealists *cannot* avail themselves of those non-time-relative facts. Given our limited accessibility to the events in the temporal series, they are in a position to explain why having experience *e* excludes having *e'*, but not to explain why they are having experience *e* rather than *e'*. If there is no objectively privileged present that can differentiate the mental events that happen at *t* (when *e* happens) from those that happen at *t'* (when *e'* happens), by making those happening at *t* the only available, it's difficult to see what could explain this experiential disparity.

Difficult, or better tricky, but not impossible. An antirealist has at least two kinds of rejoinder. The first is to stick to the general idea that when we talk or think of what happens, including talking or thinking of finding oneself at one time rather than another, we have to consider the time at which we make those assertions or entertain those thoughts. I find myself at time *t*, simply because *t* is the time at which I assert or think that I am finding myself at. In order to explain why it is this time *t* rather than another time, there is no need to introduce the metaphysically loaded idea of availability. The phenomenological prominence of the present is not its consequence of happening at some metaphysically privileged moment, and it is entirely due to our limited accessibility to the events in the temporal series. Each moment is prominent in this sense *relative to our experiencing it*, because our experience is *limited* to it; we do not experience anything more than it. If the realist insists that she wants to know what are the experiences that we have *simpliciter*, and not relative to a time, the answer is that all experiences that I had, am having, and will have at some time or other are experiences that I have *simpliciter*. The 'sensation' that I have that the present experience is the only one around does not force me to believe a metaphysics in which it is objectively present.

The second is to concede that the antirealist has an explanatory problem, but argue that it entirely depends on certain implicit *assumptions about personal identity through time* in the argumentation, and that by endorsing a different account of persistence she can give an answer that is based on the same key point of the realist's, namely that we experience *simpliciter* only certain experiences. Parsons (2015), Balashov (2015), and Skow (2015), writing in favour of an antirealist solution, maintain that the *endurantist* fares the worst. According to the endurantist, I (as anyone else) am wholly present at each moment of my existence, hence there is nothing in *me* that can distinguish my experiences of today from those of any other day. And, by assumption, there is nothing in the time at which my present experience is happening that can explain that either. Hence the explanatory *cul-de-sac*. Here again is Balashov:

I am wholly present at night, and am also wholly present during the day. This immediately *connects* me with my pain as well as my pleasure. My relations to both are equally robust. No metaphysically significant feature of my relation to my current pleasure is missing from my relation to my last night's pain. In that respect, my pain is ontologically on a par with my pleasure. But they are not on a par as far as my experience goes. I am enjoying the pleasure, but I am not having the pain. Why? (Balashov 2015: 62)

Contrariwise, a stage theorist maintains that I am a plurality of virtually instantaneous persons, each existing at a different time and, if conscious, having their own experiences *simpliciter*. The person who exists at *t* and has experiences *e* is not identical to the person who exists at *t'* and has experience *e'*, hence the problem of explaining why the first is not having the experience of the second (and *vice versa*) does not arise: the only experiences that the person who exists at *t* has *simpliciter* are *e* and not *e'*. The stage theorist has to revise our ordinary understanding of identity through time and soften it *à la* Parfit. I am *severally but not jointly* (that is, I am not them in the sense of being their sum) all those persons, and therefore for me to survive from *t* to *t'* it is enough that the person who exists at *t* bears the right type of connection with the person who exists at *t'*.[19]

Although the second rejoinder is worth considering and discussing, I think that the antirealist should insist on some version of the first one. This is *not* because endurantism is preferable as a theory of persistence. However, the second rejoinder seeks an account of the *phenomenology* of our experience by appealing to *metaphysical* claims that only apparently are explanatorily satisfactory. This is my rationale. Describing my experiences as occurring *simpliciter* undoubtedly captures something important about the way I experience the various moments of my life. The phenomenal present is a full house, it does not contain—but in the form of present memories and anticipations, past or future experiences.[20] As already noted, we are in some sense directly aware of this fact, as if the phenomenal present came with a 'that's all' clause, namely it has a phenomenology of synchronic fullness. However, it is doubtful that a metaphysical antirealist with respect to presentness can capture this

[19] Parsons (2015) and Balashov (2015) argue that the stage theorist has an advantage not only over the endurantist, but also the perdurantist. Skow (2015) seems to think that a perdurantist version of the view is viable. Prosser (2016: 31–2) disagrees with all of them, and defends a position closer to mine, according to which the perdurantist and the endurantist are not worse off than the stage theorist in accounting for the temporal location problem.

[20] Cf. 'Past and future things are not accessible except through present experience [...]' (Hoy 1978: 270).

phenomenological fact in terms of the thesis that, given her theory of personal persistence, a subject has experiences *simpliciter* in a more fundamental and direct way than having them at various times.

Firstly, the '*simpliciter*' of the realist and the '*simpliciter*' of the antirealist are different. According to the realist, the fact that a subject *S* experiences *simpliciter* depends on facts about the nature of time—the existence of an objective present and its 'effects' on subjects with experiential capacities. That is why if you consider earlier and later times you won't find any other subject (no matter how strictly related to *S*, indeed not even *S* herself as multilocated) having experiences *simpliciter* (you will find only subjects who had and will have experiences). Contrariwise, according to the antirealist, the fact that *S* experiences *simpliciter* depends on her being confined to *one* temporal location.[21] That is why if you consider earlier and later times, they may contain other subjects (possibly, some of them linked in the proper way to *S*, so that we can say that *S* has survived until that moment, or was already alive then) having experiences *simpliciter*.

Secondly, remember that the endurantist does *not* need to deny that I am having today's experiences *simpliciter*. Her main problem is rather to account for the fact that I mistakenly think that those are the *only* experiences that I am having *simpliciter*. But is providing an account of such a mistaken belief so difficult for her? Consider endurantism in its *locational* formulation. According to this theory, to persist through time is to be *exactly located* at different times (cf. Gilmore, Costa, and Calosi 2016). Therefore, I am temporally multilocated, and relative to different times I have different properties, among which experiential properties. As of each time I think that the experiences that I am having are the only ones that I have, but I am mistaken. Each of my temporal locations has certain locality constraints that explain why, even if I have several experiences *simpliciter*, they are not *unified* in a phenomenal present; I do not apprehend 'all at once' the experiences that I have at the various different temporal locations that I occupy.[22]

---

[21] Notice that the stage theorist here has a lot of dust under the carpet. Is this temporal location literally instantaneous? If so, it seems difficult that she can have experiences at all, given that it seems plausible to maintain that in order for a subject to have an experience, temporally extended neural processes must take place. If they are 'virtually' instantaneous, and thus have a short temporal extension after all, then how is temporal extension determined? By the amount of time required to have one coherent experience? Is this amount settled by fundamental metaphysical facts, or is it grounded on physical facts? To my knowledge no stage theorist has provided clarifications of those issues.

[22] I have argued more in detail about this point in Spolaore and Torrengo (2019: 9–12). Balashov (2015) protests that insisting on this relativization is based on accepting an unwarranted analogy with the modal case. I agree that we should distinguish carefully how an individual can be located at different points in the temporal dimension and how they can be located at different points of the 'modal dimension' (see Torrengo 2010). However, if we have to look for an analogy here, it should not be

Unlike the realist, the antirealist has no reason to think that *all* the things that we are presented with *simpliciter* are parts of a whole which we are presented with. There are local constraints that limit the content of my experience at a given time *regardless* of how I account for my persistence through time (and compatible with the thesis that there is no objective present). But then, what exactly would be the contribution of the thesis that I am *severally and not jointly* my stages to solving the temporal location problem? The fact that I lack evidence to think that I have, at other temporal locations, other temporal experiences does not mean that I have evidence that I do *not* have such experiences.[23] The existence of local constraints, which is independently motivated (and indeed, quite uncontroversial), *explains* why I do not have evidence of those other experiences.

This argument against the stage view solution can be replicated into a parallel one against the metaphysical realist solution. This is not surprising, since, as I have already pointed out, both the realist and the stage theorist crucially appeal to having experiences *simpliciter* to solve it. However, dialectically the two parallel arguments play a different role. While the stage theorist and the endurantist share, as metaphysical antirealists with respect to presentness, an explanation of the phenomenological prominence of the present based on the local accessibility constraints and part company on how to solve the temporal location problem, the realist aims at solving the temporal location problem *through* her construal of the phenomenal prominence as metaphysical privilege. But her stone misses, rather than hits, two birds, since her explanation is bad in both cases. The fact that I have no experiential evidence of my past and future experiences does not support that I have no past and future experiences *simpliciter*, since past and future experiences are *not accessible* to me from the temporal location that we are considering. I am not claiming that therefore it is impossible for us to come to know which metaphysical hypothesis is true. There may be very indirect reasons to abductively prefer one hypothesis over the others. However, providing a better explanation of the alleged presentness of our experience *cannot* be one of those.

---

the modal case, but rather the multi-location of a subject in a multiverse. If we are so located *in the actual world*, then even 'synchronically' we are mistaken about how many experiences we are having *simpliciter*. Cf. also Skow (2015).

[23] If you are not convinced, think of a spatial analogue. Sometimes lack of evidence *is* evidence of a lack. If I am walking down the Rambla in Barcelona, my lack of evidence that it is raining in Barcelona is evidence that there is no rain in Barcelona now. However, my lack of evidence that it is not raining in Hobart in this moment (assume I don't have a mobile with me, and I am walking in Barcelona), it is *not* evidence for a sunny day in Hobart. Local constraints are 'evidence defeaters' (Section 1.4) both in the spatial and in the temporal case. See also Spolaore and Torrengo (2019).

Finally, the first strategy prevents the antirealist also against a more general objection that both the realist and the stage theorists can raise. The idea is that temporally extended wholes, or four-dimensional worms as they are sometimes called, are not the right bearer of the *kind* of experience that we have.[24] Whatever is to have an experience that is spread across time for a whole stream of consciousness is not to have the experiences that human subjects have. This objection to the perdurantism equivocates on the notion of having experience. It is true that the way a worm has experience is not the way we have experience, and this is surprising since we are the worm. But the worm, as us, has *this* or *that* experience only relative to temporal positions. The type of temporally localized experience that the worm has is the familiar type of experience that we ordinarily have. The fact that the type of experience of the whole worm is alien to us (as it is to the worm, unsurprisingly, since we are the worm) is just a consequence of the local constraints. The experience of the worm as a whole is not accessible to the worm. Think of a non-experiential case. A table displays an inlay of longitudinal stripes, alternating black and white ones. Being striped is a property that the whole table has, but that the single parts of the inlay lacks, and being white or black all over is a property that only the parts have but not the table as a whole. If there are local constraints, having an experience of the ordinary type is more like being white or black all over, rather than being striped. But this should not be something that counts against identifying us with the worm, rather than its parts. After all, the table *is* black or white all over relative to its parts, and indeed being striped as a whole just is being black or white relative to its parts. The fact that as a whole a four-dimensional worm has an alien type of experience should not worry us (namely, the worm), since that experience is not accessible to us. Only the experiences of the ordinary type are accessible to us, relative to their temporal positions.

To sum up Section 6.2, I have first argued that there is no abductive evidence in favour of an objective present to which our experience is reactive and that can be used to explain an experience of the passage of time. Second, I withstood the location problem. Why I have *this* experience *rather than* a past or a future one is not a question that has an answer if we do not specify the moment that we are considering, and once we have, the answer is trivial. And why I have this experience *at the exclusion* of all others is something that is explained by the existence of local accessibility constraints. The wave model is explanatorily vacuous because it cannot resort to an objective present that plays the roles

---

[24] Cf. Parsons (2015: 238); Goff (2017: 269); Tullio (*ms*).

required by the theory and thus the purported explanation cannot get off the ground.[25]

6.3 The sunshine model

Philosophers who take the wave model as more intuitive and closer to common sense often point at the Special Theory of Relativity as the turning point in history where the idea of an objective present and the flow of time as an absolute becoming began losing their attractiveness.[26] I do not know how accurate those historical insights are. However, it is true that already in the early decades of the twentieth century certain scholars familiar with the idea of a relativistic universe note not only that relativity suggests a radically new understanding of temporal reality, but also that it forces us towards a radically new understanding of temporal experience.

For instance, in a famous passage, Arthur Eddington writes: 'Events do not happen; they are just there and we come across them. "The formality of taking place" is merely the indication that the observer has on his voyage of exploration passed into the absolute future of the event in question; and it has no important significance. We can be aware of an eclipse in the year 1999, very much as we are aware of an unseen companion to Algol. Our knowledge of things *where* we are not, and of things *when* we are not, is essentially the same—an inference (sometimes a mistaken inference) from brain impressions, including memory, *here* and *now*' (Eddington 1920: 46).

In this passage Eddington is more worried about establishing the determinacy of each event in space-time, and thus dismissing the idea of an open future as opposed to a fixed past, but in so doing he inevitably raises the question of how we can square the fact that we seem to be aware of the unfolding of our experience with the fact that our life is a collection of mental events along a time-like curve. However, the only thing that Eddington tells us is that the observer's situation 'has no important significance'. But this is puzzling since, from an experiential point of view, it is hardly without significance that our life appears to constantly 'pass into the future' of what we are experiencing.[27]

---

[25] In Cassaghi and Torrengo (2021) we argue against the A-theoretic interpretation of the update view (see Section 5.4.1). A consequence of those results is that even if we could track the present in some sense, we would not have a good explanation of our experience of passage.

[26] A typical example is Bigelow (1996).

[27] Eddington (1927 [1948]) will say something more, by defending a theory of introspection as capable of revealing the true nature of time somehow directly. Cf. 'Our knowledge of space-relations is indirect, like nearly all our knowledge of the external world—a matter of inference and interpretation

Hermann Weyl seems to be more aware of the puzzle, when he writes: 'The objective world simply is, it does not happen. Only to the gaze of my consciousness, crawling upwards along the lifeline of my body, does a section of this world come to life as a fleeting image in space which continuously changes in time' (Weyl 1949). Weyl draws a clear contrast here: there is something off between experiencing life as in constant flux, and reality not containing any such flux. Suggestive as Weyl's words can be, he does not tell us what the truth behind the 'coming to life' metaphor is, and how the 'image' in question can be 'fleeting' at all, since it is presumably part of the objective world, and thus simply is, rather than happens.[28]

What such quotes and similar ones teach us is that if one takes seriously the idea of the block universe, when speaking strictly and philosophically, they should not say that they are having now an experience—looking at a peony while hearing a viola playing in the distance, say—but rather that there is (*simpliciter*, one may want to add, to stress the lack of temporal viewpoint) an experience of theirs somewhere in space-time. This may be easier to say than to do, though. As we all know, we experience our outer and inner worlds always from a particular temporal (and personal) perspective. And even if, as I have argued, the view-pointedness of experience as a whole comes from our narrative thoughts rather than from perception, we are dramatically aware that our position in time proceeds inexorably towards the future. So even when we say that at coordinate such and such in space-time there is an experience of ours concerning a peony and a distant melody, we say it when we are having a certain experience (possibly the very same one), and thus from the temporal perspective that we happen to inhabit when we say it or think it. We can act as if this fact is not 'of important significance', for instance because we firmly believe that it does not reflect how reality is, but with that we have not yet explained it. Which is what we should do, among other things, if we aim at providing an account of temporal experience.

of the impressions which reach us through our sense-organs. We have similar indirect knowledge of the time-relations existing between the events in the world outside us; but in addition, we have direct experience of the time-relations that we ourselves are traversing—a knowledge of time not coming through external sense-organs but taking a short cut into our consciousness. [...] That is why time seems to us so much more mysterious than space. We know nothing about the intrinsic nature of space, and so it is quite easy to conceive it satisfactorily. We have intimate acquaintance with the nature of time and so it baffles our comprehension. It is the same paradox which makes us believe we understand the nature of an ordinary table whereas the nature of human personality is altogether mysterious' (1927 [1948]: 25–6). An early (and sharp) criticism of Eddington's semi-mystic conception of temporal experience is in Susan Stebbing (1937).

[28] Already in *Raum-Zeit-Materie* (1919: 5), Weyl discusses the difference between how we experience time and how experiences themselves are located in space-time as something 'obscure and perplexing to our minds'. See De Bianchi (2020: 188–9) for an illuminating discussion.

Notice that the issue here is not the (false) claim that in the block there is no change. No B-theorist wants to deny that there is qualitative variation across the temporal dimension, and thus change (cf. Rovelli 2018). The issue is that, as existentialist philosophers noted on various occasions, we *know* in some very intimate and deep sense that we cannot avoid being 'thrown' in time, and thus having a shifting temporal viewpoint.[29] It is not something that we learn from theorizing (as we know that the peony is a genus of flowers), and it is not something that we know on the ground of what we perceive, in some immediate and automatic manner (as we know that the thing over there is of a certain dark shade of pink). Empirical information of any sort seems to be irrelevant to this knowledge. If that is right, what does it mean then to take seriously the idea that the 'perspective from nowhen', as Huw Price (1996) puts it, is the fundamental one, the only perspective there is, and we should thus discard the embedded perspectives as deceitful?

If we keep both our intimate belief that we experience always from the point of view of the now, and our theoretical belief that there is no such thing as the point of view of the now, we end up embracing a contradiction. Of course, one may stress that there is nothing contradictory in believing that reality is in a certain way, but it appears to us in another. Galileo was not advocating for dialetheism[30] when arguing that bodies always appear to us as coloured even though they only have primary properties. The fact that they appear coloured does not entail that they are coloured, and indeed, given that they merely appear coloured, they are not coloured. But temporal properties are peculiar. Time appears to be both inside us and outside us. It is not just events around us but also our experiences that appear to inhabit the temporal dimension. Therefore, it is more difficult to make Galileo's manoeuvre in the temporal case. The question is thus whether there can be a dynamic mode of experience without experience being itself dynamic.

I hope that it is clear from what I have argued for in the previous chapter that appearances can be dynamic even if there is nothing dynamic in their bearers. However, I do not deny that understanding what it is for beings like us to exist in a block universe while experiencing a dynamic time requires some effort. It requires us to go beyond the suggestive images of Eddington and Weyl. And if we go all the way down that rabbit hole, we end up with a view that has

---

[29] See also Chappell (2022: Chap. 4) for an interesting reflection on the temporal nature of our experience.

[30] The position in philosophy of logic according to which there are *dialetheias*, namely propositions that are both true and false, which often takes the form of a theory admitting true contradictions. Cf. Priest (2006).

something mystical to it. But if such a view has some shot at being the truth, so be it. In the rest of this final chapter, I will say something more about it.

6.3.1 Illusion, error, and projection

It should be clear from what I have argued in Chapter 5 that it would be a mistake to consider our experience of temporal passage in a block universe as a perceptual illusion. There is nothing that we misperceive or systematically fail to track when it comes to temporal aspects of the world. We can, of course, be subject to many illusions with respect to temporal features, as we can with respect to spatial ones, and to colours, temperatures, and so on. But experiencing passage and being aware of the succession of our own experiences is not having a non-veridical perceptual experience, even if there is no passage or objective flow. Rather, the mistake we make is cognitive. We believe that time passes, or at least that there is a constant renewal of our experiences, when there is only a world-line of conscious mental events, a tenseless sunshine of consciousness along a succession of mental events. And, if I am right, we believe that time passes because there is something in our phenomenology that strongly suggests that it is so.

In accordance with recent results in experimental philosophy, I do not think that the Priorian belief in an absolute movement of the objective present is constitutive of experience.[31] However, I am inclined to think that a metaphysical lightweight belief in the renovation of our own experience is inextricably connected to the way we experience our life, and it reflects a deep aspect of our phenomenology. More precisely, it reflects that the overarching phenomenology that makes us aware of our experiences being in succession is inherently progressive and dynamic. This is the fundamental way our temporal experience is. Even when we are not attentive, or we are mind-wandering, or meditating, we can always postdictively reconstruct what we were experiencing as having occurred along with an awareness of time passing.

But what does it mean that we are aware of time passing, if it does not mean that we have an experience that prompts us to embrace the Priorian belief in an objective flow? Here the notions of direct and indirect projection come in handy (cf. Section 1.5). Perhaps if one holds the Priorian belief in the passage of time, what happens is that they directly project the phenomenal modifier on the events accessible to them through perception. They interpret the awareness

---

[31] Cf. Section 5.5. See also Balcells (2019) and Everett et al. (2023).

that there is something dynamic connecting our experiences in succession as an experience presenting us with a feature of the world, namely the inherent dynamicity of the events that we see, feel, smell, and touch. And if the sunshine model is correct, the succession of our experience is just another series of physical events along a time-like curve among others, and thus there is nothing objectively dynamic about it either. However, direct projection may not be the most natural way to understand the cognitive error at stake here. The way our awareness happens, with overarching phenomenology of dynamically modified feelings, primarily suggests that our experiences are inherently dynamic. And if the sunshine model is correct, *that is a mistake no less than believing in a Priorian universe.* It may be then that, if we believe that time objectively passes, or *if it seems to us that our experience suggests so*, this is so because of an indirect projection of our feeling of time passing onto the word. That is, we first interpret the phenomenal modifier phenomenology as telling us that our experiences succeed one after the other in an inexorable way. And then in order to make sense of what we believe about our experience, we implicitly infer that the world is equally dynamic—the underlying rationale being that our experience is dynamic simply because it is part of a dynamic world.

In a sense, we are directly projecting dynamicity on our own experience, and then indirectly projecting on the world in which our experience happens. If not everybody has the Priorian belief, then perhaps not everybody makes the implicit abductive inference, or they resist it upon reflection on the ground of what they know from physics, or meditation, or some other source. Although it is curious to think that we can project a feature of our experience on our own experience, thereby making a cognitive mistake, it is not something surprising if we think of the feature in question. The phenomenal modifier is an aspect of experience that makes us aware of the connection between our experiences. By directly projecting such a feature on the succession of our experience we interpret the way we are aware of their succession as a way the succession is. But what makes us aware of the succession of experiences is a feature of individual experiences, and not of the succession itself. More precisely, it is the way the experience we are presently having makes us aware of being connected to others. Therefore, if the sunshine model is correct, it is a mistake to project it onto the succession of experience, even if we restrain to (indirectly or directly) projecting it on the external world. Here is the quasi-mystical aspect of the view: only if we are aware that not even our own experiences are in flux, specifically that the experience that I have now does not come from a previous one and it is not going to be substituted by a new one, do we correctly understand the connection between experience and reality. Only when we emancipate thought, and not just reality from the past and the future, the difficulty is solved, and we do not succumb to an obstinate mistake.

Consider the following analogy concerning three pictures in a sequence. In picture (a) you see a frog about to leap. In picture (b) the frog is mid-air while leaping, and in (c) it is landing after the leap. There are certain intrinsic features of picture (b), the positions of the legs, the tension of the muscles, which suggest that the sequence represents a frog leap. Therefore, picture (b) suggests something about the whole sequence, but it would be a mistake to attribute whatever features (b) is responsible for to the whole sequence. Analogously, just because each experience has a phenomenology that suggests that experience is constantly renovating, we should not conclude that the succession of experiences we are going through *is* constantly renovating. According to the sunshine model, it is a succession of events in space-time as the ones that do not involve consciousness. We are hardwired to react to our modified overarching phenomenology each time it is in the focus of our attention with the thought that the experience that we are having comes from an old one and is going to give way to a new one, namely with the metaphysically lightweight belief in the passage of time. But reality is not how this reaction suggests. This is, in a way, disturbing. There is no difference, not even in consciousness, between the first and the last moment of our life, and all those in the middle. At every moment, we have the impression that our experience is in the process of renovating, but that impression is misleading. Not one of my experiences is renovating, each is located in its location in the sequence, and each 'thinks' that it is the last arrived and is about to be substituted by the next. But they are all wrong.

Finally, I want to briefly explore an alternative route to the connection between the belief in the passage of time and the phenomenal modification. We are aware of the succession of our own experiences in a way that generates the belief in the constant renewal of experience. We do not track such a renewal as we arguably track colours and movements, because there is, literally, nothing to track in this case, if the metaphysics of the sunshine model is correct. Although I take the mechanism that generates the belief as simply a matter of hardwiring, I have also insisted that the phenomenology of the passage of time is cogent. When we talk of time passing, we describe indirectly our experience in a cogent way, it is not merely a matter of interpretation. However, one may wonder why the phenomenology and the belief are so related, given that according to my theory the belief is hardwired into the phenomenology, rather than the phenomenology providing rational justification for the belief, as in ordinary cases of tracking (e.g. the phenomenology of my visual experience provides me with a rational justification to believe that there is a pink peony in front of me). We cannot exclude that we are hardwired to form the belief independently of any phenomenology, and as a consequence of entertaining such a belief, we tend to describe our phenomenology as suggesting that time passes. In other terms, if the metaphysically lightweight belief is so central to the structure of our experience, we cannot exclude that the phenomenal modification in question may be an effect of such a constitutive belief.

Perhaps the narrative thoughts that allow us to think about the temporal distribution of the events that constitute our lives have a role that somehow percolates into the phenomenology of the passage of time. This may sound as yielding to the deflationist model of the experience of passage and embracing a position similar in spirit to misdescriptivism or inferentialism. But that is not true. According to sophisticated deflationism, the belief in the passage of time has not a structural origin, it is a consequence of certain conceptual elements embedded in our language, which in turn are there for evolutionistic reasons. According to this alternative take on the sunshine model, the belief is part of the structure of our experience; it comes from the narrative thoughts that constitute the skeleton of our temporal cognition. And because the belief in the passage of time is so central to an important aspect of our cognitive life, it is reflected in an aspect of our phenomenology.

6.3.2 Timelessness

Briefly before concluding, I want to add a few words on the possibility that the metaphysics in the background of the sunshine model is even more sparse than that of the block universe. According to certain models of quantum gravity, fundamental reality is genuinely timeless. Our world has no temporal structure at all, not even as an emergent or derivative phenomenon. At a low-energy regimen, as the one in which our lives are located, reality approximates a spatiotemporally ordered reality, but spatiotemporal relations never obtain in reality, not even at a low-energy regimen, and not even at that regimen spacetime somehow emerges. Sam Baron, Kristie Miller, and Johnathan Tallant, in an exciting book (Baron et al. 2022), have argued that, as long as we can talk of locations, we can make sense of our rational agency even if the locations of our actions and experiences are not spatiotemporal at all. Roughly, their idea is that agentive thoughts require belief in some sort of temporal structure in the world. Therefore, if we were to discover that there is no such structure in reality, we should endorse a fictionalist stance, and make believe that the world is temporal, even if we know it is not.

With respect to the beliefs and narrative thoughts involved in temporal experience according to my atomist dynamic model of temporal experience, I suppose that, if indeed our best physic tells us that there is no temporal structure after all, and if such thoughts and beliefs play a certain role in our ordinary interaction with the world, a fictionalist attitude would be the natural option as well. However, one may wonder whether the explanation of temporal experience that I have given is compatible with a background metaphysics in which there are no temporal locations and relations. My atomist model requires experiences to be physical processes, and thus to be virtually instantaneous rather than genuinely unextended. There is a tension between the assumption that experiences have temporal structure, and the claim that there is no temporality. However, as long as physical processes are compatible at all with the quantum gravity timeless reality (cf. Huggett and Wüthrich 2013), this is not a problem for the model as such. Molecular models as well are in tension with the fundamental lack of temporal structure of reality. They may resist the charge of incompatibility by saying that the approximation that we reach at a low-energy regimen is all we need to have experiences structured in the appropriate ways. Analogously, the atomist model can appeal to the same approximations to say that the timeless reality makes room for experiences as processes.

However, note that according to molecularism, it is somehow the structure of experience itself that is illusory, in the sense that it *appears* as it is not, namely temporally structured. According to my model, our temporal position does not appear as temporal, or as temporally extended, and thus at least certain aspects of our temporal phenomenology are not illusory, even if we live in the timeless world. True, we have a phenomenology that is hardwired to a belief that is erroneous, not only in projecting temporal passage, but also in picturing a temporally structured reality. Yet, it is only at the level of cognition that we misrepresent reality. The awareness of succession and feeling of passage as such are misleading only insofar as they are indirectly projected outside, or directly inside, but they do not require a temporal structure themselves. Therefore, *as appearances* they do not require something that is ruled out in the timeless universe. The same goes for our perception of change and motion and the expectations with respect to the past and the future that the phenomenology of dynamic state properties triggers.

One last point: according to the atomist dynamic model, we are reactive to temporally extended stimuli. But in a timeless universe, that there are such temporally structured stimuli is simply false. Is it a problem? I am not sure. First, if it is, it is a very general problem of any account of temporal experience, since it is hard to deny that the seemingly temporal structure of the stimulus is sometimes relevant for our experiences. Second, our lives happen in locations at a low-energy regimen, therefore the stimuli around us can approximate spatiotemporal structures. It turns out thus that what we are reactive to is an approximation of that kind. Again, the atomist dynamic model predicts an error at the cognitive level, rather than in our phenomenology, since it is not the case that the stimulus appears as temporally structured. Rather, what is presented to us in a temporally unstructured experience creates certain deeply mistaken expectations, which entail that there is a temporal structure in the world, and that our experiences, as denizens of the world, are also so temporally structured.

6.4 Conclusions

If we look back at our past, we may wonder where the years we have lived so far are. The skull in the folk song of the epigraph at the beginning of this chapter says, 'they are gone, but I do not know where'. This may be just a rhetorical way to say that one regrets not having used one's time in a better way, or that time has passed too quickly. But regret has meaning only if the past is unable to give us opportunities, if it is gone for good. According to the wave model, the past is gone because only the present can give us opportunities, if the future complies. The past is radically different from the present, and there is not a thing that we can do about it. According to the sunshine model, the past is gone because every temporal location has its past and is the past of some other. The past is not radically different from the present, and yet it is gone for good, because like the future it is not, and cannot be, where we are. So, even if the past is gone, the past years have not gone anywhere. This is a consequence of taking both the block universe and our temporal phenomenology seriously. It is not just the conscious subject that is misled by appearances; it is the very way a conscious subject is located in time and how time appears at each temporal location that misleads every version of us, past, present, and future.

Bibliography

Almäng, J. (2014) 'Tense as feature of perceptual content', *Journal of Philosophy*, 7: 361–78

Alwishah, A. (2013) 'Ibn Sīnā on Floating Man arguments', *Journal of Islamic Philosophy*, 9: 49–71

Ansorge, U., Klotz, W., and Neumann, O. (1998) 'Manual and verbal responses to completely masked (unreportable) stimuli: Exploring some conditions for the metaconstrast dissociation', *Perception*, 27: 1177–89

Arstila, V. (2012) 'Time slows down during accidents', *Frontiers in Psychology*, 3: 196

Arstila, V. (2015a) 'Keeping postdiction simple', *Consciousness and Cognition*, 38: 205–16

Arstila, V. (2015b) 'Defense of the brain time view', *Frontiers in Psychology*, 6, Article 1350 (https://doi.org/10.3389/fpsyg.2015.01350)

Arstila, V. (2015c) 'Theories of apparent motion', *Phenom Cogn Sci*, 15(3): 337–58 (DOI 10.1007/s11097-015-9418-y)

Arstila, V. (2018) 'Temporal experience without the specious present', *Australasian Journal of Philosophy*, 96(2): 287–302

Arstila, V. and Lloyd, D. (2014) *Subjective Time: The Philosophy, Psychology, and Neuroscience of Temporality*. Cambridge, MA, MIT Press Ltd

Bach, K. (1997) 'Engineering the mind: Review of naturalizing the mind by Fred Dretske', *Philosophy and Phenomenological Research*, 57(2): 459–68

Balashov, Y. (2005) 'Times of our lives: Negotiating the presence of experience', *American Philosophical Quarterly*, 42: 295–309

Balashov, Y. (2015) 'Experiencing the present', *Epistemology and Philosophy of Science*, 54(2): 61–73

Balcells, M. (2019) 'The dynamic block universe and the illusion of passage', in A. Bardon, V. Arstila, S. E. Power, and A. Vatakis (eds.), *The Illusions of Time: Philosophical and Psychological Essays on Timing and Time Perception*, London, Palgrave Macmillan: 35–52

Bardon, A. (2023) 'The passage of time is not an illusion: It's a projection', *Philosophy*, 98(4): 485–506

Baron, S. (2017) 'Feel the flow', *Synthese*, 194(2): 609–30

Baron, S., Miller, K., and Tallant, J. (2022) *Out of Time: A Philosophical Study of Timelessness*. Oxford, OUP

Bayne, T. (2010) *The Unity of Consciousness*. Oxford, OUP

Bayne, T. and Montague, M. (eds.) (2011) *Cognitive Phenomenology*. Oxford, OUP

Benovsky, J. (2013) 'From experience to metaphysics: On experience-based intuitions and their role in metaphysics', *Noûs*, 49(3): 684–97

Bergson, H. (1889 [2003]) *Time and Free Will: An Essay on the Immediate Data of Consciousness*. London, Routledge

Bigelow, J. (1996) 'Presentism and Properties', *Philosophical Perspectives*, 10: 35–52

Blackmore, S. (2002) 'There is no stream of consciousness', *Journal of Consciousness Studies*, 9: 17–28

Block, N. (2003) 'Mental paint', in M. Hahn and B. Ramberg (eds.), *Reflections and Replies: Essays on the Philosophy of Tyler Burge*, Cambridge, MA, MIT Press: 165–200

Boghossian, P. A. and Velleman, J. D. (1989) 'Color as a secondary quality', *Mind*, 98: 81–103

Boroditsky, L. (2000) 'Metaphoric structuring: Understanding time through spatial metaphors', *Cognition*, 75(1): 1–128

Bourne, C. (2005) *A Future for Presentism*. Oxford, OUP

Braddon-Mitchell, D. (2004) 'How do we know it is now now?', *Analysis*, 64(3): 199–203

Braddon-Mitchell, D. (2013) 'Against the illusion theory of temporal phenomenology', *CAPE International Workshops, 2013. Part II: The CAPE International Conference 'A Frontier of Philosophy of Time.'*

Brogaard, B. (2000) 'Presentist four-dimensionalism', *The Monist*, 83: 341–54

Burge, T. (2010) *Origins of Objectivity*. Oxford, OUP

Butterfield, J. (1984) 'Seeing the present', *Mind*, 93: 161–76

Byrne, A. (2001) 'Intentionalism defended', *Philosophical Review*, 110: 199–240

Byrne, A. (2009) 'Experience and content', *The Philosophical Quarterly*, 59(236): 429–51

Callender, C. (2008) 'The common now', *Philosophical Issues*, 18(1): 339–61

Callender, C. (2017) *What Makes Time Special?* Oxford, OUP

Cameron, R. (2015) *The Moving Spotlight: An Essay on Time and Ontology*. Oxford, OUP

Campbell, J. (1994) *Past, Space and Self*. Cambridge, MA, MIT Press

Cappelen, H. and Dever, J. (2014) *The Inessential Indexical: On the Philosophical Insignificance of Perspective and the First Person*. Oxford, OUP

Carson, D. M. (1999) 'Temporal distortions and the ejection decision', *Flying Safety*, 55(6): 4–7

Casati, R. (2000) *La Scoperta Dell'Ombra*. Milan, Mondadori (Eng. Trans. 2003, *The Shadow Club*, NY, Knopf)

Casati, R. and Torrengo, G. (2011) 'The not so incredible shrinking future', *Analysis*, 71(2): 240–4

Castañeda, H. (1967) 'Indicators and quasi-indicators', *American Philosophical Quarterly*, 4(2): 85–100

Chalmers, D. (2006) 'Perception and the fall from Eden', in T. S. Gendler and J. Hawthorne (eds.), *Perceptual Experience*, Oxford, OUP: 165–96

Chalmers, D. (2015) *Constructing the World*. Oxford, OUP

Chalmers, D. (2021) 'Finding space in a nonspatial world', in B. Le Baptiste, N. Huggett, and C. Wüthrich (eds.), *Philosophy beyond Spacetime*, Oxford, OUP: 165–96

Chappell, S. G. (2022) *Epiphanies: An Ethics of Experience*. Oxford, OUP

Chess, S., Fieste, M. P., and Eagleman, D. M. (2007) 'Does time really slow down during a frightening event?', *PLoS ONE*, ii, 12: e1295, doi: 10.1371/journal. Pone.0001295

Chuard, P. (2011) 'Temporal experiences and their parts', *Philosophers' Imprint*, 11(11)

Chuard, P. (2017) 'The snapshot conception of temporal experiences', in I. Phillips (ed.), *Routledge Handbook of Philosophy of Temporal Experience*, London, Routledge: 121–32

Comrie, B. (1985) *Tense*. Cambridge, Cambridge University Press

Connor, A. and Smith, J. (2019) 'The perceptual present', *The Philosophical Quarterly*, 69(277): 817–37

Correia, F. and Rosenkranz, S. (2018) *Nothing to Come: A Defence of the Growing Block of Time*. New York, Springer

Costa de Beauregard, O. (1981) 'Time in relativity theory: Arguments for a philosophy of being', in J. T. Fraser (ed.), *The Voices of Time*, second edition, Amherst, MA, The University of Massachusetts Press, 417–33

Craig, W. L. (2000) *The Tensed Theory of Time: A Critical Examination*. Dordrecht, Kluwer Academic Publishers

Crane, T. (1988) 'The waterfall illusion', *Analysis*, 48(3): 142–7

Crane, T. (2009) 'Intentionalism', in Ansgar Beckermann, Brian P. McLaughlin, and Sven Walter (eds.), *The Oxford Handbook of Philosophy of Mind*, Oxford, OUP: 474–93

Crowther, T. and Soteriou, M. (2017) 'Time in dreams', in I. Phillips (ed.), *Routledge Handbook of Philosophy of Temporal Experience*, London, Routledge: 184–200

Dainton, B. (2000) *Stream of Consciousness: Unity and Continuity in Conscious Experience*. London, Routledge

Dainton, B. (2008a) 'The experience of time and change', *Philosophy Compass*, 3(4): 619–38

Dainton, B. (2008b) 'Sensing change', *Philosophical Issues*, 18, Interdisciplinary Core Philosophy: 362–84 [non-modal/modal ret.]

Dainton, B. (2014) 'The phenomenal continuum', in Valtteri Arstila (ed.), *Subjective Time: The Philosophy, Psychology and Neuroscience of Temporality*, Cambridge, MA, MIT Press: 101–38

Deasy, D. (2015) 'The moving spotlight theory', *Philosophical Studies*, 172(8): 2073–89

De Bianchi, S. (2020) 'Weyl's Raum-Zeit-Materie and the philosophy of science', in S. De Bianchi and C. Kiefer (eds.), *One Hundred Years of Gauge Theory*, Fundamental Theories of Physics Book Series, Volume 199, New York, Springer: 185–96

Debord, G. (1967) *La société du spectacle*. Paris, Buchet-Chastel

Debus, D. (2007) 'Being emotional about the past: On the nature and role of past-directed emotions', *Noûs*, 14(4): 758–79

Deng, N. (2013) 'Fine's McTaggart, temporal passage, and the A versus B-debate', *Ratio*, 26(1): 19–34. doi: 10.1111/j.1467-9329.2012.00526.x

Deng, N. (2019) 'One thing after another: Why the passage of time is not an illusion', in Adrian Bardon, Valtteri Arstila, Sean Power, and Argiro Vatakis (eds.), *The Illusions of Time: Philosophical and Psychological Essays on Timing and Time Perception*, London, Palgrave Macmillan: 3–16

Dennett, D. (1991) *Consciousness Explained*. New York, Back Bay Books

Dennett, D. and Kinsbourne, M. (1992) 'Time and the observer: The where and when of consciousness in the brain', *Behavioral and Brain Sciences*, 15(2): 183–201

Dolev, Y. (2007) *Time and Realism: Metaphysical and Antimetaphysical Perspectives*, Cambridge, MA, MIT Press

Dretske, F. (1995) *Naturalizing the Mind*. Cambridge, MA, Bradford Books

Dretske, F. (2003) 'Experience as representation', *Philosophical Issues*, 13: 67–82

Droit-Volet, S., Bigand, E., Ramos, D., and Bueno, J. L. O. (2010) 'Time flies with music whatever its emotional valence', *Acta Psychologica*, 135(2): 226–32

Droit-Volet, S. (2019) 'The temporal dynamic of emotion effects on judgment of durations', in A. Bardon, V. Arstila, S. E. Power, and A. Vatakis (eds.), *The Illusions of Time: Philosophical and Psychological Essays on Timing and Time Perception*, London, Palgrave Macmillan: 103–26

Dummett, M. (1969) 'The reality of the past', *Proceedings of the Aristotelian Society*, 69: 139–58

Durgin, F. H. and Sternberg, S. (2002) 'The time of consciousness and vice versa', *Consciousness and Cognition*, 11: 284–90

Dyke, H. (2013) 'Time and tense', in H. Dyke and A. Bardon (eds.), *A Companion to the Philosophy of Time*, Oxford, Blackwell: 328–44

Eagleman, D. M. and Sejnowski, T. J. (2000) 'Motion integration and postdiction in visual awareness', *Science*, 287(5460): 2036–8. doi: 10.1126/science.287.5460.2036

Eddington, A. S. (1920) *Space, Time and Gravitation. An Outline of the General Relativity Theory*, Cambridge, Cambridge University Press

Eddington, A. S. (1927 [1948]) *The Nature of the Physical World: Gifford Lectures*. Cambridge, Cambridge University Press

Eker, B. (2023) 'Perspectivalism about temporal reality', *Synthese*, 202(2): 1–29 (online first)

Evans, G. (1982) *The Varieties of Reference*. Edited by John Henry McDowell. Oxford, OUP

Everett, B., Latham, A. J., and Miller, K. (2023) 'Locating temporal passage in a block world', *Ergo*, 10(9): 237–73

Falk, A. (2003) 'Time plus the whoosh and whiz', in A. Jokić and Q. Smith (eds.), *Time, Tense, and Reference*, Cambridge, MA, MIT Press: 211–50

Fara, D. G. (2001) 'Phenomenal continua and the Sorites', *Mind*, 110: 905–35

Farr M. (2020) 'Explaining temporal qualia', *European Journal for Philosophy of Science*, 10: 8

Forrest, P. (2004) 'The real but dead past: A reply to Braddon-Mitchell', *Analysis*, 64(284): 358

Frischhut, A. (2013) 'What experience cannot teach us about time', *Topoi*, 1: 1–13

Frischhut, A. (2014) 'Diachronic unity and temporal transparency', *Journal of Consciousness Studies*, 21(7–8): 34–55

Frischhut, A. (2017) 'Presentism and temporal experience', in I. Phillips (ed.), *Routledge Handbook of Philosophy of Temporal Experience*, London, Routledge: 249–61

Frischhut, A. (ms.) 'Awareness without time'.

Gallagher, S. (2003) 'Sync-ing in the stream of experience: Time-consciousness in Broad, Husserl, and Dainton', *Psyche*, 9(10)

Gallagher, S. and Zahavi, D. (2008) *The Phenomenological Mind: An Introduction to Philosophy of Mind and Cognitive Science*. London, Routledge

Gentner, D. (2001) 'Spatial metaphors in temporal reasoning', in M. Gattis (ed.), *Spatial Schemas and Abstract Thought*, Cambridge, MA, MIT Press: 203–22

Gibson, J. J. (1966) *The Ecological Approach to Visual Perception*. Boston, Houghton Mifflin [1986, Taylor and Francis]

Gilmore C., Costa D., and Calosi, C. (2016) 'Relativity and three four-dimensionalism', *Philosophy Compass*, 11(2): 102–20

Goff, P. (2017) *Consciousness and Fundamental Reality*. New York, OUP

Gow, L. (2016) 'The limitations of perceptual transparency', *The Philosophical Quarterly*, 66(265): 723–44

Gow, L. (2019) 'Everything is clear: All perceptual experiences are transparent', *Eur J Philos*, 27: 412–25

Graziani E., Orilia F., Capitani E., and Burro R. (2023) 'Common-sense temporal ontology: An experimental study', *Synthese*, 202: 193

Green, E. J. and Schellenberg, S. (2018) 'Spatial perception: The perspectival aspect of perception', *Philosophy Compass*, 13: e12472 (https://doi.org/10.1111/phc3.12472)

Grünbaum, A. (1967) *Modern Science and Zeno's Paradoxes*. Middletown, Wesleyan University Press

Grush, R. (2005) 'Internal models and the construction of time: Generalizing from state estimation to trajectory estimation to addresses temporal features of perception, including temporal illusions', *Journal of Neural Engineering*, 2: 209–18

Grush, R. (2006) 'How to, and how not to, bridge computational cognitive neuroscience and Husserlian phenomenology of time consciousness', *Synthese*, 153(3): 417–50

Grush, R. (2007) 'Brain time and phenomenological time', in A. Brook and K. Akins (eds.), *Cognition and the Brain: The Philosophy and Neuroscience Movement*, Cambridge University Press : 160–90

Grush, R. (2016) 'On the temporal character of temporal experience, its scale non-invariance, and its small scale structure', doi: 10.21224/P4WC73

Hancock, P. A. and Weaver, J. L. (2005) 'On time distortion under stress', *Theoretical Issues in Ergonomics Science*, 6(2): 193–211

Hartle, J. (2005) 'The physics of now', *American Journal of Physics* 73(2): 101–9

Hawley, K. (2001) *How Things Persist*. Oxford, OUP

Hestevold, H. S. (1990) 'Passage and the presence of experience', *Philosophy and Phenomenological Research*, 50: 537–52

Heywood, C. and Kentridge, R. W. (2009) 'Akinetopsia', in T. Bayne, A. Cleeremans, and P. Wilken (eds.), *The Oxford Companion to Consciousness*, Oxford, OUP: 35–6

Hilgevoord, J. and Atkinson, D. (2011) 'Time in quantum mechanics', in C. Callender (ed.), *The Oxford Handbook of Philosophy of Time*, Oxford, OUP: 540–87

Hoerl, C. (2013) 'A succession of feelings, in and of itself, is not a feeling of succession', *Mind*, 122(486): 373–417

Hoerl, C. (2014) 'Do we (seem to) perceive passage?', *Philosophical Explorations*, 17: 188–202

Hoerl, C. (2015) 'Seeing motion and apparent motion', *European Journal of Philosophy*, 23(3): 676–702

Hoerl, C. (2017) 'Temporal experience and the philosophy of perception', in I. Phillips (ed.), *Routledge Handbook of Philosophy of Temporal Experience*, London, Routledge: 171–83

Hoerl, C. (2018) 'Experience and time: Transparency and present', *Ergo*, 5(5): 127–51

Hoerl, C. P. (2023) 'The mechanics of representing time', *Timing & Time Perception* (published online ahead of print 2023). https://doi.org/10.1163/22134468-bja10087

Hoerl, C. (forthcoming) 'The flow of time: Rationalism vs. empiricism', *Australasian Philosophical Review*

Hohwy, J. (2013) *The Predictive Mind*. Oxford, OUP

Hohwy, J., Paton, B., and Palmer, C. (2016) 'Distrusting the present', *Phenomenology and the Cognitive Science*, 15: 315–35. https://doi.org/10.1007/s11097-015-9439-6

Hoy, R. (1978) 'Becoming and persons', *Philosophical Studies*, 34(3): 269–80

Huggett, N. (2014) 'Skeptical notes on a physics of passage', *Annals of the New York Academy of Sciences*, 1326: 9–17

Huggett, N. and Wüthrich, C. (2013) 'Emergent spacetime and empirical (in)coherence', *Studies in History and Philosophy of Modern Physics*, 44: 276–85

Hume, D. (1739) *A Treatise of Human Nature*

Hutto, D. (2008) *Folk Psychological Narratives: The Socio-Cultural Basis of Understanding Reasons*. Cambridge, MA, The MIT Press, Bradford Books

Iaquinto, S. and Torrengo, G. (2022a) *Fragmenting Reality: An Essay on Passage, Causation, and Time Travel*. London, Bloomsbury

Iaquinto, S. and Torrengo, G. (2022b) 'Materiality, parthood, and possibility', *Erkenntnis*, 87: 1125–31 (DOI: 10.1007/s10670-020-00233-4) [online 2020]

Ismael, J. (2007) *The Situated Self*. Oxford, OUP

Ismael, J. (2012) 'Decision and the open future', in A. Bardon (ed.), *The Future of the Philosophy of Time*, London, Routledge: 149–69

Ismael, J. (2016) *How Physics Makes Us Free*. Oxford, OUP

Ismael, J. (2017) 'Passage, flow, and the logic of temporal perspectives', in B. Christophe and H. Philippe (eds.), *Time of Nature and the Nature of Time*, Cham, Springer Verlag: 23–38

James, W. (1890) *The Principles of Psychology*, New York, Henry Holt and Company

Jones, L. A. (2019) 'The perception of duration and the judgment of the passage of time', in A. Bardon, V. Arstila, S. E. Power, and A. Vatakis (eds.), *The Illusions of Time: Philosophical and Psychological Essays on Timing and Time Perception*, London, Palgrave Macmillan : 53–68

Kail, P. (2007) *Projection and Realism in Hume's Philosophy*. Oxford, Clarendon Press

Kant, I. (1782 [1989]) *Critique of Pure Reason*. Translated and edited by P. Guyer and A. W. Wood, Cambridge, Cambridge University Press

Kaplan, D. (1989) 'Demonstratives: An essay on the semantics, logic, metaphysics and epistemology of demonstratives and other indexicals', in J. Almog, J. Perry, and H. Wettstein (eds.), *Themes from Kaplan*, Oxford, OUP: 481–563

Kelly, S. D. (2005) 'The puzzle of temporal experience', in A. Brooks and K. Akins (eds.), *Cognition and the Brain: The Philosophy and Neuroscience Movement*, Cambridge, Cambridge University Press: 208–38

Kentridge, B. and Brogaard, B. (2013) 'The functional roles of attention', in B. Nanay (ed.), *Current Controversies in Philosophy of Perception*, London, Routledge: 139–47

Kiverstein, J. and Arstila V. (2013) 'Time in mind', in A. Bardon and H. Dyke (eds.), *Blackwell Companion to the Philosophy of Time*, Oxford, Wiley-Blackwell: 444–69

Kriegel, U. (2015) 'Experiencing the present', *Analysis*, 75(3): 407–13

Lachter, J. and Durgin, F. (1999) 'Metacontrast masking functions: A question of speed?', *Journal of Experimental Psychology: Human Perception and Performance*, 25(4): 936–47

Latham, A. J., Miller, K., and Norton, J. (2020a) 'Do the folk represent time as essentially dynamical?', *Inquiry*, 66(10): 1882–913

Latham, A. J., Miller, K., and Norton, J. (2020b) 'An empirical investigation of purported passage phenomenology', *Journal of Philosophy*, 117(7): 353–86. https://doi.org/10.5840/jphil2020117722

Latham, A. J., Miller, K., and Norton, J. (2021) 'Is our naïve theory of time dynamical?', *Synthese*, 198: 4251–71 (https://link-springer-com.pros.lib.unimi.it:2050/content/pdf)

Lee, G. (2014a) 'Temporal experience and the temporal structure of experience', *Philosophers' Imprint*, 14: 3

Lee, G. (2014b) 'Extensionalism, atomism and continuity', in N. Oaklander (ed.), *Debates in Metaphysics of Time*, London, Bloomsbury: 150–73

Lee, G. (2015) 'Experiences and their parts', in D. Bennett and C. Hill (eds.), *Sensory Integration and the Unity of Consciousness*, Cambridge, MA, MIT Press: 287–321

Lee, G. (2018) 'Explaining away temporal flow: Thoughts on Prosser's "Experiencing Time"', *Inquiry: An Interdisciplinary Journal of Philosophy*, 61(3): 315–27

Lee, G. (2019) *Hoerl's Commentary*. Ann Arbor, MI, Ergo

Lee, R., Shardlow, J., Hoerl, C., O'Connor, P. A., Fernandes, A. S., and McCormacka, T. (2022) 'Towards an account of intuitive time', *Cognitive Science* (online first: https://doi.org/10.1111/cogs.13166)

Le Poidevin, R. (2007) *The Images of Time: An Essay on Temporal Representation*. Oxford, OUP

Le Poidevin, R. (2019) 'The experience and perception of time', SEP

Lewis, D. (1979) 'Attitudes de dicto and de se', *The Philosophical Review*, 88: 513–43

Lucas, J. R. (1973) *A Treatise on Time and Space*. London, Methuen & Co.

Markosian, N. (2004) 'A defense of presentism', in D. Zimmerman (ed.), *Oxford Studies in Metaphysics*, Volume 1, Oxford, OUP: 47–82

Martin, M. (1992) 'Sight and touch', in T. Crane (ed.), *The Contents of Experience*, Cambridge, Cambridge University Press: 196–215

Martin, M. (2002) 'The transparency of experience', *Mind and Language*, 4(4): 376–425

Masrour, F. (2012) 'Phenomenal objectivity and phenomenal intentionality: In defense of a Kantian account', in T. Horgan and U. Kriegel (eds.), *The Phenomenal Intentionality Research Program*, Oxford, OUP: 312–45

McAdams, D. (2019) 'First we invented stories, then they changed us: The evolution of narrative identity', *Evolutionary Studies in Imaginative Culture*, 3(1): 1–83

McKenna, C. A. (2020) 'Don't go chasing waterfalls: Motion aftereffects and the dynamic snapshot theory of temporal experience', *Review of Philosophy and Psychology*, https://doi.org/10.1007/s13164-020-00511-8

Mellor, H. (1998) *Real Time II*. Cambridge, Cambridge University Press

Merino-Rajme, C. (2022) 'The fragmentation of felt time', *Philosophers' Imprint*, 22(02)

Merricks, T. (2007) *Truth and Ontology*. Oxford, OUP

Metzinger, T. (2020) 'Minimal phenomenal experience: Meditation, tonic alertness, and the phenomenology of "pure" consciousness', *Philosophy and the Mind Sciences*, 1(I): 7

Meyer, U. (2015) 'Consciousness and the present', in Y. Dolev and M. Roubach (eds.), *Cosmological and Psychological Time*, Berlin, Springer: 143–53

Michaelian, K. (2016) *Mental Time Travel: Episodic Memory and Our Knowledge of the Personal Past*. Cambridge, MA The MIT Press

Michotte, A. (1946) *La perception de la causalité*. Paris, Vrin

Miller, I. (1984) *Husserl, Perception, and Temporal Awareness*. Cambridge, MA, The MIT Press

Miller, K. (2019) 'Does it really seem as though time passes?', in A. Bardon, V. Arstila, S. E. Power, and A. Vatakis (eds.), *The Illusions of Time: Philosophical and Psychological Essays on Timing and Time Perception*, London, Palgrave Macmillan: 17–34

Miller, K., Holcombe, A., and Latham, A. J. (2020) 'Temporal phenomenology: Phenomenological illusion vs cognitive error', *Synthese*, 197(2): 751–71

Millikan, R. G. (1991) 'Perceptual content and Fregean myth', *Mind*, 100(4): 439–59

Mitrani, L., Shekerdjiiski, S., and Yakimoff, N. (1986) 'Mechanisms and asymmetries in visual perception of simultaneity and temporal order', *Biological Cybernetics*, 54(3): 159–65

Mozersky, J. (2006) 'A tenseless account of the presence of experience', *Philosophical Studies*, 129: 441–76

Nagel, T. (1986) *The View from Nowhere*. New York, OUP

Nagel, T. (2012) *Mind and Cosmos: Why the Materialist Neo-Darwinian Conception of Nature Is Almost Certainly False*. Oxford–New York, OUP

Nanay, B. (2010) 'Attention and perceptual content', *Analysis*, 70(2): 263–70

Noë, A. (2006) 'Experience of the world in time', *Analysis*, 66: 26–32

Núñez, R., Motz, B., and Teuscher, U. (2009) 'Time after time: The psychological reality of the ego- and time-reference-point distinction in metaphorical construals of time', *Metaphor and Symbol*, 21(3): 13–46

Oaklander, L. N. (2004) *The Ontology of Time*. Amherst, MA, Prometheus Books

O'Callaghan, C. (2011) 'Against hearing meanings', *Philosophical Quarterly*, 61: 783–807

O'Callaghan, C. (2015) 'Speech perception', in M. Matthen (ed.), *Oxford Handbook of the Philosophy of Perception*, Oxford, OUP: 235–56

O'Regan, J. K. (2002) 'Change blindness', in *Encyclopaedia of Cognitive Science*, Oxford, Wiley

O'Shaughnessy, B. (2000) *Consciousness and the World*. Oxford, OUP

Papineau, D. (2021) *The Metaphysics of Sensory Experience*. Oxford, OUP

Parsons, J. (2004) 'Distributional properties', in F. Jackson and G. Priest (eds.), *Lewisian Themes: The Philosophy of David K. Lewis*, Oxford, Clarendon Press: 321–55

Parsons, J. (2015) 'A phenomenological argument for stage theory', *Analysis*, 75(2): 237–42

Paul, L. A. (2010) 'Temporal experience', *Journal of Philosophy*, 107: 333–59

Peacocke, C. (1999) *Being Known*. Oxford, Clarendon Press

Peacocke, C. (2004) *The Realm of Reason*. Oxford, OUP

Peebles, G. (2017) 'Temporal experience and metaphysics', *Manuscrito*, 40(1): 145–82

Pelczar, M. (2010) 'Must an appearance of succession involve a succession of appearances?', *Philosophy and Phenomenological Research*, 81(1): 49–63

Perry, J. (1979) 'The problem of the essential indexical', *Noûs*, 13(1): 3–21

Perry, J. (1986) 'Thought without representation', *Proceedings of the Aristotelian Society: Supplementary*, 60: 137–51

Perry, J. (2001) 'Time, consciousness and the knowledge argument', in L. N. Oaklander (ed.), *The Importance of Time: Proceedings of the Philosophy of Time Society, 1995–2000*, Dordrecht, Kluwer Academic: 127–52

Perry, J. (2013) 'Temporal indexicals', in H. Dyke and A. Bardon (eds.), *A Companion to the Philosophy of Time*, Oxford, Blackwell: 486–507

Phillips, I. (2011) 'Indiscriminability and experience of change', *The Philosophical Quarterly*, 61: 808–27

Phillips, I. (2012) 'Afterimages and sensations', *Philosophy and Phenomenological Research*, 87(2): 417–53

Phillips, I. (2013) 'Perceiving the passing of time', *Proceedings of the Aristotelian Society*, 113: 225–52

Phillips, I. (2014a) 'Experience of and in time', *Philosophy Compass*, 9(2): 131–44

Phillips, I. (2014b) 'The temporal structure of experience', in V. Arstila and D. Lloyd (eds.), *Subjective Time: The Philosophy, Psychology, and Neuroscience of Temporality*, Cambridge, MA, MIT Press: 139–58

Popper, K. R. (1935) *Logik der Forschung. Zur Erkenntnistheorie der modernen Naturwissenschaft*. Vienna, Julius Springer

Popper, K. R. (1982) 'Quantum theory and the schism in physics', in the *Postscript* to *The Logic of Scientific Discovery*, London, Hutchinson

Predelli, S. (2009) *Contexts: Meaning, Truth, and the Use of Language*. Oxford, OUP

Price, H. (1996) *Time's Arrow and Archimedes Point: New Directions for the Physics of Time*. Oxford, OUP

Priest, G. (2006) *Doubt Truth to Be a Liar*. Oxford, Clarendon Press

Prior, A. N. (1959) 'Thank goodness that's over', *Philosophy*, 34: 12–17

Prosser, S. (2012) 'Why does time seem to pass?', *Philosophy and Phenomenological Research*, 85(1): 92–116

Prosser, S. (2016) *Experiencing Time*. Oxford, OUP

Prosser, S. (2017) 'Rethinking the specious present', in I. Phillips (ed.), *Routledge Handbook of Philosophy of Temporal Experience*, London, Routledge: 146–56

Quinton, A. (1962) 'Spaces and times', *Philosophy*, 37(140): 130–47

Rashbrook-Cooper, O. (2011) 'The continuity of consciousness', *European Journal of Philosophy*, 21(4): 611–40

Rashbrook-Cooper, O. (2016) 'The stream of consciousness: A philosophical account', in Bruno Mölder, Valtteri Arstila, and Peter Øhrstrøm (eds.), *Philosophy and Psychology of Time*, New York, Springer: 117–34

Recanati, F. (2007) *Perspectival Thoughts*. Oxford, OUP

Reichenbach, H. (1938) *Experience and Prediction: An Analysis of the Foundations and the Structure of Knowledge*. Chicago, Univ. of Chicago Press

Reid, T. (1785 [2002]) 'Essays on the intellectual power of man: A critical edition', edited by D. Brookers and K. Haakonssen, *The Edinburgh Edition of Thomas Reid*, Edinburgh, Edinburgh University Press

Rensink, R. A. (2002) 'Change detection', *Annual Review of Psychology*, 53(1): 245–77

Richardson, L. F. (2014) 'Space, time, and Molineaux's question', *Ratio*, 27(4): 483–505

Richardson, L. F. (2019) *Reply to Hoerl*. Ann Arbor, MI, Ergo

Ricoeur, P. (1984) *Time and Narrative*. 3 vols., trans. Kathleen Blamey and David Pellauer, Chicago, University of Chicago Press

Rovelli, C. (2018) *The Order of Time*. London, Allen Lane

Russell, B. (1913[1992]) *Theory of Knowledge: The 1913 Manuscript*. London, Routledge

Sattig, T. (2019a) 'XIII—the flow of time in experience', *Proceedings of the Aristotelian Society*, 119(3): 275–93. https://doi.org/10.1093/arisoc/aoz014

Sattig, T. (2019b) 'The sense of temporal flow: A higher-order account', *Philosophical Studies*, 176(11): 3041–59. https://doi.org/10.1007/s11098-018-1162-z

Savitt, S. (2011) 'Time in the special theory of relativity', in C. Callender (ed.), *The Oxford Handbook of Philosophy of Time*, Oxford, OUP: 216–31

Schechtman, M. (1996) *The Constitution of Selves*. Ithaca, Cornell University Press

Schlesinger, G. N. (1991) 'E pur si muove', *Philosophical Quarterly*, 41(165): 427–41

Shardlow, J., Lee, R., Hoerl, C., McCormack, T., Burns, P., and Fernandes, A. S. (2020) 'Exploring people's beliefs about the experience of time', *Synthese*, 198: 10709–31 (s11229-020-02749-2)

Sider, T. (2001) *Four Dimensionalism*. Oxford, OUP

Siegel, S. (2006) 'Subject and object in the contents of visual experience', *Philosophical Review*, 115(3): 355–88

Siegel, S. (2010) *The Contents of Visual Experience*. New York, OUP

Sizer, L. (2000) 'Towards a computational theory of mood', *The British Journal for the Philosophy of Science*, 51: 743–69

Skow, B. (2015) *Objective Becoming*. Oxford, OUP

Smart, J. J. C. (1949) 'The river of time', *Mind*, 58(232): 483–99

Smith, A. D. (2002) *The Problem of Perception*. Cambridge, MA, Harvard University Press

Smith, B. and Varzi, A. C. (2000) 'Fiat and bona fide boundaries', *Philosophy and Phenomenological Research*, 60(2): 401–20

Smith, Q. (1985) 'The mind-independence of temporal becoming', *Philosophical Studies*, 47: 109–19

Smith, Q. (1986) *The Felt Meanings of the World: A Metaphysics of Feeling*. West Lafayette, Purdue University Press

Smith, Q. (1988) 'The phenomenology of A-time', *Diálogos. Revista de Filosofía de la Universidad de Puerto Rico*, 23(52): 143–53

Solomyak, O. (2019) 'Presentism and the specious present: From temporal experience to meta-metaphysics', *Dialectica*, 73(1–2): 247–66

Soteriou, M. (2011) 'The perception of absence, space and time', in J. Roessler, H. Lerman, and N. Eilan (eds.), *Perception, Causation and Objectivity*, Oxford, OUP: 181–206

Soteriou, M. (2013) *The Mind's Construction: The Ontology of Mind and Mental Action*. Oxford, OUP

Spolaore, G. and Torrengo, G. (2019) 'The moving spotlight(s)', *Inquiry: An International Journal of Philosophy*, 64(7): 754–71 (onlinefirst: https://doi.org/10.1080/0020174X.2019.1610046)

Stanghellini, G., Ballerini, M., Presenza, S., Mancini, M., Raballo, A., Blasi, S., and Cutting, J. (2016) 'Psychopathology of lived time: Abnormal time experience in persons with schizophrenia', *Schizophrenia Bulletin*, 42(1): 45–55. https://doi.org/10.1093/schbul/sbv052

Stebbing, S. (1937) *Philosophy and the Physicists*. New York, Dover Publications

Strawson, G. (2020) 'On the use of the notion of narrative in ethics and psychology', in E. Nahmias et al. (eds.), *The Natural Method: Essays in Honor of Owen Flanagan*, Cambridge, MA, MIT Press: 119–55

Synofzik, M., Vosgerau, G., and Newen, A. (2008) 'Beyond the comparator model: A multifactorial two-step account of agency', *Conscious. Cogn*, 17: 219–39

Tallant, J. (2014) 'Defining existence presentism', *Erkenntnis*, 79(3): 479–501

Tipples, J. (2011) 'When time stands still: Fear-specific modulation of temporal bias due to threat', *Emotion*, 11(1): 74–80

Torre, S. (2009) 'Tense, timely action and self-ascription', *Philosophy and Phenomenological Research*, 80(1): 112–32

Torrengo, G. (2010) 'The modal dimension', *Humanamente*, 19: 105–20

Torrengo, G. (2017) 'Feeling the passing of time', *Journal of Philosophy*, 114(4): 165–88

Torrengo, G. (2018) 'Perspectival tenses and dynamic tenses', *Erkenntnis*, 83(5): 1045–61

Torrengo, G. and Cassaghi, D. (2021) 'The way of presentness', *Erkenntnis* (online first: http://link.springer.com/article/10.1007/s10670-021-00477-8)

Torrengo, G. and Cassaghi, D. (2022) 'Flow and presentness in experience', *Analytic Philosophy* (online first: 10.1111/phib.12264)

Travis, C. (2004) 'The silence of the senses', *Mind*, 113: 57–94

Tullio, E. (ms.) 'Conscious worms: On perdurantism and phenomenal consciousness'

Tye, M. (2003a) *Consciousness and Persons: Unity and Identity*. Cambridge, MA, MIT Press

Tye, M. (2003b) 'Blurry images, double vision, and other oddities: New problems for representationalism?', in Q. Smith and A. Josic (eds.), *Consciousness: New Philosophical Perspectives*, Oxford, OUP: 7–32

Tye, M. (2009) *Consciousness Revisited: Materialism without Phenomenal Concepts*. Cambirdge, MA, MIT Press

Valberg, J. J. (1992) *The Puzzle of Experience*. Oxford, OUP

van Fraassen, B. C. (1980) *The Scientific Image*. Oxford, OUP

Varzi, A. and Torrengo, G. (2006) 'Crimes and punishments', *Philosophia*, 34: 395–404

Velleman, J. D. (2006) 'So it goes', *The Amherst Lecture in Philosophy*, 1: 1–23

Vendler, Z. (1957) 'Verbs and times', *The Philosophical Review*, 66: 143–60

Viera, G. A. (2019) 'The fragmentary model of temporal experience and the mirroring constraint', *Philosophical Studies*, 176(1): 21–44

Vosgerau, G., Schlicht, T., and Newen, A. (2008) 'Orthogonality of phenomenality and content', *American Philosophical Quartely*, 45(4): 309–28

Watzl, S. (2013) 'Silencing the experience of change', *Philosophical Studies*, 165(3): 1009–32

Wearden, J. (2016) *The Psychology of Time Perception*. London, Springer

Weyl, H. (1919) *Raum-Zeit-Materie. Vorlesungen über allgemeine Relativitätstheorie*. Berlin, Julius Springer

Weyl, H. (1949) *Philosophy of Mathematics and Natural Science*. Princeton, Princeton University Press

Williamson, T. (2000) *Knowledge and Its Limits*. Oxford, OUP

Windt, J. (2015) *Dreaming: A Conceptual Framework for Philosophy of Mind and Empirical Research*. Cambridge, MA, MIT Press

Wu, W. (2013) 'Attention and perception: A necessary connection?', in B. Nanay (ed.), *Current Controversies in Philosophy of Perception*, London, Routledge: 148–62

Young, N. (2022) 'Agents of change: Temporal flow and feeling oneself act', *Philosophical Studies*, 179(8): 2619–37

Young, N. and Calabi, C. (2018) 'Can movement be depicted?', *Phenomenology and Mind*, 14: 170–9

Zahavi, D. (2007) 'Self and other: The limits of narrative understanding', in D. Hutto (ed.), *Narrative and Understanding Persons*, Cambridge, Cambridge University Press: 196

Zakay, D. (1992) 'On prospective time estimation, temporal relevance and temporal uncertainty', in Françoise Macar, Viviane Pouthas, and William J. Friedman (eds.), *Time, Action and Cognition*, Dordrecht, Springer: 109–17

Zimmerman, D. (1996) 'Persistence and presentism', *Philosophical Papers*, 25: 115–26

Zimmerman, D. (2005) 'The A-theory of time, the B-theory of time, and "taking tense seriously"', *Dialectica*, 59(4): 401–45

Index

258   INDEX